African Textiles and Dyeing Techniques

African Textiles and Dyeing Techniques

CLAIRE POLAKOFF

Routledge & Kegan Paul
London and Henley

First published in Great Britain in 1982
by Routledge & Kegan Paul Ltd
39 Store Street, London WC1E 7DD and
Broadway House, Newtown Road,
Henley-on-Thames, Oxon RG9 1EN
Printed and bound in Great Britain by
William Clowes (Beccles) Limited,
Beccles and London

ISBN 0-7100-0908-9

For all my friends and family, especially
Paul, Stacey, and Alexandra

Contents

INTRODUCTION ix

ACKNOWLEDGMENTS xii

1 *American Interest in African Fabrics* 1

2 *African Fabrics* 11

3 *The Art of Tie and Dye in Africa* 15

4 *Wax and Paste Resist Patterning—"Batik"* 55

5 *The Hand-printed Adinkra Cloth of Ghana* 83

6 *Bokolanfini—The Mud Cloth of Mali* 131

7 *Korhogo Cloth of Ivory Coast* 155

8 *Traditions/Transitions: Working with African Textiles Today* 187

EPILOGUE 218

APPENDIX: *Indigo—The Legend and Technique* 221

GLOSSARY 239

BIBLIOGRAPHY 243

PHOTOGRAPHY CREDITS 251

INDEX 255

Introduction

The word "indigo" brings to mind many images—deep blue and seemingly timeless. These images are sometimes caught in the shifting blue lengths of fabric which flow from the heads and shoulders of mysterious nomads as they endlessly trace and retrace ancient trails across the Sahara. Yet this stark African scene is complemented by a more contemporary concept of indigo. Like Duke Ellington's personal midnight, "Mood Indigo," it is both earthy and tangible as the blues of the soul, intense and elusive as one's innermost longings. Wrapped in this range of blues are all the village tones and city rhythms coloring African life . . . the blues of sky, sea, and soul are reflected on the people themselves in the shimmer of copper-glazed indigo and glittering adornments. I suggest readers delve into indigo within this mood of multiplicity, although the colors and moods of this book will not only be blue. I hope to include many of the moods and activities related to African traditional methods of dyeing and patterning cloth which are part of the contemporary art scene both in Africa and America.

In a sense, the subject of this book is joy, although at first glance it may appear that fabric design techniques are the dominant theme. Actually, there are several deeper themes in the book. The techniques described simply give access to the joyful experience that creative achievement can be. The finished fabric is the tangible product of that special process through which the human spirit finds nourishment and pride. The fabric itself has a value in its beauty and usefulness, but the spiritual fulfillment experienced by participants in fabric design groups is equally valuable.

This book grew out of my own experiences. I have been involved in American fashion and fabric design since my undergraduate days at the University of California at Los Angeles. My interest in African textiles began when I was living in Libreville, Gabon, where my husband was director of the American Cultural Center from 1966 to 1968. I designed exhibits for the Center and conducted informal art classes for Gabonese and French children. My interest in African fabrics deepened during a year at UCLA where I worked for a master's degree in textile and costume design in the Department of Art (which I completed in 1977) while my husband did graduate work at the African Studies Center. From California we went to Washington, D.C., where we found the interest in African art and crafts flourishing. In Washington, I reveled in the availability of African textiles in museums, private collections, and newly opened commercial boutiques. This, plus the expanded contact with people interested in African art—Peace Corps volunteers, curators, scholars, diplomats, and the personnel of various private and governmental agencies—enabled me to continue my studies. From what I learned, I was inspired to organize and conduct a series of experimental workshops on "Fabric Design in Africa" at the Smithsonian Institution in Washington, D.C., during the winter and spring of 1970.

In this book I will attempt to give an overview of some aspects of current work in fabric design using African methods. I do not intend to cover the entire field of African textiles, either in their traditional or contemporary forms, but have restricted myself to resist dyeing, painting, bleaching, and hand printing. Other important methods such as weaving, embroidery, appliqué, and various forms of looping and knotting are cited in the Bibliography as sources of design inspiration to enrich the variety of patterns available. They cannot be taken up in detail here. This book is not being offered in order to create a nation of tie-dyers and batik artists, but to provide people with a means to understand another culture similar to the way one might approach the study of architecture or linguistics. The economic and social aspects of Africa are as important as the technical aspects of fabric design.

At this point, I would like to say a few words about my own experience with indigo dyeing—a preface to my comments later in the Appendix. I came to indigo as a complete neophyte, fascinated by its incredible blue depths and shimmering surfaces. Little by little, experiment after experiment (and frequently failure after failure), I built a small store of knowledge and ability, vastly inferior to that of the traditional African artists whose splendid work had inspired me. I continue to seek a better understanding of this extraordinary dyestuff in the hopes of perfecting the techniques required to bring forth its beautiful blues. I can only hope that at some point in the future I may truly master this process and be capable of communicating to others a comprehensive understanding of indigo's complex and mysterious ways.

Acknowledgments

I would like to thank the many people whose involvement helped bring this book to fruition. Invaluable contributions have been made by my research associates: Helen Anderson-Bauer, Gloria Freeman, Aminata Konaté, Rita Warpeha, and Mimi Wolford. Museum curators have been extremely generous with their time, and I am especially grateful to Mme. Francine Ndiaye, Head of the Department of Black Africa, the Musée de l'Homme, Paris, France; Dr. Gordon D. Gibson, Curator of African Ethnology, Smithsonian Institution, National Museum of Natural History, Washington, D.C.; and Dr. Renée Boser-Sarivaxévanis, Chief Curator of African Art and Textiles, Museum für Völkerkunde und Schweizeriches Museum für Volkskunde Basle/Musée d'Ethnographie et Musée Suisse de Folklore Bâle,* Switzerland, as well as the many others who so gracefully supplied information and photographs. The staff of the Smithsonian Associates, under whose auspices my fabric design workshops have been formed, continues its work with tireless enthusiasm, and I wish to thank them for their long support of these programs, particularly the former director Mrs. Susan Hamilton and her associate, Ms. Carolyn Hecker, who now operates her own workshops and lectures through the American Crafts Council and the Greenwood Gallery, Washington, D.C.

* The Museum's full title, whether it appears in German or French, is not used throughout this book. Instead, I use shortened forms such as the Musée d'Ethnographie, the Museum für Völkerkunde, the Basel Museum, or others. Similarly, I use the simpler version of Dr. Renée Boser-Sarivaxévanis' name—Dr. Boser—which she herself uses now, both personally and professionally.

I greatly appreciate the encouragement and continuing supportive criticism of my editor, William Strachan, and am much obliged to Margo Viscusi and Robin de Silva for help in organizing and refining the manuscript. I would also like to thank Robin Haft Lee and Carolyn Potter for their assistance in photographing my fabric collection, and Esther Warner Dendel, Ida Talalla, Francine Ndiaye, and Helen Anderson-Bauer for their extremely helpful comments upon reading my manuscript midway through its conception.

There are some other special people I wish to mention: My deepest appreciation to Dr. Joanne B. Eicher and Dr. Robert F. Thompson for their comments on the galleys just before the manuscript finally became a book. I also extend my gratitude to Dr. Leon Siroto for suggesting certain research sources as well as appropriate linguistic alternatives to phrases that might be puzzling to nonspecialized readers. I would like to thank Professor Emeritus Madeleine Sunkees and Professor Alice M'Closkey who were my instructors at UCLA when I was an undergraduate as well as my mentors for the master's degree I undertook some twenty years later. Chapter 5 on the *adinkra* cloth of Ghana is an edited and revised version of the master's thesis that complemented my creative work in textile and costume design, and I am indebted to both professors for their considerable guidance and patience during the time it took me to complete my work.

In addition to the various acknowledgments in the text, there were so many teachers, colleagues, museum associates, workshop participants, and textile enthusiasts in America, Europe, and Africa who have contributed to this project that it is impossible to mention each one separately, so I would like to offer them a collective thank-you. I hope they find pleasure in the following pages and are reminded of the sense of adventure and discovery we often shared in the pursuit of our varied goals.

MAURITANIA
CAPE VERDE ISLANDS
SENEGAL
Dakar
Rufisque
WOLOF
GAMBIA
N
W
E
S
GUINEA-BISSAU
GUINEA
Bamako
BELEDOUGOU
BAMBARA
Mopti
Djenne
0 Miles 400
0 Km 400
SIERRA LEONE
SENUFO
Korhogo
Atlantic Ocean
LIBERIA
IVORY COAST
Abidjan

ALI

NIGER

CHAD

OLTA

Ouagadougou

HAUSA

NIGER RIVER

Kano

BENIN

GHANA

NIGERIA

TOGO

YORUBA

Oshogbo

Ibadan

Abeokuta

HANTI

nasi

Lagos

Accra

EJAGHAM

BAMUN

Foumban

CENTRAL AFRICAN
EMPIRE

CAMEROON

GULF OF
GUINEA

EQUATORIAL
GUINEA

UBANGI RIVER

CONGO

GENYA

GABON

CONGO RIVER

ZAÏRE

KUBA

ANGOLA

African Textiles and Dyeing Techniques

1

American Interest in African Fabrics

Today we are learning that the real story of Africa is her people and their cultures. With the emergence of the independent African nations in the late 1950s and early '60s came a healthy curiosity about the vast and mysterious continent. Modern technology —notably air travel and the media—made Africa accessible to the world as the world became accessible to Africans.

Various forms of exchange have encouraged a new insightfulness about Africa and have often helped change outmoded and false concepts of Africans and their countries. These multilevel exchanges have also helped ameliorate the painful experiences of the colonialization of Africa, slowly replacing exploitation with respect and serious interest.

International diplomatic relations with the newly formed African republics opened areas of awareness which provided more realistic concepts of these countries. Many universities' African Studies Centers featured exchange programs and extensive fieldwork in Africa. Government and private agencies subsidized study grants in Africa and sponsored programs enabling Africans to study abroad. People from international volunteer organizations such as the Peace Corps went to live with Africans in remote villages, small towns, and crowded urban areas. In addition, tourists and businessmen began to visit Africa as never before. These exchanges made an immediate contribution toward a more rapid dispersal of information and ideas within Africa as well as on other continents.

These visitors and their families—some of whom stayed for years—came home from Africa, sharing their treasures as well as their experiences. Craft forms, as simple and salable as carved and painted calabashes, beads, and, of course, fabrics, were displayed in homes which had once housed only the familiar bric-a-brac of their own national manufacture. Some of the rather startling collections of African objects included complete costumes used in initiation rites, ingeniously designed rural mousetraps, and basketry devices for catching fish. Some people brought back and wore indigenous African clothes, such as the *bou-bou,* the *gele* head tie, and the wraparound *pagne* of French-speaking Africa.

Fabrics were a direct way people could relate to African cultures. Textiles—the stuff clothes are made of—are almost a universal experience. There is no language barrier with fabric—it speaks directly to the senses, and we can wrap ourselves in its sensuality and special textures, densities, and movements. To put on someone else's clothes is to take on, as an actor does, a bit of the wearer's personality. With fabrics we can feel close to the culture as well as the craftsman.

Sporadic and peripheral international interest in African decorative art had been expressed in writing by missionaries and explorers for centuries. Arab scholars wrote about African fabrics as early as the eleventh century. In the nineteenth century the journals of European explorers often featured descriptions of fabrics, apparel, and accessories. Through the first half of the twentieth century some scholarly interest was occasionally expressed and various aspects of African culture were recorded, particularly by colonial district officers and certain eccentric anthropologists whose observations were not always acceptable to the academic viewpoints of that period.

By the late 1960s, however, a growing interest in African studies was revealed on a number of levels. Original research was carried out among scholars in Europe, America, and, of course, Africa. Some museum curators developed an interest in extending and reclassifying their collections as experts increasingly regarded African art—once a curiosity brought back by missionaries, commercial agents, and explorers—as one of the world's great art forms. A number of private connoisseurs, who had previously confined their interests in African art to masks and sculptured figures, extended their collections to include some of Africa's decorative arts. Textiles—along with jewelry, ceremonial costumes, and pottery—were bestowed new prestige by the experts.

This change in appreciation of the decorative arts was aided by a revolutionary change in the definition of African art itself. The long and dreary dialogue separating anthropological and ethnographic "material culture" (those objects—called "artifacts"—formed by the technology of everyday life) from the world of "art" was coming to an end. The conflict lay in the contemporary Western idea that an art object may be of value purely for its aesthetic form and expression, while most of the African objects regarded as art by Western experts were, to their African creators, functional utilitarian objects. They were, by definition, artifacts. Yet they were aesthetically pleasing, as art, to Western eyes. The distinction between art and artifact had blurred, broadening the meaning of art.

Thousands of these objects—so highly charged with the energies and vitality of their own societies—lay dormant for years in the dusty basements of natural history museums in various countries. Finally, eager and insightful art historians recognized these hidden treasures and brought them to the surface. Curators, anxious to revitalize their study collections, made these specimens available to scholars, students, and the public. At last these humble items had come to be recognized as objects worthy of exhibition with the "classic" art of Africa—those masks and figures which inspired Picasso, Modigliani, Epstein, and others, themselves collectors.

African textiles were among the items given a new significance. They, too, are being moved from museums of natural history into the museums of fine and decorative arts. Textile curators are now careful to preserve surviving examples of ancient African fabrics as they expand their present collections.

Historically, beautiful fabrics and elegant attire have always been venerated. They are regarded with respect by people of the most varied cultural backgrounds; they bring pleasure through their beauty and craftsmanship and their historical and social significance. Persons of esteem everywhere honor each other with gifts of intricately fashioned textiles and national dress as nonverbal tributes of the highest order. Fabrics have been used as currency in many societies and have often served as marriage tender—both as "bride wealth" in Africa and as the similar "dowry" in Western societies.

It would seem natural, then, to assume that traditional handcrafted fabrics occupy a place of esteem within the newly formed African nations. Only recently, however, has this been the case. During the colonial period in Africa, emphasis was placed on imported fabrics as "prestige" items, with cheap, machine-printed European cottons serving the general population for daily wear. The Africans sought to emulate the dress of their European rulers and adapted Western styles and fabrics in an attempt to reflect the prestige and social positions of their colonial overseers. Concurrently, European and American missionaries were busy converting Africans not only to Christianity but to Western clothing as well.

Textiles played an important part in the economics of colonial power. As the slave market dwindled, profits were replaced by the incredibly lucrative European textile market which the Africans themselves supported. They bought thousands of yards of bright, poor-quality cotton prints from European traders—prints which soon replaced their indigenous handwoven and dyed fabrics. Ironically, the cotton from which these imported materials were woven was often African in origin—produced by exploited labor and then sold back to the Africans as materials of the cheapest quality at exorbitant prices.*

However, with independence came new attitudes. Leaders of individual African states have renewed national pride in traditional textiles and attire, which they wear themselves. African diplomats

* Extremely high-quality, well-designed, and excellently dyed cottons known as wax prints were an exception to this practice and continue in use among Africans today, who often prize them as heirlooms and value them above indigenous handwoven cloth. For detailed information on wax prints, see *The History and Development of Wax-printed Textiles Intended for West Africa and Zaïre* and *African Wax-Prints—An Exhibit from the Nielsen and Eicher Collections,* both by Ruth Nielsen. (See Bibliography.)

wear robes similar to those which clothed the sovereigns of ancient kingdoms. These sumptuous cloaks and ensembles have inspired international admiration and acclaim. This, in turn, has stimulated the wearing of traditional garments of handcrafted textiles by more and more Africans at home as well as abroad, though in Africa one still sees Western apparel mingled with the traditional.

This renewed interest in African textiles has spread to African museums. Many of these institutions seek to reinforce a sense of national pride and identification by displaying traditional costumes and accessories and by setting up exhibits on handcrafted textiles of all kinds. Some museums have workrooms or courtyards where craftsmen and craftswomen demonstrate weaving and dyeing techniques; finished items are then sold by the museum. A number of European and American museums feature similar exhibits and many more are in the planning stages.

Gradually, the enormous textile industry, which until recently has serviced Africa almost exclusively from abroad, is finding its way back to the African soil, whence its original staple—cotton—first came. Many of these African factory-made fabrics take their design inspiration from the early handcrafted textiles. Unfortunately, much of the appeal of the original fabrics is lost in the poor quality of the manufactured cloths. With better factory methods of reproduction and with greater care for the fineness of original designs, even industrialized Africa could take part in preserving and perpetuating the cultural significance of handcrafted cloth. Ultimately, the coordinated efforts of craft centers, museums, technical trade schools, designers, and manufacturers may preserve the beauty of this aspect of the African heritage.†

As Africans themselves developed a renewed interest in their traditional decorative arts, a number of social, political, economic, and cultural developments in the United States worked to encourage an interest in African textiles and the adoption of African styles in textiles and fashion on an astonishing scale.

Many black Americans, reaching toward Africa for cultural

† Senegalese artist Iba Ndiaye has proposed a design center with a collection of traditional motifs for contemporary African artists who seek inspiration from the designs of their ancestors.

identity, found in the various forms of national dress a ready expression and fulfillment of those desires. In an eloquent statement of black pride, they stepped forward and enveloped themselves in Africa—quite literally—with the clothing of the continent. White Americans who were interested in African and Afro-American culture were led back to Africa, too—in search of sources as well as solutions. They expressed this intellectual, emotional, and sometimes realistic voyage by adapting the African style of dress.

Meanwhile, rigid dress codes in the United States had relaxed and a casual lifestyle was becoming the fashion. Most notably, the youth in America and elsewhere began to assert its own way of life—one characterized by, among other things, an extreme individuality of dress. Along with traditional Indian, Indonesian, Latin-American, and Native-American styles, African dress (and Western-style clothing made of African textiles) became popular with the young. The flowing, languid lines of loose-fitting garments and the lovely colors of traditional African textiles—plus their intricate patterns and inviting textures—gave exotic expression to this new informality.

This attraction to the exotic in dress and fabrics coincided with a unique international fashion trend—that is, the tendency for fashion to move upward from the streets rather than downward from the *couturiers* or, as in earlier times, from the upper classes. For example, no couturier decreed that worn and faded jeans should be bought by Paris boutique owners and resold at incredible markups to fashionable Parisians. This unusual trend reflected a complete change in the concept of "fashion."

The standard view of fashion was disintegrating. It had decentralized from a massive, self-perpetuating dictatorship, based primarily in New York's garment district, to something as hard to merchandise as a state of mind. In fact, the new fashion was based on whimsy, emphasizing individuality of expression and personalization of style. The question of "fashion" per se arose. Merchandise sat on shelves while businesses floundered and the ultimate demise of the fashion industry seemed at hand.

There were psychological as well as financial reasons for this progression. People's priorities, aspirations, and experiences had changed so much that the dictates of New York not only didn't matter, they didn't fit into people's lives. High fashion no longer made sense and consequently had no power. For another, rising costs motivated people of every age group to make their own clothes—either sewing them from scratch or creating them from recycled or ready-made, cut-rate clothes.

People turned to the colors and embroidered cottons of India, North Africa, and the Near East found in bargain-priced import shops. They sought the eccentric and often quite beautiful old clothes from the exquisite dress of the *belle époque* or from the provocative 1920s. They found them not in Paris or New York boutiques, but at the Paris flea markets or at secondhand clothes carts in London. Lovely bits of antique lace, graceful tassels, charming buttons and buckles could also be found in thrift shops across the United States, at barn sales in New England, or at outdoor swap meets in Southern California. These shops, stalls, and barns all had a sense of crowded, carnival-like bargaining activity not unlike that of an African marketplace.

But Americans were not only adopting a new form of dress; another subtle but very important psychological change was taking place in their lives. Though it remains somewhat undefined to many people, some experienced it as a general feeling of disorientation caused by loss of control over what we do in our daily lives. Many of us work to obtain food, shelter, clothing, and leisure (which is part of the point of labor-saving devices), but we work with abstractions such as paper and assembly-line parts. There is no connection between what we do for a living and what we live for. Nor is there a direct relationship between our work and what we get with our wages.

We shop at a giant supermart and purchase food that is so sanitized, processed, and packaged it looks as if it's been produced mechanically; there is no sign that it ever grew anywhere. We buy clothes and household furnishings at a huge department store—ready-made, prefabricated, abstract. It could be that a part of the reason for the return to the handcrafted has to do with the unfulfilled feelings of people who live their lives abstractly. Even the return to natural foods is a move away from abstraction toward the concrete—the reality of the earth for growing food, tools and wood for building shelter, fibers and dyes for making fabrics and clothing.

This, plus the increasing mobility of families to the point that they don't belong to any community, adds to disorientation and alienation. People have an inherent need for some sense of community, maybe in contradiction to their need for freedom but true, nevertheless. Perhaps there is still a yearning for the community in which the old and the very young participated throughout their lives. The very young used to do simpler chores and the very old did the milder ones—along with being keepers of history and explaining heritage. All of these things related to the quality of life one experienced every day.

By being part-time craftsmen and making many of the things we use, we turn our leisure into a way to feel accomplishment—and gain some control over an otherwise synthetic life. We are able to experience a sense of community with people in a group craft experience that we can no longer otherwise enjoy because of the disintegration of natural communities. Like the Africans, who are in transition from a rural agricultural economy to an urban industrial one, we, too, are in a transition from the traditional community based on blood and location to a new and necessary one based on common need, interest, cooperation, and fulfillment.

The strong need for individual expression, so blatantly expressed in the exotic dress and lifestyles of the late 1960s and early 1970s, is largely a reaction to the worldwide phenomena of technology. It is the same technology that made the world more accessible to the peoples in it. But Americans were so impressed with technology's precocious childhood they let it annihilate many of the more human qualities of their lives—not too unlike the Africans' threatened loss of their traditional art and crafts.

What remains to be resolved in contemporary industrialized society—whether in America, Africa, or elsewhere—is the delicate balance between satisfying man's need for technologically advanced methods of production, which lighten life's burdens and allow for more meaningful pursuits in work and leisure (technology's great advantage), and the threat of a technological take-over where man loses his own vital involvement in the mechanics of his culture.

People now want to retrieve from technology the basic sense of participation in their own lives. They want manual involvement and the satisfying texture of exchange between individuals in a group. So Americans have gone from acquiring things to making things. Now, for example, some of the many people who have collected African fabrics are starting to master the techniques Africans used, by taking workshops in textile design and production. At the same time, they are participating in a communal setting still prevalent in Africa but largely lost in America.‡

An American tradition that fits in with craft involvement is that of night school. Night school—or the idea of "taking a class"—is a way of life so integrated into our society we take the idea for granted. Although night school has existed in France since the end of the nineteenth century, the contemporary concept of the workshop as it is experienced in the United States is only modestly appreciated in most European countries. In America, night school readied Americans for the idea of workshops.

Recently, people in the United States have been influenced by the art and craft traditions that existed in this country before their ancestors arrived. These were the arts and crafts of the original Americans—the Native Americans. Their skills in jewelry-making, beading, weaving, pottery, and leatherwork have been much admired, and traditional Indian designs have had a profound effect on contemporary American painting and sculpture.

These varying forms of appreciation of American art/craft have many manifestations. We want to explore the American interest in African textiles and especially the joy in mastering techniques used to dye and pattern these textiles. In part, the growing attraction to African culture accounts for this interest, as does the departure from "fashion" to a new individuality and informality in dress, and a renewed respect for all things handmade.

But there is perhaps a deeper current connecting the American who decides to master African techniques of, say, tie and dye and

‡ For a brief introduction to the history of crafts in the United States, see the Epilogue.

the African artisan who turns out tie-dyed textiles as a vocation. The American may well be searching to recapture a tradition of self-expression through community-based endeavor that has both social and economic significance, once such a strong strain in the American experience. This tradition is still alive in Africa, particularly in rural areas where the maker of useful and beautiful objects remains strongly integrated into his or her society's social and economic structure.

In contemporary Africa, however, traditional methods of producing textiles, along with many other art and craft forms, are seriously threatened by increasing urbanization and industrialization. These arts/crafts may disappear, as they almost did in America, if the vital personal, religious, social, and aesthetic needs they can fulfill are not recognized adequately and in time.

The African textile artist has a great deal to teach the American who wants to create beautiful textiles. But perhaps the American who treasures the handcrafted African textile and the social wisdom that fosters its creation can also help the African avoid the mistake American society made in casting aside traditions whose loss is so poignantly felt by a postindustrialized nation.

2

African Fabrics

Fabric and fabric design have fascinated scholars of every discipline from art and archaeology through the social sciences and into the world of tomorrow's technology. Today, the phenomenal interest in handcrafted textiles in the United States—most notably the exciting and inventive techniques of tie and dye, batik, painting, and hand printing—has focused attention on the many parts of the world where these innovative approaches to textile design have been practiced for many centuries.

At last the intricacies of African fabrics have warranted the art world's attention. Unfortunately, their complete and accurate documentation is made immeasurably difficult by the perishable nature of the cloths themselves, coupled with the extremely humid climatic conditions of tropical Subsaharan Africa, where much of the textile activity of the continent is centered. Slowly and painstakingly, specialists in African textiles, working in Nigeria, Ghana, Senegal, Ivory Coast, Mali, and other countries, are beginning to penetrate some of the mysteries involving the origins of these fabric designs and techniques. Until such time as these further studies have been concluded and published, we must rely on the information presently available, such as documentation by some of the same scholars who at this very moment are readdressing themselves to the many questions brought forth by their earlier research.

Currently, the outlook for new insights into the history of African textiles is encouraging. Many textile scholars are producing texts which promise enlightenment on design origins—the recurrence of various motifs and similar themes in a variety of techniques which appear in different parts of the continent. Brigitte Menzel's monumental three-volume edition on the textiles of Africa, *Textilien aus Westafrika,* 1972–73, written for Berlin's Museum für Völkerkunde, has been published, with a fourth and final volume expected soon. Dr. Renée Boser-Sarivaxévanis, curator of African Textiles and Art at the Musée d'Ethnographie, Basel, Switzerland—who published her first volume, *Les Tissus de l'Afrique Occidentale* in 1972, and presented a magnificent exhibition of African textiles and costumes at the Basel Museum—spent eighteen months of intense fieldwork in West Africa in 1973–74 in preparation for her second volume. She was accompanied by Bernhard Gardi who assisted with the documentation while photographing their findings. While at Michigan State University, Dr. Joanne B. Eicher published her latest work, *Nigerian Handcrafted Textiles,* through the University of Ife Press, Nigeria, in 1976. Professor Eicher is now head of the Department of Textiles and Clothing, College of Home Economics, at the University of Minnesota. Esther Warner Dendel's *African Fabric Crafts,* featuring off-loom weaving and plaiting techniques, was published in October 1974. Many other scholars are also at work as well—in the field and at universities and museums throughout the world. Their current and future efforts will result in more profound coverage of specific textiles in museum collections as well as all-encompassing theoretical studies on the validity of diffusionist concepts of design distribution. More enlightening books and pamphlets will emerge with the publication of essays in anthropological quarterlies and other magazines such as the University of California at Los Angeles' *African Arts,* which has featured a growing number of excellent articles on the textile arts of Africa.

Here, a comment on defining African fabrics is appropriate. Just how does one recognize an "African" fabric, and how does one distinguish handcrafted textiles "made in Africa" from machine-printed cloths bearing the same label? The question is valid because in America, particularly, a great flood of European and Asian adaptations of African designs have been mixed in with African machine-printed imitations of nearly identical cloths. To further complicate the matter, many of these European representations of African prints are as much Indonesian in origin as they are African. This situation can be traced to the international textile trade of Holland centuries ago. Handcrafted batik designs were brought back from Java, translated into the famous machine-made "Dutch wax prints" in Holland, and then popularized to a phenomenal degree in African marketplaces. Meanwhile, the British textile magnates took old African motifs to the manufacturing centers of Manchester and made fantastic fortunes in Africa by selling these reproductions. In this roundabout way, various Indonesian and African motifs from the original handcrafted textiles of both cultures became intermixed, copied, and recopied until the contemporary African machine-printed textile—whether manufactured in Europe, Asia, or Africa itself—is often a conglomeration of these early intracultural design motifs with more than a dash of added contemporary flavoring. Some of the design additions feature photo-processed reproductions of political heroes, sports stars, and orbiting spacemen in their unearthly crafts.

Are these fabrics African? They are certainly considered just that in countless department stores and boutiques throughout the United States and Europe. Salespeople in these shops are often surprisingly ignorant of the finer points that distinguish the design techniques and are equally inadequate in their abilities to differentiate between handcrafted and machine-printed fabrics, both of which are often labeled "made in Africa." It's hardly surprising that the innocent shopper is frequently disappointed to find that the fabric she had thought a one-of-a-kind original turns out to be available on countless store counters. Unfortunately, it takes a person with good textile experience to analyze the difference between a handcrafted fabric and an excellent reproduction. For this reason, the uninitiated should rely on the reputation of the merchandising agent to determine the true nature and value of the textile. Many cities feature fine boutiques and museum shops where the owners and salespeople take great pride and enjoyment in their knowledge of the fabric's country of origin, the type of technique employed, and the kinds of dyes utilized. There is nothing wrong with buying European or African-styled machine-printed fabrics that are manufactured for sale in Africa—particularly since the Africans have been wearing them for years. The point that machine-made copies of African fabrics are widely sold is made so that the purchaser not be misled. One is much less likely to feel disappointed and cheated afterward if one knows the facts beforehand. For those readers who are really interested in this aspect of African fabrics, an amusing and enlightening afternoon can be spent sleuthing at the local department stores and even the more elegant African boutiques, inquiring of the clerks the exact sources of the materials as well as the techniques by which they are manufactured. It will certainly serve as an eye-opening introduction to the study of African fabrics.

With these few introductory remarks in mind, let us now look at the various techniques employed to pattern African textiles and attempt to place them in a historical perspective.

3

The Art of Tie and Dye in Africa

The techniques popularly known as tie and dye are believed to have been practiced at some time in history by craftsmen and craftswomen of almost every country in the world. China, Japan, India, Indonesia, the Philippines, Russia (it was a Jewish craft before the revolution), pre-Columbian Peru, Bolivia, the United States (the Pueblo Indians of New Mexico), and Africa all produced examples of varying skill and beauty. Yet no one knows when or where the technique began in Africa. Much of Africa's history is known only orally; that is, it is passed down within ethnic groups from older to younger members in the form of myths or family traditions that are sometimes acted out and not understood by outsiders. Until this history is written and can be studied, we must say that we don't know the true origins of African tie and dye. We can offer scattered pieces of information gathered by scientists, anthropologists, art historians, and observant visitors to Africa. Perhaps many such scatterings will someday form a whole picture, but at present, most textile scholars credit China as the innovator of tie and dye.

Dr. Renée Boser offers some history of tie and dye in Africa that is more substantial than our conjectures.[1] She notes that the Portuguese landed on the west coast of Africa during the middle of the fifteenth century and that in the Senegal-Gambia area they discovered, developed, and exploited the indigenous industries of weaving and dyeing cotton. When they colonized the Cape Verde

Islands, they deported hundreds of black slaves of different origins from the continent to the islands, to make them work in weaving and dyeing installations on cotton and indigo plantations. The Portuguese, it seems, perfected the native techniques, and the islands rapidly became an important fabric-production center. The Cape Verde Island cottons became famous on the coast and were used as exchange currency for the slave, gold, and ivory trade that came from the interior.

Dr. Boser tried to trace the diffusion of five related tie and dye techniques found in Senegal, Gambia, Guinea, Liberia, and Ivory Coast, and she discovered that

> The designs by specific resists (including those obtained by *froissage* [crinkling]) don't seem to be diffused—except in instances—by progressive transmission from one people to another. Their techniques have been obtained and assimilated on the spot in the region of Cap Vert (Senegal)* by indigenous peoples like, for example, the Wolof, and by certain Sudanese peoples present in Senegal. In the present case they were diffused in West Africa by their affiliates the Soninké (Sarakolés) and the Manding (Malinké) and their migrations and journeying through Gambia, Ivory Coast, Sudan (present-day Mali), etc.[2]

Techniques

Tie and dye is a resist method of patterning fabric that is achieved by withholding dye from certain areas of the fabric. This leaves the original undyed area as a background for the design in the dyed area (or vice versa). Among the Yoruba people of Nigeria the technique has been perfected to an everyday art form; it is called *adire,* meaning, quite literally, "to take, to tie and dye." In Yorubaland the term *adire eleso* indicates a design achieved by tying and sewing, as distinguished from *adire eleko,* where the design is formed by the application of a cassava-paste resist.

An excellent example of the techniques used in creating this Yoruba fabric design is shown in the following figures, where

* Near Dakar.

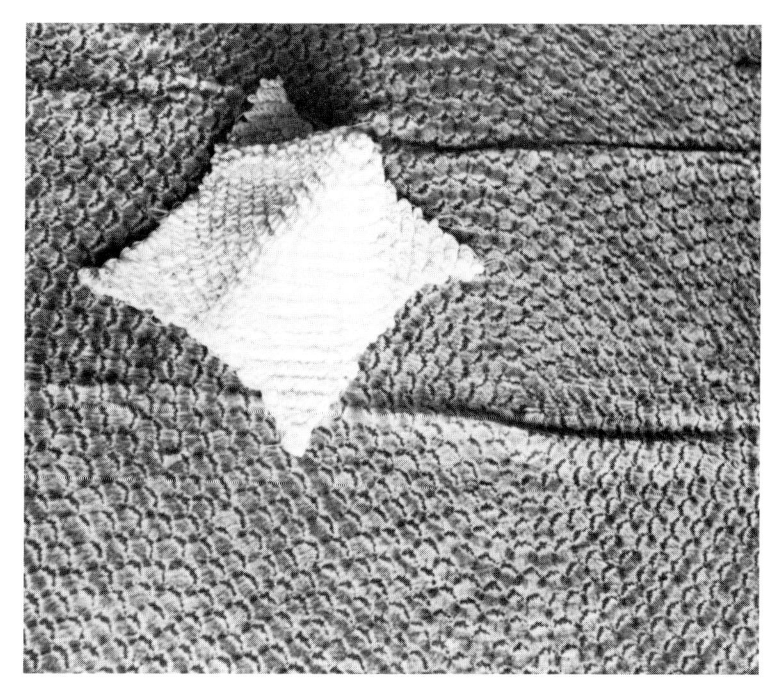

Figure 1. *Yoruba circular pattern tied in little circles before dyeing (small white piece of fabric), resting on the finished cloth after being dyed and having ties removed.*

one can see the technique employed in the process of tying and dyeing. The figures show sewing and tying with cotton and raffia threads and the resulting patterns where some of the threads have been removed. Figure 1 shows a contemporary Yoruba tied piece before dyeing and the resulting finished design. Figures 2 through 5 were taken in Dakar, Senegal, at the textile-dyeing co-operative, directed by Peace Corps volunteer Helen Anderson-Bauer, and show various stages of preparing, dyeing, and finishing the cloth, which include folding, pleating, tying, binding, knotting, and sewing.

We see details of a typical Yoruba adire eleso from Ibadan, Nigeria, in Figure 6. The results of two distinct techniques are discernible: 1) tying the fabric around the index finger to form each small circle, and 2) folding a slight tuck into the material, rolling

Figure 2. *Sewn and bound pieces from the Dakar cooperative, undyed, resting on an example of the pattern produced on fabric by this technique.*

Figure 3. *Adja Traoré of the Dakar cooperative soaking tied and bound pieces of fabric.*

Figure 4. *Threads knotted around small circles of fabric, locally called "Nyombos," before dyeing, at the Dakar cooperative.*

Figure 5. *Finished example of designs produced by knotted Nyombos technique.*

Figure 6. *Detail of a Yoruba* adire eleso *from Ibadan, Nigeria.*

Figure 7. *Indigo-dyed, intricately embroidered resist technique patterning from Senegal.*

a ridge of fabric over the tucked area, and, finally, sewing a whipping stitch over the design and pulling it taut before dipping. The resulting pattern is exquisitely detailed. One still sees a few strands of raffia clinging to the perfect design.

Figure 7 shows the delicacy that can be achieved by using fine embroidery as a resist. This indigo-dyed imported damask cloth is from Senegal. Though this particular fabric is relatively recent (1962), the same embroidery technique and its characteristic designs have a definite history among the Manding peoples of Senegal and probably the Wolof and Soninké as well. A similarly patterned piece in the British Museum dates from the celebrated Beving Collection made in 1880. Originally, most of these tie and dye techniques were used on handwoven fabrics, with the cotton fibers spun into threads on spindles still seen in use in certain areas of West Africa today.

One can only speculate on the numerous dyeing accidents that lead to the discovery of these techniques . . . perhaps cloths were twisted in the dyeing process, perhaps playing children tied their pebble toys in cloths and no one noticed until the cloths were dyed and dried. One could easily imagine an accidental circumstance for each of the techniques of folding, pleating, binding, sewing, and inserting fabric between wooden sticks—all methods seen in Africa today. Since the forerunners of today's fabrics have perished in the tropical regions that concern us, our imaginations must serve in lieu of tangible evidence.

Traditional Dyes

In connection with resist methods of forming patterns, one must consider the natural dye indigo, for it has been the most common and popular source of color throughout West Africa for centuries. Renée Boser's studies show that the first written evidence of indigo dyeing in West Africa appeared in the sixteenth century (which does not negate the possibility that its use occurred centuries before that; expeditions in Mali have revealed indigenous woven designs of indigo threads close to eight hundred years old). Dr. A. Bühler notes that over fifty plants are known to contain indigo and that further research would probably reveal more.[3]

Indigo dyeing is a vast subject. A look at the indigo dyeing processes of the Yoruba of southwest Nigeria will show how this long and arduous process provides the rich color found in traditionally dyed textiles, a richness somehow missing in fabrics made with modern chemical dyes.

Indigo is not soluble in water and must be reduced (the oxygen removed) and dissolved in an alkaline solution before it will adhere to the fabric. When a fabric is soaked in the dye solution long enough to absorb the potential color, the material is removed and hung to dry. Exposure to the air causes reoxidation and brings out the blue color. The dye has then been absorbed by the fibers of the fabric, is again insoluble, and therefore colorfast.

The indigo used in Yorubaland grows wild and is called *elu* (*Lonchocarpus cyanescens*). The entire process (picking the young leaves, pounding them with a mortar and pestle, forming them into balls, drying them in the sun, making the alkaline ash water, and performing the actual dyeing) is done by women.

In the book entitled *Adire Cloth in Nigeria*, edited by Jane Barbour and Doig Simmonds, Nancy Stanfield writes,

> The process of indigo dyeing is a lengthy one. The dye is obtained from a plant and a mordant is also made by the dyer herself to mix with the colour in the water. The actual preparing of the ingredients is hard work and the process of dyeing is exacting and tedious. The entire process is carried out by the women. They share the labours and carefully divide the results between themselves. Any surplus materials they produce are sold in the market.
>
> The plant used for the dye in Western Nigeria is a species of *Lonchocarpus*, a climbing shrub, called *elu* in Yoruba. The mordant is the salt in wood ash and this the dyer gets by dripping water through it.[4]

Stanfield points out that while indigo dyeing in Western Nigeria is always done by the women, in other areas this is not so. In Northern Nigeria, men do the dyeing; and instead of earthenware dye pots sunk into the ground, they use deep cement pits, which in Kano are a large tourist attraction (Plate 1, see insert). Drawing on Stanfield's essay, I will describe the way dyeing was, and often still is, done in the ancient Yoruba tradition.

Nothing in indigo dyeing is easy. Even maintaining the mud kilns for the preparation of mordant ash is hard work. Any cracks in the thick walls are repaired before each use. Layers of wood, from dry sticks to green boughs, are layered on top of a sieve that lies about a foot from the top of the kiln. Then, balls formed of old ash from the salt-ash pots, wood ash from house cooking fires, and the water left over from the last dyeing are placed on top of the sticks. When these form a big pile, rising above the walls of the kiln, the sticks are ready to be lighted.

The kiln is prepared on one day and the firing is done on the next. The fire is kept burning for about ten to twelve hours or until all the wood turns to ash. The ash is collected continuously, to be formed into balls that are left to dry. Any ash balls not used are taken to the market or saved. When all the wood has burned, the kiln is left to cool for a night and a day.

To prepare the mordant water, the dyer uses a pot with a good-sized hole in the side and one with a hole in the bottom. The pot with the hole in the side is put into a shallow hole in the ground so that it doesn't tip over. The pot with the hole in the bottom is put over this. Dry sticks, old dye-leaf fibers, and the broken-up ash balls are arranged over the hole in the bottom, forming a sieve. Water is poured into the top pot; the water drains through the ash taking the salt with it. The dyer collects this salt water by passing a bowl through the hole in the side of the bottom pot and transferring this salt water to the dye pot.

The dyer pounds the fresh green elu leaves with mortar and pestle until they form a pulp, which is then formed by hand into tennis-ball-sized globes of dye. Nothing is wasted in this ancient procedure—the dye solution left after a fabric has absorbed all the color in the water is used to form the ash balls. The leaf fibers that float from the indigo balls to the top of the dye pot are used as part of the sieve in making the salt-ash water.

The number of indigo balls used depends on the color the dyer wants—more balls are used for deeper colors. Up to a hundred fifty would make a blue-black shade. For a good, popular blue, about fifty balls are used. (Stanfield tells us that a "particular dyer uses fresh dye for each dipping of a cloth.")

The balls are broken up before being put into the pot. The mordant water is then poured over the dye and the entire mixture is left to stand for about three days; it is stirred occasionally. As the water is absorbed by the cloth during the dyeing process, more of the salt-ash water is added. The dye will keep for only about five days, as it develops an unpleasant smell that is often passed on to the dyed cloths.

Stitched and tied cloths to be dyed are totally immersed in the solution and gently squeezed by hand three or four times for about two minutes at a time. Between dippings they are left on the draining board next to the pot. Then they are left in the sun to dry. This series of dippings and dryings is repeated five or six times, depending on the strength of the dye and the color desired. The pots are kept covered and are never stirred. When the cloths are first taken out of the pots they are a greenish color that quickly changes to blue as seen in Plate 1 (see insert).

For a cloth that is patterned with starch resist, the process is slightly different. It is folded gently into thirds, the sides and middle carefully held by the dyer. The cloth is dipped into the dye and held still for about three minutes. Then it is lifted out and placed on the draining board to be folded in a slightly different place before being redipped. The entire cloth is dyed in this manner.

Dyed cloths are never rinsed, whether they have starch on them or not; they always drip dry. To get the starch off, the cloth is hung on a bamboo pole; buckets of water are thrown on the hanging cloth, and the starch, which turns into a kind of blue mud, is then scraped off with a stick. However, there is always a little dye left on the starched parts; this slowly disappears with repeated washings, leaving the design progressively sharper.

The finishing is done by beating the cloths, a process with which men and children often help. The cloths are folded in thirds and stretched out on a board between two people who hit the cloth with heavy mallets. One of the beaters pulls the cloth toward him until the entire piece is at one end. The cloth is folded again and beaten and the process repeated until the cloth is folded into a twelve-inch square.

In 1974 I visited a typical dyeing compound in Ibadan, with earthenware pots sunk slightly into the ground, as shown in Figure 8. I was told that one hundred balls of dried indigo are placed in the wood-ash filtered water (alkaline lye) contained in these pots. The containers are covered and left for seven days, at which time the indigo will be ready for the dyeing process. The crushed leaves can be seen lifted from the vat with the stirring stick. The dyers (*aloro*) in this compound also use a mixture of natural and

Figure 8. *Contemporary indigo dyeing compound in Ibadan, Nigeria.*

synthetic indigo which has commercial washing soda added to the liquid preparation. This type of solution sits for only five days before it is used and is considered inferior to the seven-day mixture. It is said that the five-day *adire* cloths are for the tourist market while the seven-day cloths, which are more colorfast, are made for the Yoruba clients.

Fred Gerber has spent the better part of the past fifteen or twenty years working with natural dyes and has written extensively about them, including his experiences with indigo.[5] He wrote me a letter in 1974 which offers a simplified introduction to indigo and its processes. The following excerpts with some modifications by Mr. Gerber are reprinted with his permission:

"The dye material is a transparent, perhaps yellowish, water-soluble glucoside that occurs in several plants of quite unrelated botany. The most familiar these days is indigo itself (*Indigofera*) but it was the same chemical material, or glucoside, which is found in woad (*Isatis*).

"In the West African area, the genus *Lonchocarpus* also produces the precursor of indigo. This plant is a semiwoody, shrubby vine, the leaves of which are prepared in much the same manner as were the leaves of woad, composted and made into balls, in the Middle Ages (and before and since).

"To obtain the glucoside (indican from *Indigofera*), the plant tops are soaked in water for various periods from twelve to eighteen hours. Then this water is decanted into vats where it is violently agitated to incorporate oxygen which reacts with the colorless indican and forms the oxidized blue pigment indigo. Since indigo is water *in*soluble, the pigment settles. After a settling period, the top liquid is drained off and discarded. The sediment is collected and dried—often in cloth bags or wooden flats. This is the natural indigo of commerce. In the case of woad and *Lonchocarpus*, the leaves are composted and the resulting pulp is made into balls which contain a lot of other organic matter in addition to the coloring material which is now in an oxidized, insoluble state (Figure 9).

"It is these indigo balls made from *Lonchocarpus* which one buys in some West African markets. Indigo balls made of woad were used in Europe before indigo from *Indigofera* was imported

Figure 9. *An unusual example of dried natural indigo cakes tied together with raffia in Ivory Coast.*

from the Far East, although evidence does suggest that at least some indigo was probably imported from the Far East during the Phoenician and Egyptian periods. At this point the dyers, as distinguished from the producers, enter the process, for evidence supports the contention that the producer was not generally the user of the dyestuff. (In some African villages today and in some of the islands of the South Seas, the producer may also be the user, as may be said for parts of India. Regrettably, today, even in these more unsophisticated regions synthetic indigo has largely replaced the natural.)

"The trick now is to return the indigo, insoluble and blue, to the soluble and 'white' indigo form. This must be done before the fibers of whatever kind can absorb it where, on oxidation, it may again form the permanent blue pigment. For this, a reducing agent and a dissolving agent are required. Solvents for indigo are generally considered to be strong acids or strong alkalies. However, the strength of the alkali is not critical when one considers that for millennia urine vats were used and persist in being used in some rural areas for small domestic dyeings. Fermenting urine produces ammonia, a weak base or alkali, from the breakdown of various proteins and amino acids, while the activity of the bacteria serves the reducing function.

"Of course, using stale urine offends our fastidious senses these days and the method is seldom used anymore in our more modern societies except as confirmation of old methods, or where old domestic recipes remain in use.

"It matters not what materials are used—iron sulphate, slaked lime water, household lye, sodium hydrosulphite, bran, or whatever else the recipe calls for—as long as the needs are satisfied to perform the two fundamental acts: the reduction of the indigo to indigo white and its solution in some alkali, then the application of this form of the pigment to the fibers and eventually the oxidation and return of the indigo white to the blue indigo, in place.

"The only different recipe (in principle) is that which calls for dissolving indigo in concentrated sulphuric acid, to make what we call an acid extract of indigo. (The compound is different from that of indigo.) This acid extract is sometimes partially neutralized with chalk during its preparation. The recipes, although frequent in the dye literature, have lost favor with most modern dyers who protest that the lasting qualities do not compare with the older vat methods. It was, nevertheless, very popular in those centuries just prior to the commercial synthesis of dyestuffs. Our experiences do not totally support the adverse contentions. It should not be used for kitchen or table linens which would have to be subject to prolonged and frequent washing or to those objects which might have to be exposed to long duration of sunlight. However, these limitations do not necessarily apply to the products of today's craft-weaver dyers.

"The rubbing off, or 'crocking,' of indigo from some fabrics may be the result of two different factors. First, the indigo may have been deposited on the fibers as indigo rather than as indigo white; it will then 'crock' or rub off as a result of poor dyeing. Or, secondly, under accumulations of perspiration, as may be the case in terms of North Africa's Blue Men, the indigo might behave the same way as in a urine vat and small amounts of reduced and dissolved indigo could possibly be redeposited and oxidize on the skin of the wearer. The 'crocking' of some West African fabrics is considered (locally) not only desirable but a 'test' for the 'real thing.' (The resist processes—tie and dye, paste, and wax batik—sometimes may not permit of sufficient time in the dye-bath for really reliable deposits of the indigo white. Any indigo deposited as indigo during dyeing and not removed by washing and proper finishing will eventually crock."

Unlike contemporary American craftsmen and craftswomen who always wash the excess dye from their fabric, the Yoruba never rinse theirs. The excess dye, particularly the metallic sheen which appears on unwashed indigo-dyed fabrics after the finishing process is considered an asset and a selling point in the market-place. Attempts are even made to pound powdered indigo onto the surface of the fabric before sending it to market. Cloths can be seen in the Ibadan marketplaces where indigo is caked on the fabric and can be removed by simply scraping a fingernail over the surface. This overloading of dye is discouraging to the naïve tourist who buys the fabric for its charm and finds much of the original color is lost in washing. Although many remedies are recommended to help fix indigo after the initial dyeing process has been completed—such as soaking the fabric in vinegar, salt, or alum and water—nothing can be done to save a cloth that has been inadequately dyed in the first place.

This introduction to indigo dyeing would not be complete without some reference to its ritualistic relationship to religious practices. Susanne Wenger and Ulli Beier provide this insight on the Yoruba people:

> It is significant for Yoruba culture that every activity in life has a basic religious significance. Indigo dyeing is closely linked with the worship of a goddess called "Iya Mapo." "Iya Mapo" is an important orisha, who protects all exclusively female trades like dyeing, pottery, oil pressing, soap making, etc.
>
> She is also the deity of female sex. Every fourth day is her "ose" or day of worship which happens to coincide with "jakuta," the day sacred to Sango. On this day women will bring her sacrifices of "ekuru" (made of beans), "adun" (made of maize), and groundnuts.
>
> Every fourth "ose," however, the "alaro" will stop all work on

> the dyeing pots and spend the day celebrating and worshiping "Iya Mapo." Then they will dance in the shrine and sing the praise songs (oriki) of the goddess . . .[6]

The origins of indigo and other sources of color in nature are often attributed to supernatural forces in most African societies and have a place in their religious myths, legends, and folktales. This brings the dyer and the performance of her art close to God and the spiritual essence of all natural matter.[7]

An early example of the use of indigo in a tie and dye fabric from Liberia is seen in Figure 10, which shows a detailed close-up of a late nineteenth-century shawl. This piece illustrates the use of the typical cotton fabric: narrow strips handwoven on a traditional men's loom, sewn together, and then tied with raffia around smooth pebbles—resulting in the beautiful star-burst patterns which time has made only more beautiful in its tapestrylike detail.

An extraordinary series of raffia-sewn, indigo-dyed fabrics from the Bamun peoples of Cameroon is found at the Musée de l'Homme in Paris. These fabrics were probably made at the turn of the century and the museum has very similarly designed examples of each step of production. Figure 11 shows the first step: with a brown dye, complex geometric designs have been drawn on the large, natural-colored, handwoven fabric. Like most of the early indigenous African textiles, the piece was formed by sewing narrow strips of handwoven cloth together. In the second step (Figure 12), the lines of the designs are carefully oversewn with raffia, one stitch very close to the next in order to prevent the leakage of dye into the protected area. Once the fabric has been dyed in indigo, the raffia threads stand out light against the background and the pattern appears clearly, even before the raffia stitches are removed (Figure 13). Finally, the threads are cut and removed and the intricate design is fully revealed. Figure 14 shows a portion of the cloth, providing a closer view of the variations of the designs. The cloth is quite large, measuring approximately seventy-four inches in length and fifty-three inches in width.

Many other natural dyes are used in Africa. One that is often found in combination with indigo is derived from kola nuts (the process is explained fully in the following chapter). Another im-

Figure 10. *Pebble-tied starburst pattern in natural indigo on handwoven fabric from Liberia (late nineteenth century).*

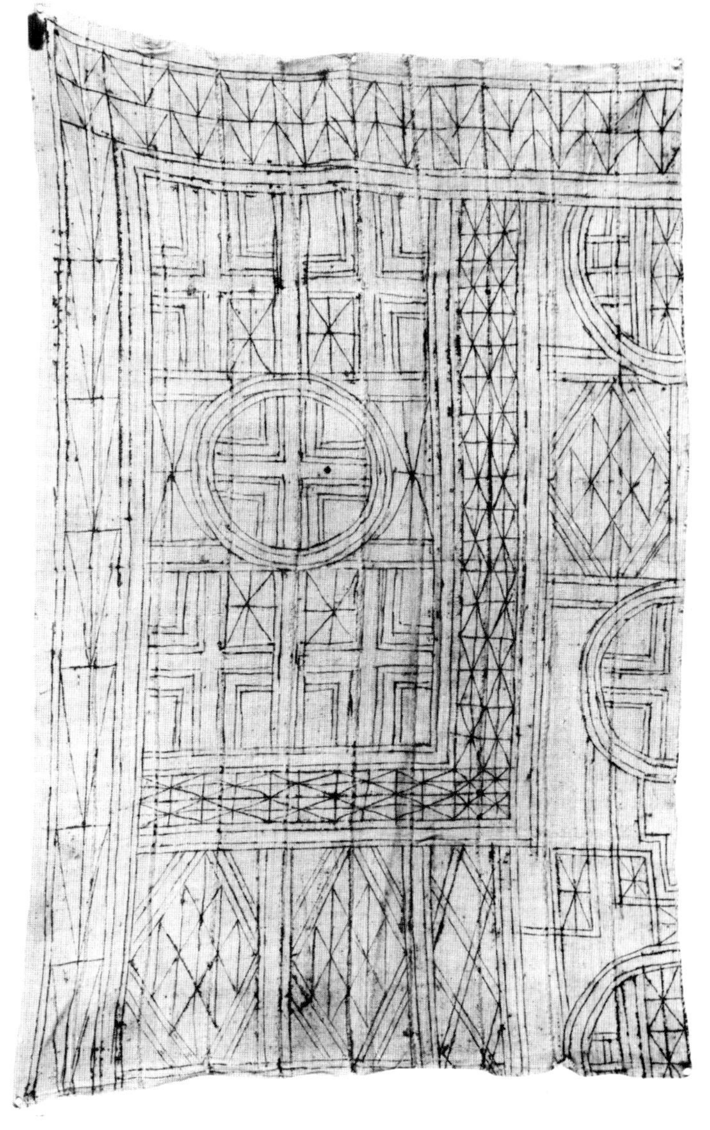

Figure 11. *Bamun textile design, first step: the pattern is traced in brown dye on natural, handwoven fabric.*

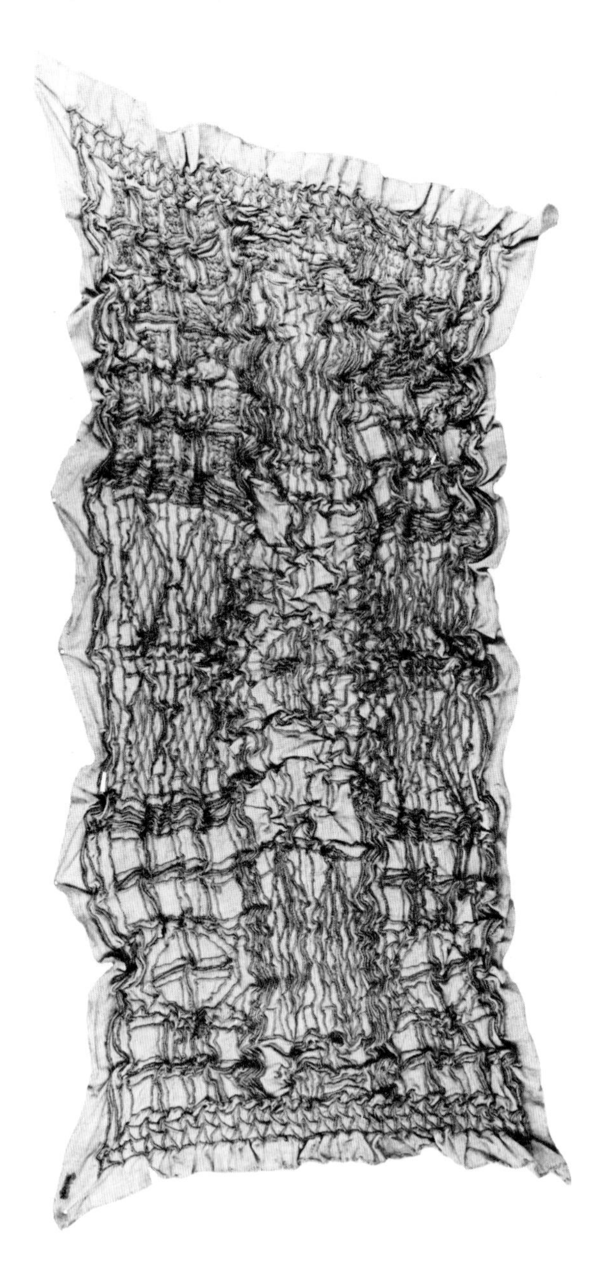

Figure 12. *Bamun textile design, step two: the pattern is very closely oversewn with raffia threads to form a resist to the subsequent dyeing process.*

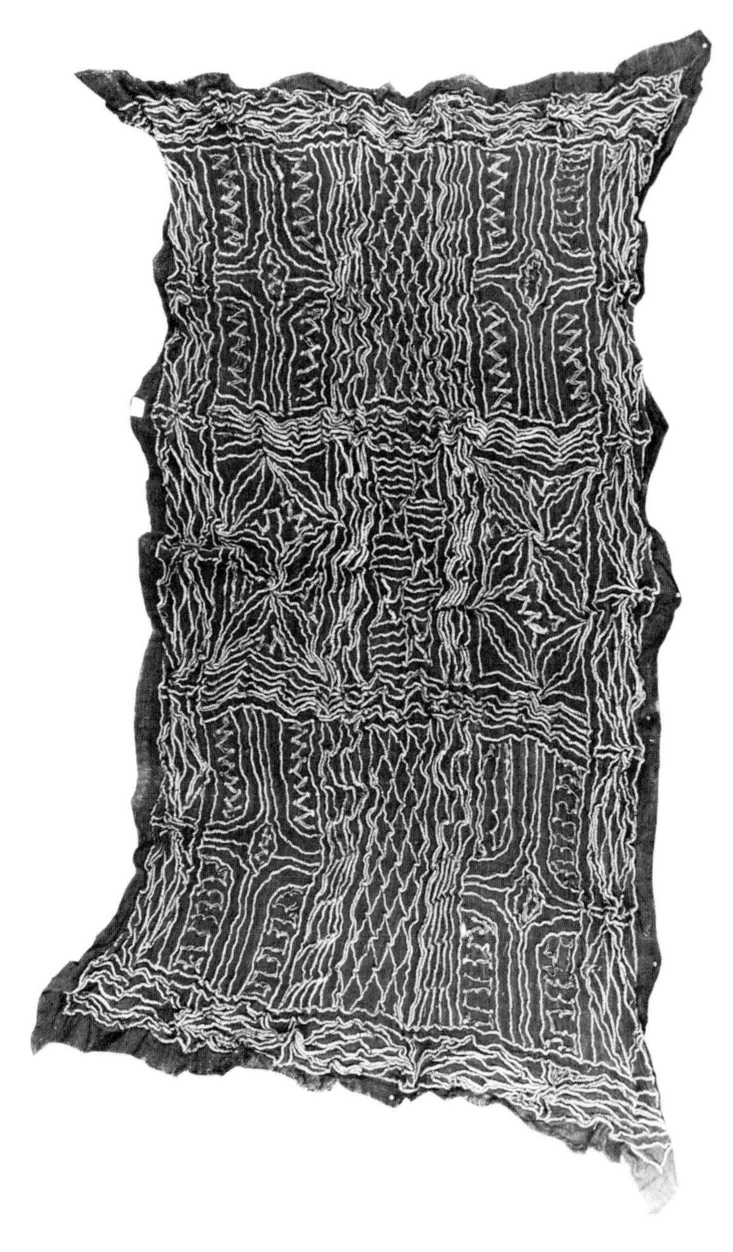

Figure 13. *Bamun textile design, step three: the fabric is dyed in indigo, showing the raffia-sewn stitches as a light pattern against the dark background.*

Figure 14. *The finished Bamun textile with the raffia sewing removed, revealing the light pattern that "resisted" the indigo dye and produced the highly intricate and exacting symbolic designs desired by the artists/craftsmen.*

portant dye used in West and Central Africa is camwood. Mrs. Esther Warner Dendel, artisan and author of several books on Africa, describes her experience using camwood for tie-dyeing in Liberia in 1944:

"When I knew that I would be leaving West Africa, after having lived in Liberia from 1941 to 1944, I decided to dye all the white cotton fabric in my house with the natural dyestuffs used by the tribal women. These women said that everything that grows has a color in it, that God made it that way, but we are not wise enough to know how to get color out of everything.

"Yardage was one of the many war-time shortages, but I did have sheets and dish towels which had been softened by much washing.

"My friend who knew how to use camwood was from the Kpelle tribe. Her English vocabulary was limited to 'Yeah, Ma, so.' She used this phrase regardless of whether she meant yes or no and she used it even if she did not understand my question. She wanted to keep a sort of soft purring of a friendship going between us and this was how she did it. My interpreter was male and was not allowed in the vicinity of the dye vat which is sacred to women in Liberia.

"The dye pot was a huge iron kettle. It represented the sole material wealth of my friend. Whether some oxidation of the iron had any effect on the color is one thing I still wonder about. The woman brought a five-gallon kerosene tin filled with water and dumped this in the kettle. Then, carefully and reverently, she built a fire beneath it. A ring of stones supported the kettle. Next she added a hamper of limes which she had reduced to a pulp by beating them in a mortar. While she did this, I busied myself with wrapping small stones in the fabric to be dyed.

"The camwood was in the form of shavings and sawdust. It had been previously boiled for some time and allowed to stand in the water in which it had been boiled.

"What information I had about camwood was gleaned from two volumes of *Liberia* by Sir Harry Johnson: page 71—'Camwood (Baphia nitida), which produces a crimson dye, was much sought after from the sixteenth to the nineteenth century'; page 104—Camwood is mentioned alongside gold, ivory, and pepper as one of the inducements which brought Europeans to West Africa during the seventeenth and eighteenth centuries; page 400—Camwood is listed as one of the exports of Liberia 'at the time of writing' (The book, now out of print, was published in 1906); page 410—'CAMWOOD—At one time—in the seventies and eighties—camwood was a most important article of export in Liberia (as with other parts of the west coast), and as much as forty pounds and fifty pounds per ton were realized; but the discovery of aniline dyes had a disastrous effect, and now, although small quantities are still shipped, the price (ten to thirteen pounds) is too low to encourage a steady export. These remarks apply to annatto and other dyestuffs, all of which have been affected by the introduction of aniline.'

"These sparse facts were my only background on camwood except for my experience carving it. When first cut into, the heartwood is the color of flame. It gradually darkens as the cut is exposed to the air.

"My friend strained the murky camwood brew through a basketlike sieve she had made for the purpose. While the temperature raised to a simmer in the pot, she immersed my rock-tied sheet in a can of plain water and let it drain over a bush. She then lowered the fabric into the pot and agitated it gently with a stick. It simmered about an hour. At the end of that time it was obvious that my friend wanted something she did not have. I brought my interpreter within shouting distance, but he sulked and was reluctant.

" 'She wants salt,' he said finally. Salt was precious in those days. It came down from the Sahara in great slabs like bacon, carried over the trails on men's heads. Our interpreter did not think salt should be wasted on cloth, when his own belly craved it.

"Muttering darkly, the man finally brought us some chunks of rather grey-looking salt. These were dissolved in a can of water. After the loose color had been rinsed from my tie-dye, it was immersed in the salt water. My friend carried it to the interpreter and instructed him to tell me to allow the cloth to 'sleep in the salt' overnight.

"The next day I dried the fabric in the sun and undid the wrappings below the pebbles. Later in the United States I used the camwood-dyed sheets for curtains and sent them to the commercial laundry without any noticeable loss of color. The color is a rust rather than a crimson and I would like to discover whether it might be a different color with an alkaline mixture rather than the acidic mixture we had from the limes. On my next visit to

Africa I hope to experiment further with camwood as a natural dye, trying various mordants."

Bamun Fabrics

Little information is available about the impressive Bamun fabrics. We do know that an extensive *artisanat* existed in the capital city of Foumban at the beginning of the twentieth century. The creative monarch, King Njoya,[8] probably is responsible for the artisanat and the six dye pits in Foumban reported to contain various colors to enrich the spectrum of available shades. Dr. Renée Boser wonders if possibly the initial introduction of indigo dyeing among the Bamun was sponsored by Njoya himself; earlier, the Bamun were known to use tying techniques with a brown dye on bark cloth.[9]

Designs

Hoping to understand the origins of the Bamun designs and the Bamun use of indigo, I consulted Professor Claude Tardits, a noted anthropologist teaching at the Sorbonne. He spent many years among the Bamun and Bamileke peoples of Cameroon and published a book on the Bamileke in 1960. He has spent the past ten years compiling a history of the Bamun kingdom and he is my source for the following information on the Bamun.

The designs featured in Figure 14 came to the Bamun as imported cloths brought from the Benue River area in Nigeria by the Hausa peoples during the latter part of the nineteenth century, when Njoya was king (or sultan).

Njoya adopted the raffia-sewn, indigo-dyed Hausa textiles as royal cloths, restricted at first to his and his mother's exclusive use. Later, with King Njoya's permission, persons of high authority within the king's court were allowed to wear the special fabrics. In their portraits of Bamun kings and their courts, contemporary Bamun artists, including one of the most celebrated, Ibraham Njoya, a descendant of the king, depict the royal per-

Figure 15. *The ancient Hausa dye pits in Kano, Nigeria.*

sonage wearing this cloth draped voluminously around his waist. It looks as though additional lengths of cloth flow from his waist and are held like a train behind him by members of his court.

Njoya gave the royal cloths a name: they were called *Ntieya.* The Hausa craftsmen were installed in the palace workshops at Foumban where they proceeded to teach the Bamun the art of indigo dyeing. In the traditional Hausa manner, the dyeing was done by men. Sunken dye pits, similar to the famous Hausa dye pits in Kano, Nigeria, were used (Figure 15). The Hausa introduced the type of indigo known as *Indigofera tinctoria,* one of the most widely used forms of indigo throughout the world. The Bamun called it *suni.*

When the Bamun craftsmen first learned the dyeing and raffia-sewn resist patterning from the Hausa, they probably repeated the same Hausa patterns given to them. These designs appear to be related to Hausa embroidery.[10] The cross within the circle and the graceful linear design forming three loops (detail, Figure 14) are apparent in Hausa embroidery. However, the meaning of the Hausa designs is obscure even to historians. Although some of the

Figure 16. *An elaborate Bamun textile with typical abstract designs and symbols.*

geometric designs on Figure 14 could be abstractions of an important Bamun theme—the double bell (Figure 16, center) and the line forming three loops might be related to a character in Njoya's alphabet[11]—chances are very slim that there is any Bamun symbolism in this cloth. It is probably Hausa in design.

However, as the Bamun artisans became more accustomed to the craft and the technique, they began to introduce typical Bamun designs into the cloths. In Figure 16 a double bell appears above and below the repeats of diamond-patterned, dotted rectangles in every row of the textile. These bell motifs (a significant Bamun symbol) represent the original metal bells which in

Bamun tradition were given only to special people within the court—high officials and the sons of the king. This is further confirmation of the fabric as a royal cloth.

The motif of the diamond-patterned rectangle, mentioned in connection with the double bells, is probably of Bamun origin (Figure 16). Its design and shape closely resemble the typical Bamun sheath used to hold a sword. Also reminiscent of the Bamun is the chevronlike rectangle in the center row at the left and right. These markings are very similar to popular designs on Bamun pottery. The white squares with dark bursts repeated regularly over the fabric may be nonrepresentational designs resulting from the dye penetrating the sewing technique—or they may represent leaves. The dotted lines bordering this fabric and interspersed among designs on the other textiles are common designs on Bamun buildings, as are various linear patterns.

Figure 17 augments Professor Tardits' theory that the Hausa textiles gradually became more and more Bamun in design. The fabric pictured is not available for study, so it is impossible to determine the techniques involved in its creation. Even when enlarged, the photographs do not give an adequate idea of the technique used. Parts of the designs appear to be related to the raffia-sewn textiles and could have been achieved through this method. However, raffia sewing would not be adequate to keep the dyes away from the large expanse of white figures and leave such a perfectly delineated edge. Paste or wax resist could achieve this effect, but supposedly these methods were not known to the Bamun. Direct painting, however, was. So parts of this large fabric may have been made through sewn resist, as in the previous fabrics, and other parts through direct painting—a combination of techniques known to both the Hausa and the Bamun. Perhaps each section was done separately and sewn together when the parts were completed.

Examination of Figure 14 showed that shades of light blue had been added to parts of the geometric designs with an almost brushlike mark. This would negate the idea that the cloths were immersed in additional dyebaths after part of the raffia sewing had been removed. Even if the fabric is not a resist pattern but

Figure 17. *A Bamun textile featuring realistic human and animal figures along with geometric and symbolic designs.*

was completely hand painted, it is relevant in showing the design progression from the original Hausa motifs to the Bamun patterns.

Although the motifs appearing in Figure 17 are of symbolic significance in Bamun cosmology, there is no legend or myth represented in the patterns on the textile. No definite story or folktale is being told. The artists who created the cloth apparently worked freely, incorporating the more realistic Bamun designs with the abstract motifs. The photographs are dated 1947, but these fabrics were no longer made in Bamun country during the 1940s. With the death of Njoya in 1931 and the increased European domination, the once active workshops of the royal palace at Foumban fell into disuse and the creation of these beautiful textiles ended.

Yale art historian Robert Thompson complements Dr. Tardits' theory on the origins of the Bamun cloth designs.[12] A combination of these men's findings reveals dual influences on the sources of these fabrics as well as on the designs and their symbolic meanings.

Dr. Thompson has conducted extensive field studies on the Bamun and on the Ejagham (or Ekoi) peoples of southeast Nigeria. He concludes that the secret *Ngbe* (leopard) society of the Ejagham was adopted by the Bamun. Further, *nsibidi,* the ancient script of the Ejagham, was incorporated into Bamun Ngbe society ritual, graphically as well as in a mime-dancing sign language. Also, trade existed between the two societies as is evidenced partly by the transport and sale of blue-and-white indigo-dyed cloth that could represent the earlier Bamun cloth.

The nsibidi signs—the ones adopted by the Bamun—are linked to designs found on ancient *akwanshi*—basalt monoliths raised in the memory of Ejagham chiefs in the Cross River valley—and to faded tattoos still visible on the faces of elderly Ejagham people. The monuments are sometimes embellished with concentric circles, spirals, squares, triangles, or circled crosses. Some such signs remain within the continuing secret scripts of the Ejagham.[13] From Dr. Thompson's chart of eight fully explained nsibidi signs, we find that two of these motifs relate directly to those found on Bamun textiles.

The dominant design on the Bamun fabrics of a cross within a circle could easily represent symbol number 8: "the Janus, a quartered circle, with one small circle within each quadrant, suggesting the meeting of the earth with the sky, or female with male, as in Janus-helmets; the four small circles standing for the four eyes of clairvoyance."[14] The second important series of designs on Bamun textiles are the many variations of small triangles which are repeated over most of the cloth, sometimes enclosed in a diamond shape; at other times included in parts of a circle; and still others used where the small triangles form separate, four-sided, swastikalike motifs. This can be directly related to symbols on the chart: number 6, "the checkerboard, representing, in stylized form, the multiplication of the spots of the leopard's pelt," and 7, "the same motif rendered as a field of shaded or solid diamonds."[15]

Dr. Thompson examined the relationship between Ejagham and Bamun masks and the Bamun textiles and concluded:

> It is significant that Grassland helmet masks may be worn with gowns of Bamun painted-resist-dyed cloth; it is significant because Bamun cloth bears signs which relate to Ejagham ideographs, hence a sign-like mask is balanced by a dress of signs. The connections linking Ejagham writing with Grassland decoration are clear, as can be evidenced by a comparison of published Ejagham *Nsibidi* signs with Grassland motifs in bead-working, divination, and wood-carving. The concordance is not absolute, and a good deal of Grasslands creativity has enriched the original fund of forms, but it is, nevertheless, substantial. To sum up, the calligraphic influence of the Ejagham may well have included the Grasslands . . . which refer back to *Nsibidi*-like Bamun textile patterns.[16]

As early as 1912, P. A. Talbot provided an appendix of Nsibidi signs, in his book *In the Shadow of the Bush*,[17] which coordinate with several of Thompson's signs. One of the motifs—the sign for the butterfly—is duplicated exactly on the Musée de l'Homme textile, as shown in detail (Figure 14). The graceful, white, triple-looped motif is repeated twice in opposite corners of the two squares within a light-dotted, dark background. The same sign in Bamun script means "the skin" (leopard skin in this case?) according to I. Dugast and M. D. W. Jeffreys' "L'Écriture des Bamun."[18]

The relationship between Ngbe societies in both countries is confirmed by David Dalby's 1968 study. Dalby said that the most extensive and elaborate recorded graphic symbols in West Africa include the Nsibidi graphic system of the Cross River tribes in Eastern Nigeria. It was probably not a coincidence that the traditional Nsibidi system belonged to the same general area as the modern indigenous scripts of Cameroon and Eastern Nigeria.[19] He continues:

> The use of *Nsibidi* does not appear to have extended far over the border into Cameroun, but appears to have reached to within at least 100 miles of Foumban, where chief Njoya devised his Bamum [sic] script. After the 'stimulus' of his dream and of the magic potion which he afterwards drank, Njoya commanded his subjects to draw simple pictures and symbols, and to name them, so that he could employ them in devising his "book" . . . Since the initial design of the Bamum characters thus appears to have been a collective enterprise, it would not be surprising indeed if it did not contain at least an echo of the neighbouring system of *Nsibidi*.[20]

Dalby provides a chart (*Table V: Comparisons Between Nsibidi and the Bamum Script*)[21] which gives conclusive evidence of relationships in design and meaning between the two scripts. He also confirms Thompson's field research by stating, "*Nsibidi* is associated also with symbols used for calabash-decoration and for tattooing, and with a code of physical gestures."[22]

The presence of the patterned indigo-dyed cloth may have been due to trading among the peoples of that area as documented by E. M. Chives.[23] Blue-and-white cloths were referred to as "stenciled," which could easily have included the sew-resist fabrics, as a variety of methods were indiscriminately referred to in French-speaking West Africa as "batik."[24] These indigo-dyed, patterned cloths could represent the Bamun fabrics restricted to royal usage in King Njoya's court, which he named Ntieya. Hausa traders handled European cloth in this area at the end of the nineteenth century, and it's possible they brought the highly valued blue-and-white decorative cloth to Njoya's court, knowing the king's interest in exotic fabrics. The Hausa traders may have encouraged indigo dyers to come from Northern Nigeria to settle in Njoya's court and set up the indigo-dyeing compounds. They established themselves among the Bamun and consequently perpetuated the sew-dye resist techniques in the textiles they brought with them.

Tie and dye is not confined to the west coast of Africa. One of the most beautiful tie-dye textiles in the African section of the Smithsonian Museum was collected in Zaïre in the mid 1890s by the Honorable R. Dorsey Mohun.[25] This stunning fabric (Plate 2—see insert) offers a variety of luscious colors: a deep, muted plum acts as a shadowy counterpart to the strips of strong orange, patterned in an intricate motif. The outermost strip is charcoal-black incorporating three pencil-thin rows of cut-pile (plush) raffia.[26] This particular piece is doubly intriguing because the cloth is attributed to the Genyan inhabitants of the Stanley Falls area of Zaïre, a people whose artisanal achievements do not include making pile cloth. Evidence shows that the creation of pile cloth in Zaïre was limited to the Kuba, Bushongo, and related peoples, who live in the area crossed by the Sankuru and Kasai rivers.[27] So the presence of pile cloth in an area which does not produce it remains a mystery.[28]

Mrs. Barbara Stuckenrath, an anthropologist at the Smithsonian, suggests that perhaps the pile-cloth section of the Genya tie and dye was originally a long, narrow, partially plain-weave, partially cut-pile raffia cloth used as currency—a common practice in the Zaïre area—and that this particular strip may have been traded from the Kasai area into the Genya territory around Stanley Falls, then incorporated in this exquisitely crafted cloth and worn by a Genya chief. Mlle. H. Van Geluwe, director of ethnology of the Musée Royal de l'Afrique Central at Tervuren, Belgium, believes that the entire piece is from the Kasai area. Her view is supported by a number of strikingly similar pieces in the textile collection of the Tervuren museum, all of which are documented as Kuba in origin. This research confirms the fact that tie and dye techniques as well as those necessary for the making of pile cloth were practiced in the Kasai area. Perhaps the Smithsonian cloth arrived in the Stanley Falls area as a gift sent to the Genya chief by a Kuba sovereign.

The sources of the dyes are less mysterious, thanks to a recent article on "Kuba Embroidered Cloth," by Dr. Monni Adams, appearing in *African Arts* magazine.[29] Dr. Adams says that all the dyes are obtained from regional plant sources and she notes that the main source of red dye is a redwood (mainly *Pterocarpus soyauxii* and *P. tinctorius*), best known in the western Zaïre region as *tukula* and called *tool* in Bushong. It is not camwood (*Baphia nitida*), which is a species that grows only in West Africa and does not occur in the Zaïre (former Congo) River basin. When the redwood dye is combined with black dye made from various plant and mineral materials, a highly prized wine-red results. Blue, mauve, and blue-violet dyes are also produced from local plants (although indigo is not mentioned). Thus, the deep plum color in this cloth may have resulted from a mixture of the available reds, blues, and blacks. Or it may be one of the color tones resulting from fading in the sun or perhaps some effect of chemical change over time, a possibility Dr. Adams suggests.[30]

Contemporary examples of the traditional use of dyes are available in abundance and offer a spectacular view of the African dyer's expertise with natural dyes. Infinite variety of color is achieved through these methods in tie and dye. With only two natural dyes—indigo (blue) and kola nut (rust)—the craftsmen and women have created patterns of great variety, ranging from the blackest blue through every subtle shade of the olive greens, clear blues, and earthy ochres (Plates 3 and 4—see insert). These designs were made by sewing diagonally across the folded fabric with a thick thread and pulling the rather widely spaced stitches together tightly. Then the stitched area was dipped in a kola-nut dye, dried, and redipped in indigo. Numerous immersions darken the blue to the desired shade. The choice of fabric affects the nuances of color—in many cases the alternately shiny and dull surface designs of an imported cotton damask offer multiple richness from one dyebath.

Both men and women are skilled in the use of natural dyes throughout West Africa. In fact, some fabrics purchased at Treichville, Ivory Coast, may very well have originated in neighboring Liberia and Guinea or nearby Sierra Leone, Senegal, and Gambia, since trading—and smuggling—from country to country is common. Various other vegetable coloring agents may have been combined with the indigo. Observations of dyeing techniques in Sierra Leone have revealed the use of avocado (seeds, fruit, and leaves) in some instances as a source of the rust-colored tones usually attributed to kola nuts. Synthetic dyes have seeped into the scene and sometimes act as a stabilizing agent in the color-adhering qualities of cloth since customarily the chemical agents which accompany these pigments contain a fixative to help make the dyes fast.

Figure 18. *A Yoruba* adire *saleswoman and her family at her stand at the marketplace in Ibadan, Nigeria.*

As we have seen from our investigation of the raffia-sewn resist textiles of the Bamun, it is difficult to trace the meaning or symbolism of many African tie and dye designs. Frequently they are simple random circular patterns or lines forming large geometric shapes. Among the Yoruba in Nigeria there is some degree of symbolization and representation in the sewn and tied designs handed down as traditional patterns. The typical Yoruba piece shown in Figure 3 is both tied and sewn, and may represent sample of original patterns that were carried by women traders along the west coast.

Generally, the Yoruba tie and dye patterns are less complex and representational than their cassava paste resist designs, mostly because the technique itself allows for less flexibility and freedom of expression. The Yoruba tie and die designs are inspired by things seen in everyday life which are simplified into symbols that are easily adapted to the technical requirements of manipulating the fabric through sewing and tying. Figure 18 shows a typical Yoruba adire saleswoman and her family in an Ibadan marketplace. One sees relatively simple patterns called "fingers," "eggs," "scissors," "full moons," and others based on ordinary objects, anatomy, and nature.[31]

The degree of sophistication in dyeing techniques with natural materials throughout Africa warrants a certain admiration. And considering the amount of pollution in rivers and lakes, caused partly by the wastes of industrial dyes, these natural dyes and processes deserve our full attention. The traditional artists of Africa who remain so skilled in this craft may value the knowledge they have preserved over the centuries and become the leaders in a worldwide reinvolvement in nature and in the crafts she has nourished.

NOTES

1. Renée Boser, "Les tissus de l'Afrique Occidentale à dessin réservé par froissage," Ethnologische Zeitschrift Zurich, January 1972, p. 54.
2. Ibid., p. 55.
3. A. Bühler, "Primitive Dyeing Methods," *Ciba Review: Dyeing Among Primitive Peoples*, No. 68, July 1948, p. 2493.

4. Nancy Stanfield, "Dyeing Methods in Western Nigeria," *Adire Cloth in Nigeria,* edited by Jane Barbour and Doig Simmonds, Institute of African Studies, University of Ibadan, 1971, p. 19.

5. See the Bibliography for a listing of Fred Gerber's publications, including *Indigo and the Antiquity of Dyeing.*

6. S. Wenger and H. U. Beier, "Adire—Yoruba Pattern Dyeing," *Nigeria Magazine,* Number 54, 1957, p. 225.

7. See Appendix: *How indigo dye came to Liberia—a folk tale,* from Esther Warner Dendel's "Blue Goes for Down," Brooklyn Botanic Garden's *Natural Plant Dyeing,* Handbook II, 1974, pp. 23–28.

8. Sultan Njoya was king of the Bamun from approximately 1883 till his death in 1931. He was extremely dynamic and creative on behalf of his people and his royal court. He developed an alphabet of ideographic script as well as a special spoken language for important personages within his court which borrowed from African dialects as well as French, English, and German.

9. Renée Boser, *Aperçus sur la teinture à l'indigo en Afrique Occidentale,* Sonderabdruck aus den Verhandlungen der Naturfoschenden Gesellschraft in Basel, Band 80/1, 1969, pp. 187, 188.

10. This relationship certainly seems possible when one views the resemblance to some of the designs seen in David Heathcote's article entitled, "Hausa Embroidered Dress," appearing in *African Arts,* Winter 1972, Volume V, Number 2.

11. See I. Dugast and M. D. W. Jeffreys, *Tables Synoptiques des Alphabets,* "L'Écriture des Bamun," I.F.A.N. Mémoires, Série: Populations, No. 4, 1950.

12. Dr. Thompson presents his research in the formidable catalogue for the exhibition of Katherine Coryton White's collection, *African Art in Motion,* 1974. The exhibition was presented consecutively at The National Gallery of Art, Washington, D.C., and at the Frederick S. Wight Art Gallery at the University of California, Los Angeles, in 1974.

13. Ibid., p. 173; p. 180.

14. Ibid., p. 180.

15. Ibid., p. 180.

16. Ibid., p. 177.

17. P. A. Talbot, *In the Shadow of the Bush,* 1912, "Appendix G, Nsibidi Signs," p. 451, figure 53.

18. I. Dugast and M. D. W. Jeffreys, "L'Écriture des Bamun," I.F.A.N. Mémoires, Série: Populations, No. 4, 1950, p. 89.

19. David Dalby, "The Indigenous Scripts of West Africa and Surinam: Their Inspiration and Design," *African Language Studies,* IX, 1968, p. 179.

20. Ibid., p. 190.

21. Ibid., p. 191.

22. Ibid., p. 190.

23. E. M. Chives, "Nineteenth Century Trade in the Bamenda Grassfields, S. Cameroons," *Afrika und Übersee,* Band XLV, Heft 4, 1962, pp. 245–48.

24. Renée Boser, in describing how designs may be painted on Bamun textiles, notes on page 188 of *Aperçus sur la teinture à l'indigo en Afrique Occidentale* that, "According to McCollock, 'several motifs can be combined to form a single design. The artisan . . . places this piece of leather in the form of a diamond triangle or rectangle on the cloth and draws the outlines with a stick dipped in blue dye.'" This technique could possibly be interpreted as a form of "stenciling."

25. R. Dorsey Mohun was commercial agent of the United States and American Consul at Boma near the mouth of the Congo River.

26. The inclusion of pile cloth as part of a fabric from the Stanley Falls area of Zaïre is a curious phenomenon, according to Dr. Gordon D. Gibson, curator of African Ethnology at the Smithsonian's Museum of Natural History. Dr. Gibson considers this tie-dyed raffia fabric from Zaïre unique among museum collections.

27. Margaret Trowell, in *African Design,* notes "that the craft cannot be traced further back than the early seventeenth century among the Bushongo, and that the Mbala tradition was that Shamba Bulongongo, the most famous king of the Bushongo, learned the art from the Pende and brought it back to his own country. Today it is considered that the origin of the craft may well have been the Lower Congo" (1966, p. 31).

28. Unless Mohun ventured into that territory during his several years' voyage along the Congo River to his ultimate goal of Stanley Falls, the pile cloth among the Genya is difficult to explain. Investigation of Mohun's communiqués to the State Department, dating from his appointment in 1892 to his return to the United States in 1894, indicates that, of necessity, he traveled the established trading route along the Congo River and its tributaries.

29. Monni Adams, "Kuba Embroidered Cloth," *African Arts* magazine, Volume XII, Number 1, November 1978, pp. 24–36; notes, pp. 106–7.

30. Ibid., pp. 34–35, 106.

31. Jane Barbour, "Nigerian 'Adire' Cloths," Baessler-Archiv, Neue Folge Band XVIII (1970), (XLIII Band), Heft 2, Ausgegeben am 31 Mai, 1971, pp. 363–81.

4

Wax and Paste Resist Patterning—"Batik"

In the contemporary world of arts and crafts, the word "batik" is universally accepted to describe the resist method of applying a substance such as melted wax or a paste of flour, corn, cassava, or rice to the surface of a fabric to form designs. The word "batik" is Indonesian in origin and means "to write with wax." When the applied substance hardens, it *resists* dyes, and when it is removed, the design of the *reserved* area remains, showing a light pattern against the dyed background.

This method of patterning fabric occurs in most countries where the tie and dye techniques are found—predominantly China, Japan, India, Indonesia, the Near and Middle East, and parts of North and West Africa. Both the resist methods—tying or waxing/pasting—probably originated in Asia early in the Christian era, according to written records and the dating of ancient fabric fragments. However, resist methods could predate written records and existing textile records.

The highest forms of fabric design with wax were achieved in Java, and many contemporary historians think that batik flourished in less extravagant forms in the Malay Archipelago long before the Indian influences penetrated the Indonesian area. Both paste and wax resist techniques have been used in Africa for centuries, although theories as to their origins are contradictory. Some authorities consider ancient Egypt as the source of wax painting on fabric, and the Egyptians, they feel, influenced Indian techniques. Others feel that although fabrics patterned with wax and clay paste dating around the fifth century A.D. have been discovered in Egypian burial grounds, the fact that there was trade between India and Egypt may well have supported an influence of Indian textiles on Egyptian designs rather than the opposite. Some textile authorities believe that resist techniques were introduced to Africa more recently by migrants from Asia. This is a possibility, particularly considering Renée Boser's early theory on weaving in West Africa, published in her major volume *Les tissus de l'Afrique Occidentale* in 1972. Dr. Boser's thesis, based on more than ten years of research, was that the basic men's looms used in various parts of Africa were closely related in structure and use to the looms used in ancient Palestine. She maintained that these looms were brought to Africa in the first centuries A.D. by a group of Semitic-Syrians who were later absorbed by the ancestors of the present-day nomadic Fulani peoples.* In turn, the Fulani traveled the continent, distributing looms and technical knowledge to the indigenous populations of each area, forming the legacy of African horizontal loom weaving as we know it today.[1]

If Renée Boser's theory on Semitic-Syrian origins is still valid, perhaps some of the early Semitic weavers and their wives may have been experienced wax resist artisans since this technique is known in their homeland. Theoretically, as the looms and weaving techniques were dispersed among the Fulanis so, too, was some understanding of resist methods (tie and dye included). The fact that the Fulani weavers' wives are renowned dyers tends to support this theory, while Renée Boser's inclusion of the Fulani as practitioners of paste resist methods, documented by the Basel Museum's collection, seems to confirm it.

Tempting as this theory may be, it is equally possible that paste and wax resist techniques were indigenous to local African populations long before the Fulani migrations. In fact, because of her findings during eighteen months of intensive fieldwork in Africa

* The theory of the Fulani descending from a Semitic-Syrian people was given wide credence in Delafosse's monumental work, *Haut Sénégal Niger*, published in 1912. For a more current view of the origins of the Fulani peoples (who are also known as the Peul) see "Qui sont les Peul?" by Yves Person, appearing on pages 60–62 of *Jeune Afrique*, No. 875, October 14, 1977.

in 1973–74, and her subsequent research, Dr. Boser now questions her earlier theory on the development of weaving in Africa. At a week-long seminar on African weaving at Michigan State University in the spring of 1977, Dr. Boser elaborated on her revised view. Her research indicates that looms were indigenous to the people who inhabited the area of the Sahara during ancient times when it was a fertile, life-sustaining land. Her findings are supported by archaeological discoveries in the Sahara, showing rock drawings of people weaving on looms and wearing woven garments. Later, as the Sahara dried up, the land became less livable, and the people were forced to take their herds southward to the Sahel where conditions were more favorable for raising cattle. Over the centuries, knowledge of the loom spread throughout the surrounding areas and gradually weaving, as we know it in West Africa today, developed.[2] Further investigations may reveal a connection between these early beginnings of weaving and the origins of paste or wax resist methods, perhaps through the discovery of designs on pottery or sculpted figures, which may be traced to resist-dyeing patterns.

In parts of West Africa—particularly Nigeria, Ghana, and Ivory Coast—there exists a tradition of bronze sculpture formed by the "lost wax" method. Some of the Nigerian sculptures have been carbon-dated as originating between the fourth and ninth centuries but many experts suspect a much earlier origin. It seems possible that wax used to decorate textiles may be related to this technique in metalwork, since in both methods the wax is ultimately "lost"—melted away. This theory is provocative in that once metal sculptures have been fixed in history by art historians and anthropologists, a truly African origin to wax resist in textiles may be ascertained.

On the other hand, the origin of wax resist cloth in Africa may simply have been the good results of a series of accidents. Perhaps a few drops of wax from a melted candle or nearby sculptor's work were carelessly spilled upon a piece of cloth awaiting its dyebath. After several dips in the indigo the spots of wax fell off, or when the fabric was placed in the shade to let the indigo oxidize, the wax spots hardened and were noticed by the dyer—perhaps with interest, more probably with vexation at the flaw on the otherwise evenly dyed fabric. Flicking aside the wax the dyer may have noticed the subtle veining patterns where the wax had cracked and had allowed very small amounts of dye to seep into the waxed area, thus producing the cherished crackled appearance characteristic of contemporary batik. Or, the artisan, disappointed in the glaring white spots on the beautiful deep indigo, may have redipped the cloth to minimize the whiteness and became entranced with the results—a lovely pale sky-blue against the midnight tones of the background.

This theory of accidental discovery of resist techniques seems even more logical when the use of paste resist is considered. Each culture using paste resist makes the paste from its most abundant food staples—cassava root in West Africa (called manioc in French-speaking countries), rice in the Orient, wheat and corn flour elsewhere. Imagine, for instance, a West African (Yoruba) woman preparing her family's daily meal of *fufu*. Bits of the sticky paste mixture fall from the bowl onto a cloth beneath it, or some of the glutinous stuff falls on her wrapper as she forms the little fufu balls and periodically readjusts her skirt panel, a typical African gesture. The paste remains on the cloth and hardens. When she decides to revitalize the color of her wrapper, she takes her cloths, including the one under the fufu bowl, to the indigo dyer. Without noticing the bits of hardened fufu clinging to the garments (or perhaps ignoring them), the dyer proceeds with the indigo process and is surprised to find that these crusts of paste on the dried cloths have prevented the penetration of the indigo into the fabric. Annoyance is followed by pleasure as the woman claiming her cloths exclaims in delight at the lyrical, spontaneous design produced by the paste spotting. Her only request, being Yoruba, is that the dyer put the fabrics into the indigo once more, please, so as to lessen the contrast and heighten the subtlety of blue on blue.

Unromantic realists may argue that the fufu substance would be unlikely to cling to the fabric during a rigorous indigo dyebath without the addition of the all-important chemical, alum. However, it could be reasoned (by romantics) that somehow, in the long process from fufu to fabric to final dyebath, nature provided a natural equivalent that performed the function of alum, forcing the pasty stuff, when dried, to adhere tenaciously to the material and act as a resist during the indigo immersion.

It is easy to speculate about the origins of resist techniques in Africa; but it is hard to accumulate facts. In his 1947 attempt to document batik methods in Africa, A. Steinmann cites a 1910 article by François de Zeltner:

> According to him [de Zeltner] a resist printing not unlike that of South East Asia is found in Senegal and on the upper Niger. Batik in these parts is a branch of the highly developed arts and crafts in the services of Princes. The indigo blue fabrics with white dots of the Bambara and Bamana tribes of the upper Niger are especially noticeable. The dots are reserved with hot wax. The Soninke people of Senegal use as a resist a tough rice paste, with which they cover the cloth spread out on a mat. The surface of the resist is then furrowed by a small-tooth comb. According to the movement of the comb the resulting design, which becomes indigo blue in the dyeing, consists of straight lines or zigzags. In both places the dyeing is exclusively women's work.[3]

François de Zeltner not only provided valuable written documentation of techniques he observed in Africa but also returned to Europe with a collection of textiles which he presented to the Musée de l'Homme, Paris, and the Museum für Völkerkunde, Basel. Figure 19 illustrates one of the early textiles he describes in

Figure 19. *Paste resist from Senegal, collected by François de Zeltner, showing typical designs resulting from furrowing through the paste with a small-toothed comb.*

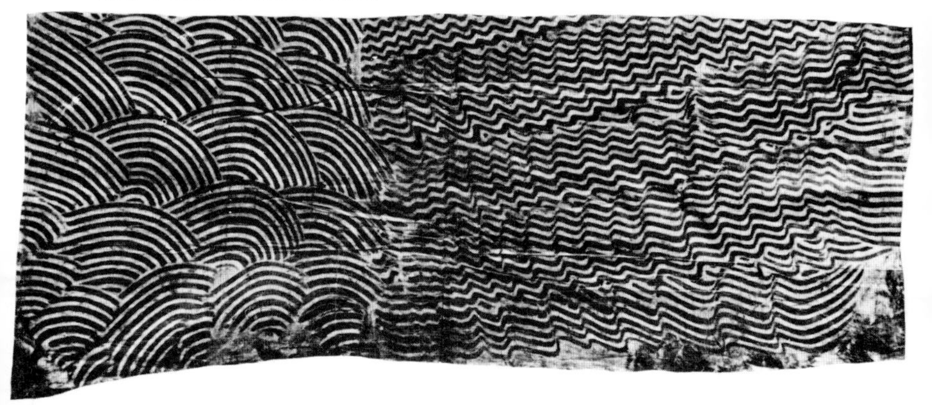

his essay. De Zeltner mentions the use of "a small-tooth comb" as an instrument for incising designs into the paste resist used on fabrics in Senegal. This method still exists, as we shall see in the following brief discussion of some of the tools employed for resist techniques in Africa and Indonesia.

Tools and Techniques

An instrument made out of a reed is said to have been used for applying hot wax to fabric in Ghana. One contemporary Ghanaian batik artist uses the stalk of an African wax rose to put the wax on as one would with a brush.[4] The tool which is most internationally associated with batik is the Indonesian instrument, the *tjanting,*† traditionally a small copper-tipped bowl with a bamboo stem which one holds in the hand like a pen. It is dipped into hot, liquid wax which flows out of a slender opening and can be drawn across fabric in quick, flowing lines to form the desired pattern. The tjanting may have as few as one opening or as many as thirteen. The circumference of the openings determines how much wax will issue from it and how fast it will flow. Thus the types of designs that may successfully be attempted are influenced by the size of the opening of the tjantings used. For example, tiny openings only permit small amounts of wax to flow slowly, allowing the designer to dawdle and make infinitely fine lines or tiny dots. A large opening flows swiftly and more fully so that work is done more quickly and spontaneously. Multispouted tjantings are often used to make flowerlike clusters of little dots. Through various government agencies and private businesses in countries like Cameroon and Upper Volta, Europeans and Americans have introduced Africans to the application of hot wax with instruments resembling the tjanting as well as with commercially manufactured brushes.

Paste resists are applied by hand with a chicken feather, broom-

† The revised Indonesian language spelling is *canting,* but I prefer to continue using tjanting since it indicates the pronunciation and is still the common term used by American craftspeople today.

LEFT, Figure 20. *Hand-carved wooden* tampon (*wax printing block*) *in abstract butterfly-like motif; commissioned by Mme. Adja Traoré in Dakar, Senegal.*
RIGHT, Figure 21. *Indonesian* tjap (*copper wax resist printing block*) *in ornate realistic butterfly design: collected in Indonesia.*

stick, or knife edge in Nigeria. Fingers, carved calabash combs, and broom twigs are used to incise designs on paste-covered fabrics in Senegal. Nigerians also use metal or leather stencils with paste.

In Senegal, Ivory Coast, and other West African countries, wax resists are applied with a hand-carved wooden *tampon*, or stamp (Figure 20), which is employed in the same manner as the Indonesian *tjap*‡ (Figure 21). The tjap is an intricate and delicately wrought copper printing stamp used in making "factory" batiks in Indonesia—a method of resist hand printing. Tjaps are often collector's items, similar to the ancient Indian and Persian carved wooden printing blocks or, in a simpler form, the abstract *adinkra* stamps of Ghana, which are carved of dried bits of calabash. (Adinkra stamps are traditionally used for printing cloth with dyes but I have used them for wax resist printing as well.)

‡ The revised Indonesian language spelling is *cap*, pronounced as in tjap, which I also choose to retain in use here.

Dyes and Designs

The Yoruba peoples of Nigeria are well known for their expertise in paste resist techniques and for the wide variety and inventiveness of their designs. Extensive studies have been made investigating the continuation of this traditional art expression. A good introduction to some of the motifs, methods of mixing and applying the paste, and dyeing techniques can be found in the book *Adire Cloth in Nigeria*, edited by Jane Barbour and Doig Simmonds, published by the Institute of African Studies, University of Ibadan, Nigeria. Although fabrics produced by paste resist patterning—adire eleko—are found locally in small towns throughout the Yoruba areas, the principal centers for their production are Abeokuta and Ibadan. Two methods of applying the cassava paste are employed. The first approach is a form of freehand painting in which the artist—*aladire*—employs a feather, continually dipping it into the bowl of paste, as she outlines and carefully fills in the traditional designs which have become part of her childhood legacy, acquired from her mother or another woman within the family compound (Figure 22).

Once the paste resist design has been completed and dried, the fabric is ready for dyeing. In larger compounds, such as those found in Abeokuta, the dyeing may be done on the premises, while in Ibadan, where the production is on a smaller scale, the fabric is usually taken to a dyer—aloro. In Nigeria today, a combination of natural and synthetic indigo is used to achieve the many blues so popular among the Yoruba. The fabrics require several days of dippings to achieve the deep midnight-blue background tones. Once the dark rich blue is acquired, the paste is scraped off, revealing the designs preserved in the original white fabric, to which some pale blue has inevitably penetrated. In order to deepen this light blue slightly and eliminate the white, contrasting areas, the fabric is passed through a final dyebath after the starch has been removed.

A typical Ibadan scene would depict several lovely adire elekos hanging to dry in the dyers' compound. A popular pattern one

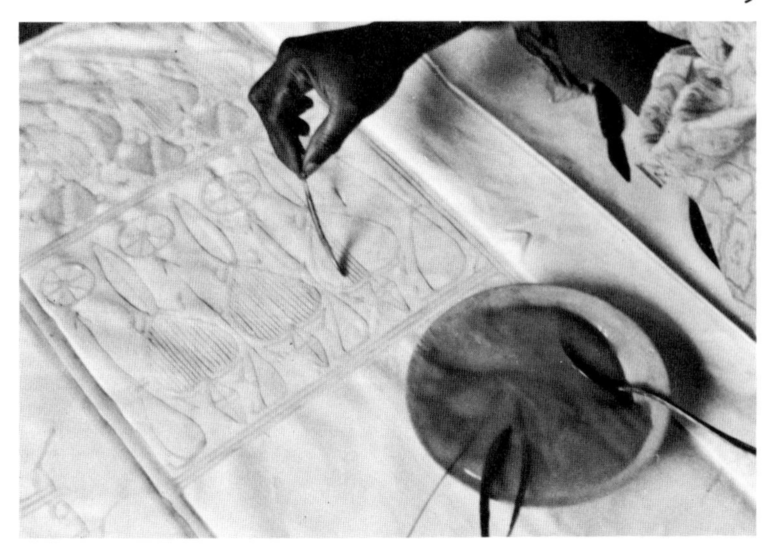

Figure 22. A *Yoruba* aladire (*paste resist artist*) *hand painting cassava resist mixture on cloth in Ibadan, Nigeria.*

often sees is the *Ibadadun*, named for the city it honors, meaning "Ibadan is pleasant." Among the many squares of typical Ibadadun designs are stylized birds, snakes, frogs, and scorpions; designs inspired by nature include different kinds of leaves, kola nuts, and stars; numerous items from everyday life include umbrellas and watches; and to a much lesser degree are designs of a purely decorative nature, not inspired by real objects. However, distinguishing the Ibadadun design from other adire eleko is the unmistakable design known as the "pillars of Mapo Hall, alternating with spoons." In her article, "Nigerian 'Adire' Cloths," Mrs. Barbour points out that "Mapo Hall stands on a hill in the center of Ibadan and is the equivalent of a town hall. It is a traditional pattern, probably forty or fifty years old."[5] According to one of Mrs. Barbour's sources, the manner in which the Mapo Hall design is executed—that is, the number of spoons alternating with the pillars—is a guide to the quality of the cloth. The more numerous the spoons appearing in the design, the more valuable the fabric is

Figure 23. *Popular Yoruba* Ibadadun *pattern paste resist cloth featuring four "spoons" and other abstract and semiabstract designs of symbolic meaning.*

judged to be. An Ibadadun cloth featuring six spoons might therefore be assessed as a finer cloth than an example which displays only three spoons. Accordingly, Figure 23, a cloth from the Musée Royal de l'Afrique Centrale, Tervuren, Belgium, showing four spoons, would be considered a more valuable piece. However, it is also said that the number of spoons in the design may be passed on from mother to daughter as she learns the craft.

Another extremely popular Yoruba design, *Olokun,* which means "goddess of the sea," is characterized by a greater use of purely decorative design motifs, but also includes stylizations of wire, snakes, birds, leaves, combs, and the popular "OK OK," as seen in this example collected in 1969 in Ibadan (Figure 24).

An infinite variety of traditional themes is found in hand-applied cassava resist cloths. Contemporary trends as well as the individual artist's innovative skills alter the traditional patterns and add new ones to the adire eleko repertoire. In Figure 25, the popular design, "My head is together," is enriched by the addition of the artist's name and profession. Within the tradition of repeated and alternating designs—enclosed within a designated number of squares and rectangles—techniques of hand painted adire eleko are used on fabrics specifically designed to be worn by Yoruba women in their conventional wrappers.

Figure 24. *Another popular Yoruba paste resist pattern entitled* Olokun, *a design easily recognized by its "OK OK" motif.*

Figure 25. *This Yoruba paste resist design, known as "My head is together," is of particular interest because the artist signed her name* (ASIRI) *and profession* (ALADIRE).

Recently two young women artists of Oshogbo, some one hundred fifty miles outside the capital city of Lagos, have transcended this traditional formula of rigidly divided space, as well as the concept of fabric designed solely as body covering. In the beautiful tapestries of Senabu Oloyede and Kekelomo Oladepo, we see a fascinating blend of traditional adire technique used to reinterpret in a contemporary and individualistic style various aspects of Yoruba life (Plate 5—see insert). In her article on the two young artists, which appeared in *African Arts* magazine, appropriately titled "New Heirs to Talent in Oshogbo," Jean Kennedy analyzes the influences the girls have experienced as the daughters of the widely respected Oshogbo artists Asiru Olatunde (father of Senabu Oloyede, who works in hammered aluminum) and Jinadu Oladepo (father of Kekelomo Oladepo, who works in welded and cast brass). The muted tones of the tapestries echo the traditional monochromatic adire elekos, though the indigo blues are sometimes supplemented with subdued tones of ochre or green.[6] Several other Oshogbo artists work in wax resist using contemporary abstract themes. These are intended as yard goods for wrappers and tailored clothes but are frequently displayed in the homes of sensitive collectors who regard them as works of art and are therefore reluctant to cut them up.

Traditionally—since the beginning of the twentieth century, but perhaps earlier—metal or leather stencils have been used to make paste resist designs on fabric in Nigeria (Figures 26, 27, 28, and 29). The paste is pushed through the openings cut into the stencil. These stenciled designs are repeated over the entire fabric, usually alternating various motifs in an attractive juxtaposition (Figure 30). One of the most famous designs in paste resist stencil has been the Jubilee Design commemorating the Silver Jubilee of King George and Queen Mary in 1935 (Figure 31). Numerous versions of this design have been produced and continue to be popular. On many of the fabrics utilizing printed letters, the legibility of the letters has been lost, since the men who cut the stencils usually do not read the Roman alphabet and frequently carve and recarve the letters from a design standpoint rather than from a literate one. Their embellishments are often aesthetic improvements. Also, when old, damaged stencils are copied, distortions

ABOVE LEFT, Figure 26. *Metal stencil used in producing paste resist patterns, usually the same design repeated as an overall motif on one cloth (double Oba—chief or king—motif). (These and the following stencils collected in Lagos, Nigeria.)*

ABOVE RIGHT, Figure 27. *Metal paste resist stencil featuring an elaborately attired Oba.*

BELOW LEFT, Figure 28. *Metal paste resist stencil with smiling angels and outstretched arms.*

BELOW RIGHT, Figure 29. *Four separate small paste resist stencils commemorating a 1973 athletic event.*

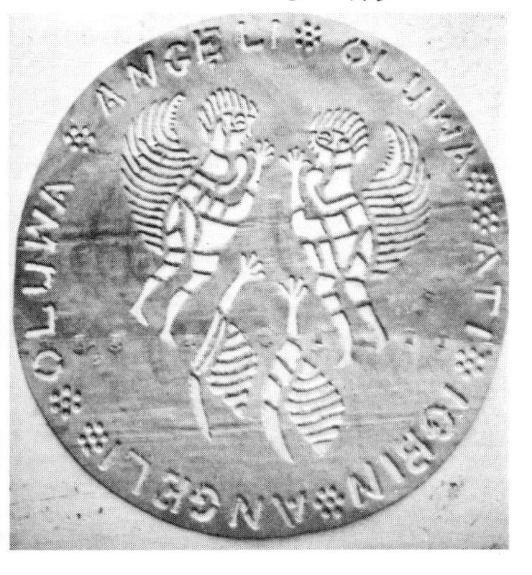

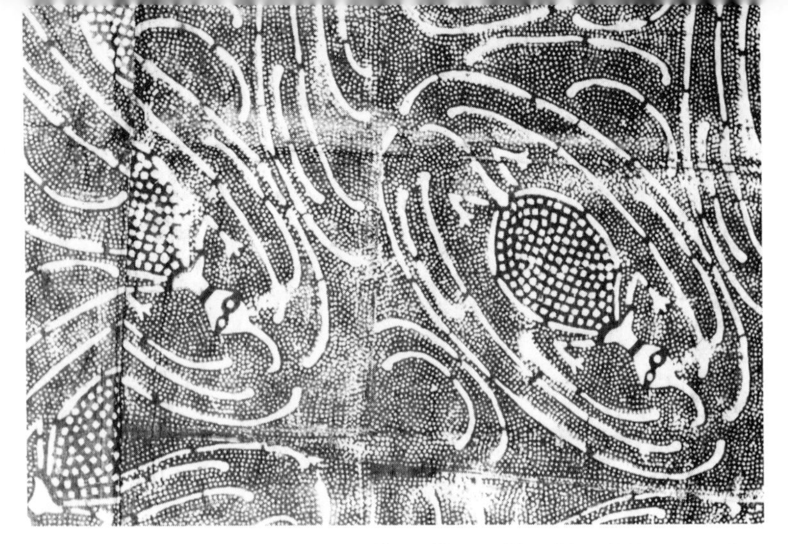

Figure 30. *Intricately designed "lizard" motif achieved by repeating one paste resist pattern over the entire cloth.*

Figure 31. *A variation of one of Nigeria's most celebrated stencil paste resist patterns, the "Jubilee Design," featuring the addition of cloudlike and textured areas over parts of the design where the stenciled motif was unclear, or where large parts of the stencil were broken. The unattractive drops of paste that passed through inspired the artist to elaborate on the details, giving the birds featherlike textures and the animals detailed fur.*

caused by broken areas are incorporated into the new designs. Combing the paste into a cloudlike pattern is common and adds a whimsical touch to the sovereigns and their surroundings.

Lois Brooks is an American artist who became deeply involved in paste resist methods of Nigeria. She spent three years researching and experimenting with various ingredients until she mastered the art of mixing a formula for paste resist containing alum like the Yoruba's, which would not disintegrate when dipped into indigo. The results were published in the August 1971 edition of *Craft Horizons*.[7]

At the cooperative in Dakar, wax resist printing with a tampon (wooden block) far exceeded the production in paste resist, probably because wax resist printing with tampons by a skilled artisan can be done faster than paste work. The process for the initial steps, as observed by Helen Anderson-Bauer (the American Peace Corps volunteer who directed the tie-dye cooperative in Dakar), is as follows: "First of all, they melt candles or they buy paraffin. They use beeswax in the bronze casting, but I've never seen it used in the batik process and I imagine it is very expensive. They melt the wax, add a large quantity of water, and when this has reached the proper temperature, they start dipping the wooden blocks in. The inevitable question is, what's the proper temperature? When it's almost bubbling on the surface they dip the tampon in only on the surface because the wax rises and the water sinks. They take it from the center and they know *just* when the temperature is right. I really couldn't do this on my own. When I try, I get splotches on my cloth."

Figure 32 shows one of the *stagiaires,* or trainees, waxing a cloth. Ms. Anderson-Bauer explains: "You'll notice the piece of cardboard running along the cloth directly in front of her. The idea in industrializing this skill was to create a certain standard of exactitude, I guess we could say. Europeans generally don't like it when the wax designs are crooked or overlapping, even if it does look more interesting to some of us. So I introduced the idea of using these cardboard guidelines and it certainly improved the alignment of designs." After the waxing is finished the fabric is dyed.

Once the wax is removed from the fabric by boiling and the

Figure 32. *Trainee patterning cloth with tampon dipped in hot wax, at the Women's Cooperative in Dakar, Senegal.*

cloth hung out to dry, the finishing process takes place. Figure 33 illustrates this procedure (with a tie-dyed cloth), which Ms. Anderson-Bauer explains: "The young girl is pounding the cloth. This acts as a kind of ironing technique and it also provides a certain shine to the surface. In one of my moments of great indus-

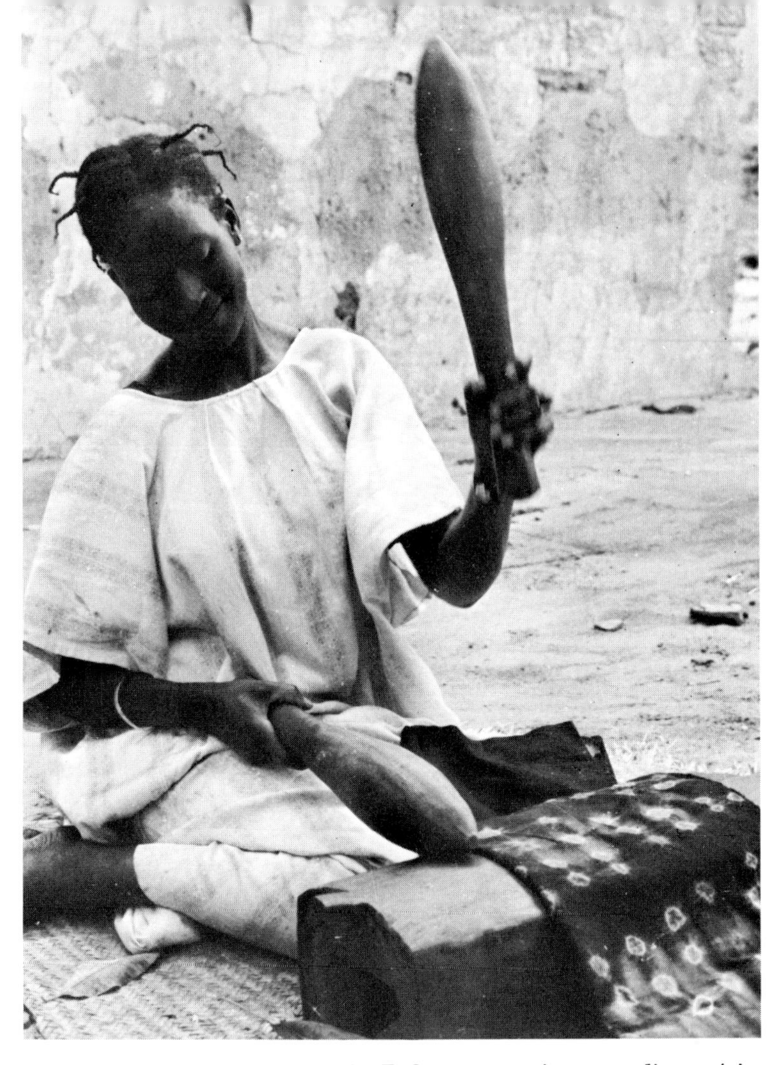

Figure 33. *Young woman, at the Dakar cooperative, pounding a (tie-dyed) cloth. The African version of ironing, this technique is very effective and adds sheen to indigo-dyed fabrics.*

trialization I tried introducing an iron and the effects were just not the same; and the women preferred to do the pounding anyway, even though they also argued over how many pieces each person had to do so it would be fair. Each hammer weighs perhaps three pounds; they're made out of very heavy mahogany."

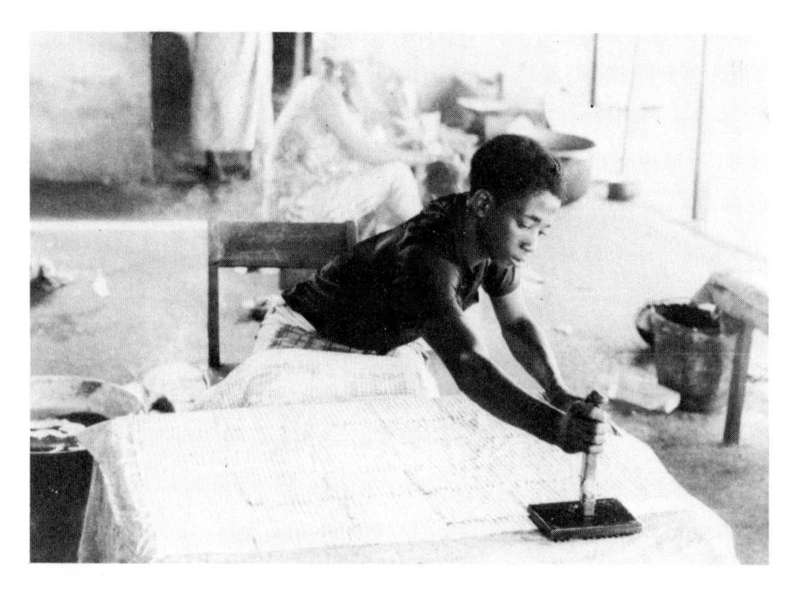

Figure 34. *A young man using a wooden tampon to pattern cloth in Treichville, Ivory Coast.*

Wax printing with wooden blocks is common in several West African countries and is particularly popular in Ivory Coast. As we see in Figures 34 and 35, the methods are almost identical to those observed in the cooperative in Senegal. However, in this case the wax printer is a young man (from Guinea), although women do wax resist printing in Ivory Coast as well. In a communal backyard not far from the large Treichville marketplace across the lagoon from the modern business section of the capital city of Abidjan, the young man practices his craft. He uses a rectangular block of wood. In this illustration, the design is a simple repeat of parallel lines (Figure 34). The melted wax at his side is kept liquid and at the proper temperature in a large bowl placed over a small stove (Figure 35). The artisan dips the carved block into the liquid wax and quickly presses it against the cloth, which has been placed over a padded table that provides a cushioned surface, making the wax adhere to the fabric more readily and evenly. On a shelf behind him are several other carved wooden blocks, most of them with simple wooden handles which project from the center of the block, allowing easy handling and a degree of uniform pressure over the surface of the stamping block.

Figure 35. *Rear view of the wax-printing craftsman, showing how he dips his tampon in the large metal bowl of wax heated from below and kept at a constant temperature to assure adherence of the hot wax to the cloth.*

When the waxing has been completed, the fabric is first dyed in kola nut, then dried on a line—sometimes rewaxed to provide an overprinted effect—and finally dipped into indigo several times. As the colors penetrate, the design becomes infinitely more interesting as the kola and then the indigo seep into small cracks in the waxed areas, altering the earlier, somewhat rigid-looking waxed grid pattern and bringing a fluid, soft-edged quality to the design.

It is possible to vary the design by alternating the placement of the patterns. A single stamp may be used to wax the fabrics, and a checkerboard effect can be achieved by leaving empty spaces alternately between the patterns. Color distribution, of course, contributes to the contrast.

The process of preparing a dyeing solution from kola nuts is similar in most West African countries. At the Centre féminin d'action, in Rufisque, Senegal, Mme. Niang, the acting director, demonstrates the full process. She is assisted by a few of the fifteen to twenty members of this women's group, which was first organized in 1971 by Mme. Cremieux, the wife of a prominent Dakar businessman. Originally, the women met as an informal social group; their first craft activity was knitting. Subsequently, Mme. Cremieux made a trip to Banjul, Gambia, and was so impressed with the batik work she saw there she began designing and carving wooden tampons herself. From this modest beginning the artisanat at Rufisque became a productive commercial center for batik and tie-dye activity. The women at Rufisque produced wax-printed, kola- and indigo-dyed articles in the following manner.

First, the cloth is spread out on the ground and stamped with tampons dipped in hot wax. The fabric is then sprinkled with water, gathered together, and tied securely into a large circular mass (Figure 36). Kola nuts, soaked in plain water for a period ranging from overnight to one or two days, are lifted from the water and placed in a large wooden mortar where they are crushed with a pestle to a rough, coffee-grainlike consistency. This strenuous work is done to a rhythmic beat of the pestle as it crushes the kola nuts against the inside of the mortar. The women interject a muscle-relieving handclap as the pestle bounces in midair; the

Figure 36. *At the Women's Cooperative in Rufisque, Senegal, a young craftswoman ties a wax resist printed fabric, which has already been crushed and gathered together into a large circular mass.*

Figure 37. *A waxed, crushed, and tied mass of patterned fabric is placed in a solution of crushed kola nuts and water at the Rufisque cooperative.*

workers relieve each other by catching the pestle and resuming the work without breaking the beat.

The crushed nuts are placed in a shallow container. Just enough cool water is added to cover the oval of waxed and tied fabric, and the kola fragments are pressed around the piece (Figure 37). After ten minutes in the solution the piece is removed from the liquid and allowed to sit for several minutes in another bowl, with the bits of kola nuts clinging to the piece. This process of dipping the piece in the kola solution is usually repeated three times. If the piece is to be dyed only in kola nut, it is untied and rinsed in tap water. If, in the West African tradition, it is to be overdyed in indigo, the piece is dried, then placed on the floor where the kola grains are brushed off and the strings readjusted. Large metal cans which serve as indigo vats—covered when not in use—are refreshed with powdered synthetic indigo made by BASF (a German-based firm). After the solution has been stirred and has rested ten to fifteen minutes, the piece is immersed. It is then removed, untied, opened, rinsed, and hung on a line to dry. Ultimately, the fabrics are sold to visitors from nearby Dakar as tablecloth and napkin sets and as traditional caftanlike Senegalese women's garments, as well as other articles of clothing and household use.

Although wax printing with tampons is a dominant medium in contemporary Senegalese design techniques, the hand-applied paste resist tradition is still an active one. A paste is made of okra—a small green vegetable often used as a design theme throughout West Africa (particularly in the hand-printed adinkra cloths of Ghana, which are discussed in the following chapter). Boxes of commercial starch are also used to make resist paste.

In the yard of the Dakar cooperative's dyeing compound were two starch-patterned pieces which exhibit a striking resemblance to de Zeltner's description of the textiles from the Museum für Völkerkunde's example (Figure 19). Both show the result of the comb or fingers, a pattern of straight lines alternating rhythmically in horizontal and vertical patterns. The crescent-shaped designs form an allover motif almost identical to the patterning of the left half of the piece in Figure 19, which was collected in the Marché de Labé, Foulbé, Fouta Djallon, Guinea, in 1956. Both museum pieces are of imported commercial cotton cloth as are the fabrics from the Dakar cooperative. In these particular co-op pieces, it is not always a comb or the fingers that are used. According to Ms. Anderson-Bauer, various methods exist: "They take their fingers or a piece of calabash—a piece of gourd—that looks like a comb, or else they take ten to fifteen pieces of a broomstick, tie them together, and make swirling designs on the cloth. It's a typical Guinean Sarakolé technique." Figure 38 shows a stagiaire heating the starch mixture on the charcoal *fourneau*, or grill. The okra *gumbo*—as the paste mixture is called (reminding us of its connections to the kitchen)—is easily made. "The dried okra flour, mixed with water, is heated. Once this gumbo starch mixture is thick like cornstarch pudding and cooled, it is ready. Whereas traditionally okra powder was used, now they buy little boxes of

Figure 38. A stagiaire (*trainee*) *heats starch mixture for paste resist on a* fourneau (*grill*).

starch and use that."* In Figure 39 the same stagiaire patterns the gumbo with her fingers, the cloth stretched out on the ground behind her.

This activity is supervised by Mme. Adja Awa Traoré. She helped Ms. Anderson-Bauer with technical advice and passed on her Guinean Sarakolé techniques to workshop participants, many

* No mention is made of the use of alum or any other chemical substance to help the simple starch paste (or the gumbo) adhere to the fabric during the dyeing process.

Figure 39. *The stagiaire patterns the starch mixture with her fingers.*

of whom are Wolof, the predominant Senegalese group. Mme. Traoré represents the Soninké tradition to which de Zeltner makes reference (Sarakolé and Soninké refer to the same group). Perhaps the "tough rice paste" he describes was, in fact, the traditional gumbo mixture. Mme. Traoré works standing straight-legged, bending directly from the waist in a yogalike stance, which only a lifetime of practice would seem to allow her to sustain.

The wax-dyeing skills of Mme. Zita Traoré were featured in the

July 15, 1969, issue of *Entente* magazine. Mme. Traoré lives and works in Bouaké, Ivory Coast. She sells directly from her dyeworks and at the Treichville marketplace where tradesmen from other African countries buy her fabrics for resale in places like Dahomey, Niger, and Zaïre. The process, again, is nearly the same. Mme. Traoré, too, stands stiff-legged over her work, bending from the waist to press the waxed tampon against the cloth, which is spread on the ground over a raffia mat. Indigo and kola are also combined. Mme. Traoré sends her fabrics to the "thrasher," who beats them with a wooden beater to bring out the sheen and to press the cloths flat. The article notes that the art of kola-dyeing "was introduced into the Ivory Coast about three years ago by Guinean craftswomen. They are very skilled and have taught the techniques of indigo-dyeing to Malian, Upper Voltan, and Ivory Coast craftswomen."[8]

Wax resist methods have also been introduced into Upper Volta through a locally sponsored government effort combined with an American Peace Corps involvement similar to those in other African countries already mentioned. In Ouagadougou, the initial impetus for this craft-revitalizing operation was through the efforts of six volunteers working at the Voltaic Arts Center. The workshops centered on the idea of promoting small business through the training of artisans and craftsmen in the traditional Voltaic arts and craft forms which have been dying out. All the volunteers had university educations in the fine arts. The results are immensely gratifying, particularly in the work of the batik artist Christophe Zemana Goudouma, who was born in 1952 in Tenkedogo. In our correspondence, M. Goudouma writes that no other member of his family is an artist; that in fact he learned to do batik from the Americans at the Centre Voltaique des Arts; that he has been an artist for over nine years now; and that he has been successfully exhibiting and selling his works. M. Goudouma uses dyes imported from Nigeria, favoring yellows, reds, blues, *l'indigo* (he adds this as distinguished from the other blues); brown, green, orange, and light red are also featured. His work has a gay spontaneity and essential truth to it, and I was struck by the universality of African life which he portrays (Figure 40).

Figure 40. *"Les Pileuses de Mil sous les Arbres"* (*"The Millet Grinders under the Trees"*), *a contemporary wax batik by C. Z. Goudouma of Ouagadougou, Upper Volta, using commercial synthetic dyes.*

NOTES

1. Renée Boser-Sarivaxévanis, *Les tissus de l'Afrique Occidentale*, Band 13, Basler Beiträge zür Ethnologie, 1972, pp. 110–11.
2. A detailed account of Dr. Boser's more recent research is forthcoming in her second major volume on African textiles.
3. A. Steinmann, "Batik Work, Its Origin and Spread," *Ciba Review, Batik*, No. 58, July 1947, p. 2109.
4. When I mentioned this to an authority on Ghanaian culture and textiles, she replied that she has neither seen nor heard of any indigenous methods in Ghana of applying wax to textiles, although, of late, a number of progressive textile artists have applied modern methods like screen printing, wax printing, etc.
5. Jane Barbour, "Nigerian 'Adire' Cloths," Baessler-Archiv, Neue Folge Band XVIII (1970), (XLIII Band), Heft 2, Ausgegeben am 31 Mai, 1971, p. 372.
6. Jean Kennedy, "New Heirs to Talent in Oshogbo," *African Arts*, Summer 1971, Volume IV, Number 4, pp. 24–27.
7. Lois Brooks, "Workshop: Adire Eleko," *Craft Horizons*, August 1971, pp. 12–15.
8. "Ivory Coast: Bouaké: Loin-cloth dyeing, a traditional art," *Entente*, No. 1, July 15, 1969, p. 55.

5

The Hand-printed Adinkra Cloth of Ghana

Tracing the origins of Subsaharan African fabrics can be a compelling challenge as well as an elusive exercise, one that echoes the enigmatic qualities inherent in the textiles themselves. Adinkra cloth,[1] as we know it today, drapes into handsome men's robes without the aid of sewing or pinning (Figures 41 and 42), using primarily hand printing and occasionally combining embroidery in its production.

Its origins are mysterious, like those of most Subsaharan African textiles, but some field research in the past century has produced documented texts and charts. Most sources agree that its origins are immersed in Ghanaian history, but we cannot accurately establish a date. The British Museum has an early example of adinkra cloth in which the symbols are printed on narrow, handwoven, natural-colored bands of fabric which were sewn together with fine stitches before the printing process took place. Figure 43 shows the fabric folded in half; it was collected by T. E. Bowdich during his celebrated expedition in 1817. In his book, *Mission from Cape Coast to Ashanti,* published in 1819, a large drawing by Bowdich himself appears, entitled "The First Day of the Yam Custom,"[2] showing celebrants wearing cloths rolled at the waist, one of the ways in which adinkra cloths are traditionally worn (Figure 44). Several of the cloths in the Bowdich illustration feature small,

Figure 41. *Ghanaian celebrant at Ashanti Durbar festival in Kumasi wearing an* adinkra *cloth (left).*

Figure 42. *An Ashanti gentleman wearing an adinkra cloth (right) as everyday apparel.*

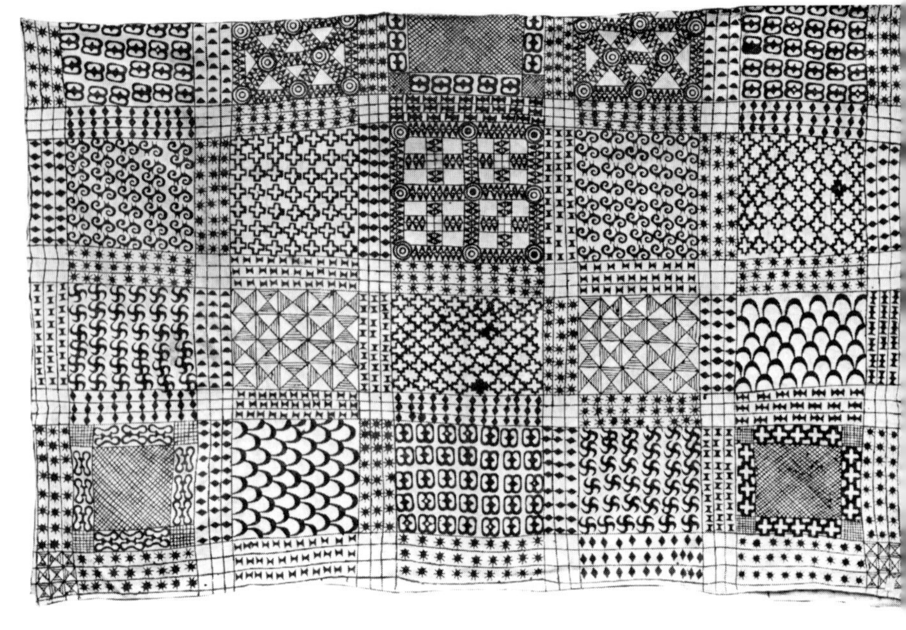

Figure 43. *Adinkra cloth collected by T. E. Bowdich in 1817 for the British Museum.*

overall repeat patterns which could be interpreted as representing adinkra cloths.

The use of adinkra cloths by chiefs can be traced through turn-of-the-century photographs of King Prempeh (1898) and Chief Kwamin Frimpon Adentin (1905). A portrait in Robert Rattray's first book, *Ashanti,* published in 1923, shows an early twentieth-century adinkra cloth in which the use of embroidery as a design element can be seen.

Several themes regarding the origins of adinkra cloth recur throughout the various documentary sources. The brief summary below should serve as a simplified introduction; more detailed investigation of each particular source follows.

Most of the research on adinkra cloth relies heavily on the investigations recorded by Captain Robert Rattray, England's colonial district commissioner. Captain Rattray documented, with great detail and accuracy, aspects of everyday life among the Ashanti in several volumes, including a book published in 1927

Figure 44. *Ghanaian wearing adinkra cloth rolled at the waistline, one of the styles in which this cloth is customarily worn in the presence of the* Asantehene (*king*).

called *Religion and Art in Ashanti,* which remains one of the most widely accepted documentations of Ashanti life and culture.

One historical assumption is that adinkra cloth first appeared in a certain battle between the Asantahene, or Ashanti king, Nana Osei Bonsu-Panyin and Adinkera, king of Gyaman (an area located in present-day Ivory Coast), in the early nineteenth century. Perhaps a variation of the plain cloth, *kobene,* acquired the name adinkra in commemoration of the memorable battle, particularly since the color red is associated with war as well as mourning. Equally possible is its eventual evolution from the plain, unprinted kobene cloth of vermilion red or russet brown; these are mourning colors in Ghana today and are still taboo for ordinary wear. Or adinkra cloth may have evolved from the dark tannish-brown cloth with black patterns, *kuntunkuni,* worn by mourners when an important person lies in state. Perhaps adinkra cloth that has been banded horizontally with ribbons of multicolored embroidery, said to be inspired by the earlier use of woven Kente strips, is related to the traditional textile called *nwumu* which the chief wore for festive occasions when in mourning. Or it may be that the word "adinkra" itself is an inversion of "*nkradie*" or "*dinkra,*" which means good-bye, an aspect of mourning the dead. Finally, the cloth could be named adinkra as a corruption of the term *adwinkena,* which means the art of designing on cloth; or because Rattray, as the first major European chronicler of Ashanti life, simply adapted the word "adinkira" to describe the process he recorded.

The similarity in the words—their repeated association with war, death, and the chiefs of vying nations—also suggests a general incorporation of all the meanings inherent in the words themselves. Much of Ghanaian life is dominated by legends and heroic folklore; there is, for instance, national recognition of the Golden Stool, symbolic of Ashanti royalty, the soul of the Ashanti people, and the powers of the state. It is possible that linking the cloth to a battle of the royalty over the use of the designs stolen from the Golden Stool of Ashanti provides a victorious type of association well suited to present-day Ghanaian nationalism.

By comparing excerpts from several sources on the origins of adinkra cloth, we can understand some of the complex historical and symbolic significance this fabric held in Ashanti ritual and daily life. It should be noted, however, that both the following sources have taken much information, as well as many of the drawings on the chart, from Rattray.

First, E. Ablade Glover, who has prepared a chart of adinkra symbolism for Ghana's University of Science and Technology at Kumasi, says that Adinkera, a famous king of Gyaman, had angered the Asantehene, Bonsu-Panyin, by attempting to copy the Golden Stool and that Adinkera was defeated and slain in an ensuing war. It has been suggested that the art of adinkra came from Gyaman, Glover noted, and he found it significant that the word adinkra means farewell or good-bye, since the special cloth is used on funeral occasions (*eyie*) to say good-bye to the departed.[3]

Another chart on adinkra cloth suggests similar origins with additional possibilities. The chart was prepared in collaboration with the Ghana Museum and Monument Board by Emerico Samassa-Mayer, who says that despite the lack of records on adinkra cloth, the Ashantis are said to have been inspired by the Muslims who had words from the Koran stamped on some of their cloths. Samassa-Mayer also relates the story that when Adinkera, king of the Gyaman, was defeated and slain, the victorious Ashanti brought back the art of stamping cloth.[4]

René Bravmann, in his book *Islam and Tribal Art in West Africa*, pictures a cloth called *karamoro-kioyolingo*—meaning Muslim cloth—as an example of one of the ways in which the Nafana peoples of west central Ghana have incorporated Islamic influences into their official regalia. This cloth is a white wrapper decorated with varying repeated blocks of Arabic script and symbols, using imported inks in red, blue, and black. Bravmann observes that its use in important festivals as well as its unique design are remarkably similar to the cloth worn by Asantehene Osei Kwame—as described by Joseph Dupuis in his 1824 book, *Journal of a Residence in Ashantee*—a large white cloth partly covering the left shoulder, studded all over with Arabic writing in various colored inks. He further notes that such Muslim cloths may be common among the Akan today, citing the experience of Professor Roy Seiber who in 1966 saw one being worn by the chief of stool-carvers in Mampong, an Ashanti town.[5]

An article in the *Ghana News*, entitled "Making an 'Adinkrah'

Cloth," suggested other possible origins, one theory being that in ancient Ghana the kings of Ashanti, Denkyira, and Tekyiman wore adinkra which their guild of designers were the first to design. Another possibility was that King Adinkera actually wore an adinkra cloth during the battle in which he lost his life, and that the cloth was taken as a trophy after he was slain. Apparently, many people claim that the kings of Ashanti wore adinkra long before the war between Ashanti and Gyaman. Supporting this is the fact that the term "adwinkena" means the art of designing on cloth, and the term "adinkra" is thought to be a corruption of it.[6]

Bowdich wrote in his journal of 1819:

> The white cloths, which are principally manufactured in Inla and Dagwumba, they paint for mourning with a mixture of blood and a red dye wood. The patterns are various and not inelegant, and painted with so much regularity with a fowl's feather, that they have all the appearance of a coarse print at a distance.[7]

Perhaps the word "adwinkena" referred to this earlier art of designing on cloth, and when the technique of printing the same or similar motifs evolved, the name "adinkra" emerged to identify it.

It might also be speculated that the example of adinkra cloth at the British Museum—identified as hand-*printed* fabric by the Museum curators as well as other European textile specialists—may well be a hand-*painted* cloth of the nature that Bowdich describes in *Mission from Cape Coast to Ashanti,* where he writes, ". . . There will be a very fair specimen in the British Museum. . . ." In fact, the Museum cloth *is* the one that Bowdich collected in 1817 during his celebrated expedition. Whether or not it is really the painted cloth to which he refers in his book requires more extensive study of the textile itself. However, the irregularities of size and shape in each individual design's repeated motifs (as seen in Figure 43) strongly suggest a hand-painted rather than a hand-printed technique, at least in some of the designs.

Relationship of Other Ghanaian Robes to Adinkra Cloth

Two important Ghanaian writers have contributed significantly toward providing a fuller view of the important textiles and attire in Ghanaian culture. A. A. Y. Kyerematen, in *Panoply of Ghana*,[8] suggests a relationship between adinkra cloth and various mourning robes of Ghanaian chiefs based on their similar fabric, dyes, and color. Kofi Antubam, in *Ghana's Heritage of Culture*,[9] examines textile symbols (*Atemadwini*), saying that the color and style of the chief's attire reflect its function and are symbolic of the feeling of the occasion.

The chart on pages 92 and 93 classifies several of the cloths mentioned by both writers. Because of their association with "mournful or solemn occasions," Kyerematen calls this group "cloth for the valiant heart."

For our purposes here and in contemporary usage, we can define adinkra cloth as a dyed fabric stamped with symbolic motifs of religious and cultural significance. Through the positioning of these stamp motifs, their symbolism and the color scheme of the cloth, a message is conveyed by the wearer.

The various cloths documented by Kyerematen and Antubam each bear a relationship to adinkra cloth as it is known and worn in contemporary Ghanaian life. The birisi, black or indigo with black stamped motifs, is identical with black adinkra cloth. Kobene, plain vermilion and terra-cotta cloths that traditionally are never stamped, are related to the adinkra cloths, which do exist nowadays, printed on vermilion and terra-cotta fabrics. Kuntunkuni, the very name of the bark of the tree from which Rattray documents the traditional source of the background dye of adinkra cloths, exists as a stamped adinkra cloth bearing that name. Both *kwasida adinkera* and nwumu cloth are closely related to the adinkra cloth of Rattray's era (the 1920s), in which strips of embroidery are used as a device to divide the cloth horizontally.

CLASSIFICATION OF

Name	Color	Fabric
birisi (K) *Birisii* (A)	Completely black or indigo with or without black stamped motifs (A)	Native-woven or imported cotton or linen (K)
Fututam (A)	White (A)	Not stated
kobene (K) *Kobene* (A)	Vermilion red (A) Terra-cotta red (A) Never stamped (K)	Native-woven or imported cotton or linen (K)
kuntunkuni (K) *Kuntunkuni* (A)	Dark burnt sienna (A) Dark tan brown with significant patterns in black (A); bark of tree from which *adinkra* cloth is dyed (R)	Native-woven or imported cotton or linen (K)
Kwasida Adinkera (A)	White or yellow with bands of yellow, black, red, and white; sometimes green or blue added (A)	Native-woven or imported cotton or linen (K)
nwomu (K) *nwumu* (K)	Horizontal lines of satin-strip embroidery; equidistant spaces between strips sometimes printed with *adinkra* designs; colors restricted to those suitable to festive occasions (K)	Imported silk or linen (K)

KEY TO SOURCES

(K) indicates the source is A. A. Y. Kyerematen, *Panoply of Ghana,* 1964, Praeger, New York, pages 67–68.

(A) indicates the source is Kofi Antubam, *Ghana's Heritage of Culture,* 1963, Kehler and Amelang, Leipzig, pages 84 and 151.

(R) indicates the source is Robert Rattray, *Religion and Art in Ashanti,* 1927, Oxford Press, London, pages 263–64.

GHANAIAN CLOTHS

Worn By	*Occasion; Significance or Symbolism; Time Worn*
Chief (K)	A passing grief or extended memory of the loss by death of a dear one. When the corpse is covered up in its coffin until the fortieth day after burial (A).
Members of the royal clan (*Adehye*) who cannot afford *Kwasida Adinkera* (A)	Fortieth day after the burial (A).
Close relatives of the chief or other important person (A)	Death of a chief or other important person (A); national calamity (K). Immediately after death (A). Traditionally taboo for ordinary wear.
Close relatives of chief (A)	Prolonged feeling of melancholy. After the corpse is laid in state (A).
Close relatives of chief (A)	The fortieth day after the burial (A).
Chief (K)	When the chief is in mourning but must appear at a festive occasion (K).

Religious and Cultural Significance of Adinkra Motifs

Adinkra designs are closely associated with daily activities, incorporating, for instance, commonly used tools as well as symbolic representations of religious and social concepts. Usually, the names given the motifs reflect their meanings.[10]

Today some fifty adinkra designs are in constant use. Ghanaian traditionalists feel that adinkra design motifs were combined so that the wearer could convey specific messages. This, then, is the proper usage of adinkra. If a man wished to convey a number of messages on one cloth, he used a selection of appropriate designs but the common practice was one design on one cloth. "Thus, if a king wished to express his fearlessness and independence of another, he wore an adinkra cloth with the 'aya' or 'fern' design (Figure 64), for the word 'aya' also means 'I am independent of you; I am not afraid of you.' If a king wore the 'Gye Nyame' design (Figure 63), his message was 'Except God, I fear none.' "[11]

Since variations in shades of red, vermilion, and rust play an important role in Ghanaian symbolism and attire, particularly in the traditional uses of adinkra cloth, it is interesting to note Antubam's observation: "All kinds of red are used to symbolize occasions of melancholy such as any loss through death of a close relation, an act of war, a national anger, sudden calamity, boisterousness, violence, and a show of dissatisfaction. This explains the reason behind the rather violent display of reds during political rallies, conventions, and upheavals even in modern Ghanaian life."[12]

We know from Eva L. R. Meyerowitz's book, *At the Court of an African King,* that Ashanti royalty not only wore adinkra cloth but sometimes were involved in the various processes of making it. Nana Akumfi Ameyaw III, king of the Bono-Tekyiman State (now called Tekyiman-Brong), whom she met in Ghana in 1944 before his enthronement, had a love for weaving and was accomplished in it.[13]

Traditional Dyeing, Printing, and Embroidery Techniques

A complete and accurate documentation of the mixing of the dyes and manner of printing adinkra cloth is found in Rattray's *Religion and Art in Ashanti.* Rattray observed and recorded the following:

> The foundation of the Adinkira cloth is a plain fabric of white cotton, or of cotton dyed russet brown (with the bark of the *Kuntunkuni* tree which is the colour of Ashanti mourning cloths). Upon this the designs are stamped. The dye used in stamping them is made from the bark of a tree called in Ashanti *Badie.* The bark is cut up and then boiled in a big pot, into which several lumps of iron slag (*etia*) have been placed. The bark and slag are boiled for several hours until two-thirds of the water has evaporated; the remainder is strained off. . . . The liquid is now called *Adinkira aduru,* i.e., *Adinkira* medicine, and is the colour and consistency of coal tar; when this has cooled, it is ready for use. A flat piece of ground is cleared and swept, and upon this the cloth to be stamped is pegged out taut with small wooden pins. . . . The stamps, cut in the various designs, are made from fragments of old calabashes, with small sticks leading from the stamp to a point which enables them to be held between the thumb and forefinger. . . .[14]

One sees in the fabric collected in 1817 by Bowdich (Figure 43) the classic adinkra cloth design—blocks of design areas composed of repetitions of the same adinkra stamps, divided by linear markings formed by dipping a comblike instrument into the dye and dragging it over the surface of the fabric. In this adinkra, neither embroidery nor Kente cloth strips have been used as a dividing device.

While the use of embroidery on adinkra cloth is not mentioned by Rattray in his account of printing the fabric, photographs of men wearing cloths in which the repeated squares of adinkra patterns are divided by embroidered strips appear in several of his books, thereby dating the use of embroidery on traditional adinkra to at least the early 1920s; it probably began well before that. Although written evidence is lacking, it is said that the brilliant colors of the embroidery are, in effect, a distillation of the intricate handwoven Kente cloth strips that were used to decorate the more elaborate adinkra cloths of the past, offering a similar effect.[15]

Kente cloth, like adinkra, was originally a royal fabric, restricted to members of the court, but nowadays it is a prestigious, expensive fabric which may be worn by anyone who can afford it. (The man in the center of Figure 42 is wearing a draped Kente cloth robe.) It has an interesting history in Ghana. According to Ashanti legend, weaving was introduced by Ota Kraban, who went to Gyaman (now Ivory Coast) and brought back the first loom which he set up in Bonwere (near Kumasi). The date is uncertain but others have suggested the seventeenth century. The name Kente appears to have been taken from the chief, Oti Akenten, who ruled the Ashanti during the period weaving was introduced.[16] Originally, Kente cloth was woven with raffia fibers; locally grown cotton was then introduced and subsequently brightly colored silk was imported.[17] Cotton, silk, and rayon from Manchester form the basic fibers of much of present-day Kente cloth. In the past the Ashanti made a practice of unraveling Dutch silk fabrics and reweaving them according to patterns of their own.[18] Woven by men on horizontal looms, the 3½-inch narrow bands are eventually sewn together to form luxurious cloths several yards in length, worn toga fashion by Ashanti men. Kente weaving incorporates tapestry or brocade techniques and is often combined with plain weaving, while picks may be made by hand for very complex patterns.[19] The intricate Kente cloth designs have symbolic meanings which relate to historical events and proverbs.

In comparing the use of Kente strips on adinkra cloth with the use of embroidery as a dividing device of horizontal strips, it is relevant to note that today Kente weavers also do the adinkra embroidery:[20] perhaps the weavers themselves were responsible for the transition from the use of Kente strips to embroidery. In fact, the Ghanaian fabric called nwumu might be considered the transitional textile that inspired the contemporary embroidery on adinkra cloth. According to Kyerematen,

> *Nwumu* is a broad piece of imported silk or linen material into which are woven in horizontal lines narrow strips of satin-stitch embroidery, having the same appearance as the weft pattern of a *kente*. The spaces between these strips of *kente* ribbons are equal, and they are sometimes stamped with *adinkra* designs. The ribbons may have straight edges or may be notched or saw-edged; the two types are called respectively *kukrubou* and *kaw*.
> . . . *Nwumu* [is] worn, not necessarily but usually, for solemn occasions, such as when the chief, being in mourning, has to turn out for a festive occasion. They are sometimes made in colours that can only be used at times of festivity.[21]

In the nwumu cloth, then, which relates to adinkra in its usage for occasions of mourning plus its occasional patterning with adinkra motifs, the embroidered strips are documented by Kyerematen as being "woven" into the imported fabric, and the strips themselves are referred to as "kente" ribbons. Two examples of this fabric are said to be in the collection of the Prempeh II Jubilee Museum, Kumasi, Ghana. Unfortunately, there are neither dates nor photographs documenting these fabrics. However, since adinkra cloths with actual Kente strips have been seen by contemporary travelers in Ghana, it may very well be that the practice of using embroidery instead of the actual Kente strips is in a state of flux, with embroidery dominating the less expensive and more readily available commercial trade in adinkra cloths.

In any case, the origins of Kente weaving and adinkra printing in Ghana appear to be related in that both are said to have been brought to the Ashanti peoples from Gyaman between the seventeenth and nineteenth centuries; the nwumu cloth implies a relationship between the two textiles which might be interpreted as transitional in the development of adinkra cloth and the usage of both Kente strips and embroidery.

Color Symbolism in Ghana

Color symbolism is extensive in Ghana and reflected in adinkra cloth usage. Kofi Antubam summarizes certain aspects of Ashanti color expressions in his chapter entitled "Akerasu Honsem" ("Notions of Colour"). While the full range of color associations in

Ashanti life is too extensive to be noted in detail, it is interesting to realize that many of the Ghanaian concepts of color relate directly to Western associations; others differ radically. White is associated with purity, virtue, joy, and the "spiritual entities [such] as God and the deified spirits of the ancestors," while black is related to deep feelings of melancholy, the devil, death, and old age. Green symbolizes "newness, fertility, vitality, and primeness in growth" while gray is related to ashes and used to personify "blame and various degrees of degradation and shame." Blue, especially indigo, is related to "love [and] womanly tenderness" and calls to mind "early dawn [and] the crescent moon." Gold in Ghana, above all, "stands for royalty . . . the presence and influence of God in society, and the rule of the king"; it also symbolizes "continuous life . . . warmth, and controlled fire." Differences in Ghanaian and Western color associations are most apparent in the uses of red "to symbolize occasions of melancholy such as . . . any loss through death of a close relation, an act of war, national anger, sudden calamity, boisterousness, violence, and a show of dissatisfaction."[22]

To bring further insight into the study of adinkra cloth, we must look at the craft as it is practiced in Ghana today.

Contemporary Adinkra Cloth in Ghana

The basic design concepts associated with early adinkra cloth are still the basis of contemporary adinkra cloth. More often than not, the cloth is stamped with more than one design, and is chosen for its aesthetic appeal.[23] Adinkra cloth is still held in high esteem by royalty and is valued for its traditional means of conveying a symbolistic message. For instance, when the present Asantehene of Ghana, Opuku Ware II (Mathiew Jacob Poku), was installed in office in 1970, he sat in state, regally attired in an adinkra cloth of one continuous design (Figure 45). The symbolism of the stamp, according to the chart created by E. Ablade Glover, is *Mframa-dan*—wind-house, or "house built to stand windy and treacherous conditions." The choice made by Opuku

Figure 45. *Asantehene Opuku Ware II, sitting in state at his installation, wearing an adinkra cloth patterned in the* Mframa-dan *motif.*

Figure 46. *Musicians of the Asantehene's court wearing adinkra cloth in a variety of patterns, including Aya, the fern (lower left corner and center).*

Ware II was especially appropriate for the stormy political mood of African countries. (Note also the men wearing adinkra cloths in the foreground of Figures 45 and 46 and the use of the fern motif which means, "I am not afraid of you; I am independent of you.")

A selection of contemporary adinkra stamp motifs, hand printed from my collection of calabash stamps, can be seen in Figures 47–77.[24]

Figure 47. Adinkrahene
The adinkra king, and "chief" of all these adinkra designs (R),*
forms the basis of adinkra printing (G).†

Figure 48. *Adinkrahene with* Ananse, *the spider.*

(*Note:* * (R) *indicates Rattray as the source;* † (G) *indicates Glover as the source.*)

Figure 49. *Adinkrahene variation.*

Figure 50. *Adinkrahene variation.*

Figure 51. *Adinkrahene variation* (*or* fofoo *flower variation; see Figure 60*).

Figure 52. *Adinkrahene variation with* musuyidie; *see Figure 59.*

Figure 53. *Adinkrahene variation.*

Figure 54. *Adinkrahene variation (central motif unknown).*

Figure 55. *Adinkrahene variation with swastika* (nkotimsefuopua); *see Figure 57.*

Figure 56. Obi nka obie.
"I offend no one without a cause" (R).
Bi-nka-bi.
Bite not one another. Avoid conflicts; symbol of unity (G).

Figure 57. Nkotimsefuopua.
Certain attendants of the Queen Mother dressed their hair in this fashion. It is really a variation of the swastika (R).

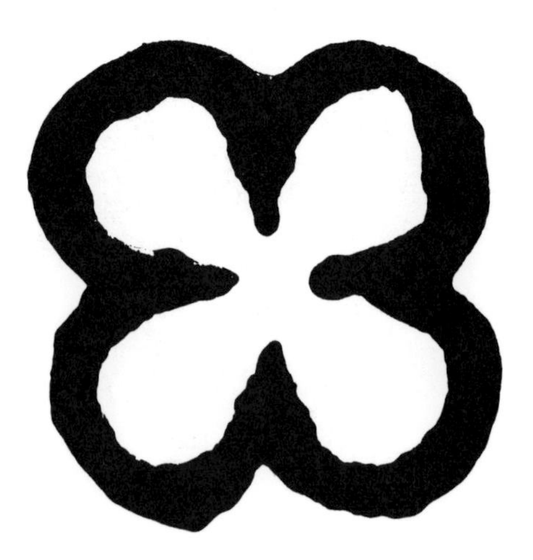

Figure 58. Kuntinkantan *variation.*
Literal meaning: bent and spread out; used in the sense of "do not boast, do not be arrogant" (R).

Figure 59. Musuyidie.
Something to remove evil; a cloth with this design stamped upon it lay beside the sleeping couch of the king of Ashanti, and every morning when he rose, he placed his left boot upon it three times (R); *symbol of spiritual cleanliness* (G).

Figure 60. *The* fofoo *flower.*
Se die fofoo pe, ne se gyinantwi abo bedie: "*What the yellow-flowered fofoo plant wants is that the gyinantwi seeds should turn black.*" *This is a well-known Ashanti saying. One of the cotton-cloth designs bears the same name. The fofoo, the botanical name of which is* Bidens pilosa, *has a small yellow flower, which, when it drops its petals, turns into a black spiky seed; said of a jealous person* (R).

Figure 61. Dweninini aben, *the ram's horns* (R); Dwani ne ahooden ne n'amen a na wo ayi no awie no—*the strength of the ram lies in its horns; once they are plucked off it is finished* (G).

Figure 62. Ohene nwa.
"In the king's little eyes," i.e., in his favor (R).

Figure 63. Gye Nyame.
"Except God, I fear none" (R).

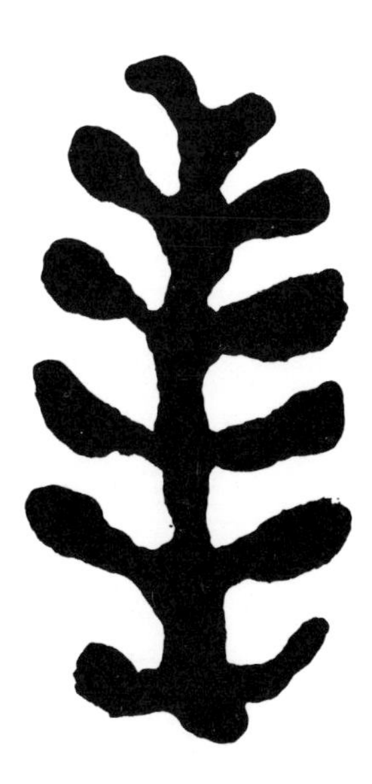

Figure 64. Aya, *the fern.*
The word means, "I am not afraid of you; I am independent of you," and the wearer may imply this by wearing it (R); *a symbol of defiance* (G).

Figure 65. Mmra Krado, *the Hausa man's lock* (R).
Krado—mmra krado; *seal of law and order, symbolizing the authority of the court* (G).

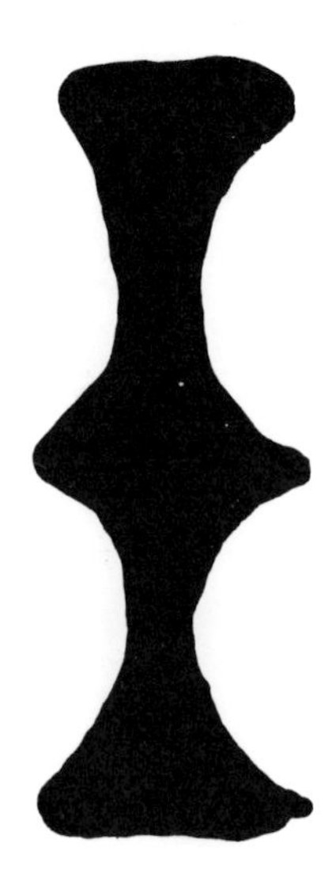

Figure 66. Dono ntoasuo, *the double dono drums* (R).

Figure 67. Osrane ne nsoroma—*the moon and star.*
Representing royal blood (king and prince), both glowing; a symbol of faithfulness (G).

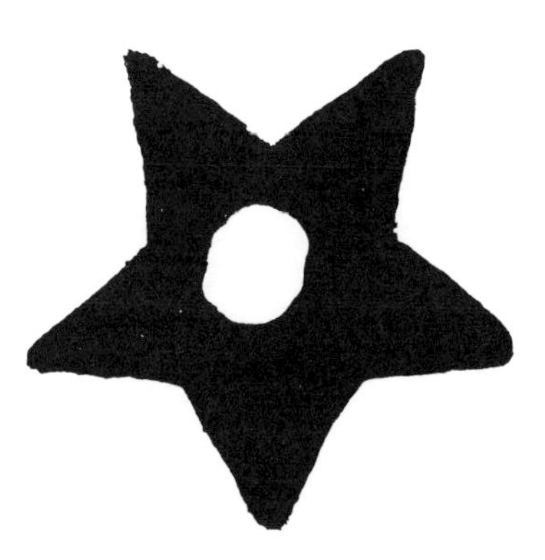

Figure 68. Nsoroma, *the star.*
Literally, a child of the sky, i.e., a star, referring to the saying: Oba Nyankon soroma te Nyame so na ho so; "*Like the star, the child of the Supreme Being, I rest with God and do not depend upon myself*" (R).

Figure 69. Akoma, *the heart* (R).

Figure 70. 'Ma te.
"I have heard what you have said"; association with design obscure (R).
Ntesie-matemasie
"I have heard and kept it"; Nyanasa bun mu nne matemasie; *symbol of wisdom and knowledge* (G).

Figure 71. Nsirewa, *cowries* (R).

Figure 72. (*Double*) Fihankra, *the circular house* (R).
The circular house or complete house; this signifies safety or security in a home (G).

Figure 73. Nsaa, *a kind of blanket.*
Nea onim nsaa na oto nago (G).

Figure 74. *Checkerboard.*

Figure 75. *Pebbles.*

Figure 76. *Okra.*

Figure 77. *Symbol of the totality of the universe, incorporating the eye, the rays of the sun, the double crescent moon, and the Ashanti stool (Kojo Baiden).*

Relationship of Adinkra Motifs to Other Ashanti Designs

Visual similarities can be found between adinkra stamp motifs and architectural designs found in seventeenth-century drawings and nineteenth- and early twentieth-century photographs depicting Ashanti life. Many structural wall sculptures appear to be directly related to traditional adinkra stamp designs. By far the most common are variations on the ram's horn motif. We also see designs which suggest a correlation to other design motifs of contemporary adinkra stamps, including the *adinkrahene;* the *fofoo* flower; *Ohene nwa,* "in the king's little eyes"; *fihankra,* the circular house; *akoma,* the heart; *nsoroma,* the star; *nsirewa,* the cowrie shell; *nsaa,* a kind of blanket; and others as seen in Figures 47–77.

There is also a similarity between calabash-carved adinkra stamp motifs and brass-cast gold-weight designs, which is evident when comparing motifs from the two media. Several examples of gold weights in Brigitte Menzel's book, *Goldgewichte aus Ghana,*[25] relate certain circular gold-weight designs to circular adinkrahene symbols, while the ram's horn and swastika gold-weight designs correspond to the same ram's horn and swastika adinkra motifs.[26]

Contemporary Adinkra Cloth

The material used in present-day adinkra cloth is a smooth-surfaced, factory-produced cotton manufactured in Ghana. Before the embroidery process is begun, the fabric is cut, washed, and dried. Frequently it is used in its original white state; sometimes it is hand-dyed. Very often solid colors of factory-purchased cottons are used, and occasionally a multicolored background; sometimes real or simulated tie and dye is seen. The colors of contemporary adinkra cloth vary considerably and are no longer confined to the traditional russet browns, terra-cottas, black, and white. In fact,

Figure 78. *Multicolored adinkra cloths on display for sale in Ntonso, Ghana.*

almost every color appears to be available, although the rust shades and vermilion continue to be taboo for ordinary wear, being confined to occasions of mourning. Green is extremely popular. Gold, mustard, and yellow are also often seen, a reflection, no doubt, of their rich association with royalty, power, and the wealth of real gold in Ghana, formerly part of the old Gold Coast. Other colors for sale in Ghana or available for export include royal blue, orchid, pink, beige, dark red, and orange. Figure 78 shows contemporary cloths on display being offered for sale in Ntonso, Ghana (a small village near Kumasi). In Figure 78, the adinkra designs on the first few cloths are created by dragging the comblike instrument across the area in one direction and then in the opposite one, making attractive, checkerboard-like squares.

The size of the cloths, once the long pieces have been embroidered together, is quite large. Contemporary cloths from Africa House in Accra measure 135 inches long and 80 inches wide, or nearly four yards by two yards. However, adinkra cloths measuring eight yards, ten yards, and twelve yards in length are available, the greater size being desirable as a sign of greater wealth and hence greater prestige.

Contemporary cloths have several variations of lengthwise designs to divide the blocks of repeated calabash-stamped motifs. Embroidery forming narrow strips of several colors is by far the most common. In its multicolored brightness, the embroidery is functional as well as decorative. It serves to attach the six, long, lengthwise widths of fabric together with a very simple but surprisingly strong, floating faggoting stitch (Figure 79). After the embroidery has been completed by the embroiderer, the cloth is hemmed and is then ready for printing.

The first step in preparing for printing usually involves the creation of parallel lines running alongside the lengthwise embroidery and dividing the width of the cloth into equal-sized blocks which will then enclose the various repeated adinkra motifs. This is accomplished by dragging a comblike instrument along the material after it has been dipped into the adinkra dye (Figure 80). The tool has the appearance of an Afro comb; however, a thread is wound around each of its six fine teeth, apparently controlling the flow of the dye so that the lines can be made with a relatively steady, flowing movement. The material is spread on a long, low wooden platform, which is only wide enough for part of the cloth to fit on. The craftsman must work section by section, creating the lines with the comblike instrument in the allotted working space, kneeling beside his work, then changing over to the calabash stamps, moving along to fill in each blocked-out area. The printing is done with a deft movement, the stamp dipped into the pail of dye for each impression (Figure 81). A padding of fabric placed between the cloth and the wooden platform cushions the stamp as it is pressed against the material. The speed of each craftsman varies with his skill and mood. Some craftsmen are very fast and can turn out a finished cloth in half an hour. However, high-quality work is not always so quickly achieved. There is a certain charm in the casual way the designs are applied, sometimes overlapping each other or the bordering lines—even covering the embroidery—often leaving little drips of dye where the stamps have been hurriedly carried over the cloth, laden with the dye mixture.

The printing of adinkra is frequently done by two people simultaneously; quite often the second person is a younger apprentice.

Figure 79. *Strips of plain cotton cloth being embroidered by Charles Ahinful in varicolored threads before the printing process is begun.*

Figure 80. *A comblike instrument is dragged over the cloth to apply dye in horizontal lines parallel to the embroidered area that joins the cloth strips.*

Figure 81. *The calabash adinkra printing stamp is dipped in the dye and quickly applied to the cloth, leaving a dark design on the white background.*

Figure 82. *Sitting under a tree, Francis Konadu, accompanied by an apprentice and friends, applies dye to an adinkra cloth.*

In Figure 82 Francis Konadu sits under a tree, his cloth nailed to the wooden board, and applies dye with the comblike instrument while a second printer works beside him. In the left foreground, embroidered adinkras await the printing process. Behind the two standing men, sun-dried adinkras are spread on the ground, the strong Ghanaian breezes having loosened them from the rocks intended to secure them.

Usually each village has a specialist to carve adinkra stamps; if not, the adinkra cloth craftsman carves his own stamps in the traditional manner from bits of broken, dried calabash (gourd). The designs closely follow the traditional motifs recorded by Rattray in 1927, with occasional regional variations that are difficult to identify symbolically. The size of the printing surface varies from 1½ to 2¾ inches; the curve of the calabash provides an area of relatively flat surface not much larger than three inches in diameter.

Contemporary photographs (1972) of the process described by Rattray show that the traditional manner of preparing the dyestuffs and carving the calabash printing stamps continues in much the same way that Rattray observed it in the 1920s. A woman peels the bark from the branches of the badie tree (which are brought to the village of Ntonso in bundles) in preparation for pounding with a large mortar and pestle. The shredded bark and iron slag are then placed in large metal cans, water is added, and the preparation is boiled. Sometimes the shredded bark is boiled and beaten several times and poured through a burlap strainer, then boiled again until, after several days, the mixture evaporates, leaving a tarrish-looking substance.

In Ntonso, the main adinkra village, an elderly man named Kwabena Anena carves all the adinkra stamps for the craftsmen. Stamps in use rest in a bowl of dye, while new, unused stamps are seen in the basket (Figure 83). As it is waiting to be used, the total stamp, including the bamboo stems which are bound together at the top with small strips of cloth to serve as a handle, is immersed in the tarlike substance. This then hardens and dries after the stamp is removed from the dye, serving as a strong coating which helps hold the stamp and its cloth-bound stems together. The results are often attractive objects valued by collec-

Figure 83. *New, unused adinkra stamps carved from bits of broken, dried calabash rest in a basket awaiting use.*

Figure 84. *Adinkra stamps of varying designs and sizes in the author's collection shown as art objects in themselves.*

tors—like many utilitarian objects in African daily life—for their aesthetic appeal rather than their function (Figure 84).

The number of repeats appearing on an adinkra cloth vary according to the size of the calabash stamps used, ranging from approximately twelve to forty-two single units within an eleven-to-fifteen-square-inch area. Sometimes the fabric is not divided into sections but is stamped all over with one particular design, such as the crescent moon and star motif. Often, the comblike instrument is used to make large "X" patterns across the whole cloth, which are then stamped in the middle with popular designs such as the fofoo flower (Figure 60) or the adinkrahene, "king of adinkra" pattern (Figures 47–50). The double *dono* drum (Figure 66) and the star (Figure 68) are sometimes used as dividers both horizontally and vertically, interspersed with each other, by themselves, or alongside the multiple lines of the comblike instrument.

It is characteristic of hand-printed adinkra that no two cloths are ever exactly alike. In fact, even repetitions of one design on a cloth vary from section to section. This is clear when we compare a section of a finished, hand-printed adinkra (Figure 85) to a machine-printed cloth (Figure 86), where the repeated designs are rigid and precise. On the factory-produced adinkra, a row of hand embroidery has been added to enhance its appearance (and perhaps mislead the naïve tourist into believing it is a hand-printed textile). The large piece has been hung over a rope so that the embroiderer can work seated in a chair before it, moving himself and the chair along as he progresses. Notice the way the blocks of repeated designs have been divided by heavy dark lines. These are copies of handmade adinkra in which rows of solid-colored cotton are appliquéd to the lengthwise, cut pieces in place of the embroidery process. Some factory-printed adinkras simulate the embroidery by printing multicolored stripes in lengthwise rows. From a distance they are very effective in giving the illusion of actual embroidery.

The similarities in adinkra cloth today and those produced early in the nineteenth century may be seen by comparing the photograph taken in Ntonso in 1972 (Figure 85) and the cloth in the

Figure 85. *A finished, hand-printed adinkra cloth displayed in Ntonso, Ghana.*

Figure 86. *An example of factory-produced adinkra cloth with hand embroidery added to give the illusion of a totally handcrafted cloth.*

collection of the British Museum (photographed folded in half), which was collected by Bowdich in 1817 (Figure 43). One sees in both pictures the classic adinkra cloth design: blocks of hand-printed areas are composed of repetitions of the same adinkra stamps. Although few of the designs from the earlier museum piece are related to those appearing on this contemporary adinkra—crescents, drums, stars, dividing lines—on many present-day adinkra cloths, motifs are found which are identical to the designs appearing on this cloth from the British Museum.

The fastness of the dyes used in adinkra hand printing is debatable. The director of The Loom, a craft boutique in downtown Accra, maintains that the cloths are washable. However, on Glover's 1974 chart appears the cautious warning that adinkra cloths are not meant to be washed. Kwasi Badu, former master drummer in residence at the University of California, Los Angeles, and Kojo Baiden, at one time director of the Museum of African Music, Howard University, Washington, D.C., both Ashanti, substantiate this view, stating that adinkra cloths are not washed after each wearing but used on special occasions, aired, and set aside for the next event. The practice of airing clothes rather than subjecting them to frequent washings which fade the colors and weaken the fibers, thereby shortening the life of the garment, is common throughout West Africa. Sometimes people bring old cloths to be redyed and restamped, according to Rita Warpeha, who visited Ntonso and Asokwa, two Ghanaian villages that produce adinkra cloth. Perhaps this is an economic measure, as it is in Nigeria where women's wrappers are retied and redyed with indigo.

Supposedly, says Ms. Warpeha, the people of Ntonso learned their craft from the Asokwans, whose work is more refined and varied in design. She observed that children from ages seven to nine participate in various parts of the processes of creating adinkra, which they learn from everyday life experiences, not from school. The dyeing and stamping may be done away from the immediate communal living area, or on the front porch of the ordinary living quarters in the compound.

In the adinkra village visited by Melvin Deal (director, African

Figure 87. *Former ethnomusicology student Jackie Peters, performing at UCLA with Melvin Deal and other students, wearing adinkra cloths designed and hand printed by the author.*

Plate 1. *Indigo dyer at the Kano, Nigeria, dye pits, raising the cloth from the solution at the moment the color oxidizes to green before changing almost immediately to deep indigo blue. (Photograph by Gerard Bonnet.)*

Plate 2. *Detail of a Genya raffia tie-dye from Zaïre, collected by Mohun in the 1890s and distinguished by its use of cut-pile embroidery edge work. (Smithsonian Collection, Natural Museum of Natural History, Washington, D.C.)*

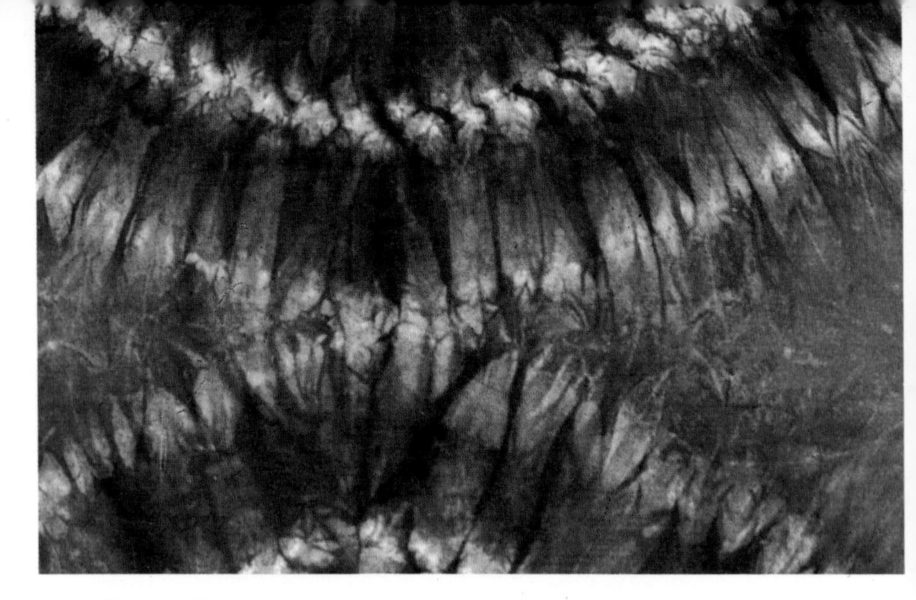

Plate 3. *Contemporary tie-dye using various subtle shadings of natural kola nut overdyed with indigo, purchased at the Treichville marketplace in Abidjan, Ivory Coast. (Photograph by John Philibert.)*

Plate 4. *Another contemporary tie-dye purchased at the Treichville marketplace, showing the variety of darker colors achieved with the same kola nut and indigo dyes as in Plate 3. (Photograph by John Philibert.)*

Plate 5. *Contemporary* adire *tapestry by Senabu Oloyede of Oshogbo, Nigeria. (Photograph by Richard F. Wolford.)*

Plate 6. *Ashanti woman (at left) wearing* adinkra-*cloth mourning dress while dancing with other women before a chief. (Photograph by Herbert M. Cole.)*

Plate 7. *An artist applies* savon de sodani *to* bokolanfini *cloth, eventually bleaching the design back to the natural color of the cloth. (Photograph by Dr. Pascal James Imperato.)*

Heritage Dancers and Drummers, Washington, D.C.) in the summer of 1970, fabric was printed in the traditional way. The large piece of cloth was pegged out on a level area of hard ground and the craftsman proceeded to dip his stamps quickly into the natural dye substance. Without premarking, he filled the spaces with repeated impressions of the same design. The craftsmen are very social and somewhat competitive, according to Mr. Deal, vying with each other to see who can appear the least concerned and still produce the most attractive results.

Adinkra cloths are popular attire among Ghanaians in high public office. Ebenezer Debrah, former Ghanaian ambassador to the United States, has been seen on numerous occasions at diplomatic functions in Washington, D.C., draped in a yellow adinkra cloth with bold appliqués of maroon cotton strips dividing the blocks of patterns both vertically and horizontally.

Traditionally, women wear adinkra cloth in two pieces—a skirt wrapper and a throw that is draped over one shoulder in a fashion similar to the man's mode of dress or wrapped and tied under the arms and over the breasts, leaving both shoulders bare, as seen on the woman at the left in Plate 6 (see insert). In traditional mourning, the woman's forehead is shaved and her hairline heightened about one inch; a black mourning band encircles the head across the brow following the curve of the head behind the ears and lower skull. The lips, too, are blackened in deep mourning and the eyes are outlined with soot and ashes. In contemporary fashion, embroidered adinkra cloth is sometimes cut and sewn into formal tailored ensembles for women.

Summary

It appears, then, that contemporary adinkra cloth continues to be designed and printed in the traditional manner as recorded by Rattray and described in his original research published in 1927. Slight regional variations and innovations occur, according to the design of the calabash stamps and the manner in which the stamps are applied to the fabric. Today, modern machine-woven fabrics in bright colors have been introduced as the basic cloth upon which the traditional designs are hand printed, and are available to all Ghanaians who can afford to buy them, without consideration of royal family origins. However, the colors russet brown and vermilion red are still reserved for mourning and regarded as taboo for wear on other occasions. The same type of hand-carved calabash stamp is used for printing the traditional symbolic designs, which vary slightly in size and exact design from region to region and from carver to carver. Usually, embroidery in five lengthwise multicolored strips holds the six long panels of fabric together by means of a close, floating faggoting stitch. The designs are printed on the pre-embroidered fabric in repeated squares averaging about thirteen to fifteen inches each, which are frequently divided by an outline of repeated designs such as the dono drum or the star. Less expensive appliqués of strips of cotton cloth in contrasting colors may be used instead of embroidery; the cotton strips may appear vertically as well as horizontally, dividing the cloth into blocks or repeated-design areas. Adinkra cloths are also hand printed without the application of embroidered strips or cotton appliqués. The size of the cloth itself varies, beginning at around four yards by two yards, and occasionally reaching a length of from ten to twelve yards per cloth. Sometimes, one overall design, a theme or message, may dominate the cloth, perhaps having been ordered especially to express the wearer's sentiments for a particular occasion. More often, the designs are multiple repeats, with symbolism chosen at random by the craftsman, although custom ordering of designs by individual clients in various multiples appears to exist as well. Although women traditionally wear adinkra cloth in two pieces, a wrapper and a throw, innovations in contemporary fashion have introduced the embroidered adinkra cloth, cut and sewn and tailored into a two-piece ensemble for formal wear. Men wear the traditional draped robe either over a loose-fitting shirt or with the right shoulder bare, as in a toga. The adinkra cloth continues to be a popular form of national dress in Ghana, enjoying favor among international figures in the diplomatic world at home and abroad while still retaining its traditional role and context when restricted to Ashanti colors of mourning.

NOTES

1. The spelling of *adinkra* cloth varies—*adinkra; adinkera; Adinkira; adinkrah; adwinkena*. The choice of adinkra is my personal preference; when variations appear, they are the result of direct or indirect quotes from cited sources.

2. T. E. Bowdich, *Mission from Cape Coast to Ashanti*, 1819, John Murray, London, Frontispiece.

3. E. Ablade Glover, Chart: *Adinkra Symbolism*, University of Science and Technology, Kumasi, Ghana.

4. Emerico Samassa-Mayer, Chart: *Adinkira Cloth*, Ghana Museum and Monument Board, Accra, Ghana.

5. René Bravmann, *Islam and Tribal Art in West Africa*, 1973, Cambridge University Press, London, pp. 88–92.

6. *Ghana News*, "Making an 'Adinkrah' Cloth," Volume 2, No. 2, March/April 1970, p. 3.

7. T. E. Bowdich, op. cit., p. 310.

8. A. A. Y. Kyerematen, *Panoply of Ghana*, 1964, Praeger, New York, pp. 67–68.

9. Kofi Antubam, *Ghana's Heritage of Culture*, 1963, Kehler and Amelang, Leipzig, p. 151.

10. Ibid., p. 151.

11. *Ghana News*, op. cit., p. 3.

12. Kofi Antubam, op. cit., p. 82.

13. Eva L. R. Meyerowitz, *At the Court of an African King*, 1962, Faber and Faber, London, pp. 68–69.

14. Robert S. Rattray, *Religion and Art in Ashanti*, 1927, Oxford Press, London, pp. 265–67.

15. While I was not able to locate any old photographs showing the use of Kente strips on adinkra cloth, in 1970 I spoke with former Ambassador Debrah of Ghana and he has confirmed the use of Kente strips as the origin and inspiration of the embroidered strips.

16. Robert Rattray, op. cit., p. 220.

17. Cheryl Plumer, *African Textiles*, Michigan State University, 1971, p. 18.

18. Elsy Leuzinger, *Africa—The Art of the Negro Peoples*, 1960, Crown Publishers, New York, p. 45.

19. Cheryl Plumer, op. cit., p. 18.

20. *The Ashanti—African Craftsmen,* documentary film, Bailey Film Corp.

21. A. A. Y. Kyerematen, op. cit., pp. 71 and 74.

22. Kofi Antubam, op. cit., pp. 75–86.

23. *Ghana News,* op. cit., p. 3.

24. Over 115 illustrations of variations in contemporary and traditional adinkra stamp designs are presented in Dr. Brigitte Menzel's *Textilien aus Westafrika,* Volume II. Volume IV, as yet unpublished, will contain details of the meanings of the designs. In personal conversation on November 11, 1976, Dr. Menzel has stated that in spite of her extended field research, she is finding it extremely difficult to offer a complete analysis of the meanings of the adinkra stamp patterns illustrating her book.

25. Brigitte Menzel, *Goldgewichte aus Ghana,* 1968, Museum für Völkerkunde, Berlin, Illustrations 126–35; 281–92; and 343–55.

26. In *The Akan of Ghana* (London: Faber and Faber, 1958), Eva L. K. Meyerowitz agrees with the usual analysis of the swastika symbol as representing the cutout design formed in the short-cropped hair of the queen mother's attendants. However, she associates the symbol itself with the moon, tracing it to a symbol of creation by the Lunar Mother-Goddess.

6

Bokolanfini—
The Mud Cloth of Mali

Among the most elusive and difficult to classify of all the fabrics in Africa—both in a technical as well as a design sense—has been the mud cloth of the Bambara (Bamana) peoples of Mali. Contemporary textile scholars are indebted to the research of Dr. Pascal James Imperato and to Marli Shamir's detailed photographic studies of the technique in process; it is on their work that much of this chapter is based.[1]

Mud cloth is variously referred to as *bokolanfini* and *bogolafini* cloth; in Mali, both words mean that the designs are made with mud. Bokolanfini is thought to have originated in Beledougou, spreading eventually through other parts of the west-central area of Mali. It is in Beledougou that the finest design work is done. The cloth itself is thoroughly indigenous to the countryside. Cotton grows locally and is combed and spun by the women. It is then woven by men into narrow strips of white cotton cloth called *finimougou,* which is sold in its undecorated state for men's and women's clothing in the cities and remote villages.

Mud cloth has confused textile historians because the designs seem to indicate procedures used in other fabric design techniques. The mud cloth patterns are produced by dyeing the fabric yellow, using a mud paste to outline the background of designs, and then bleaching some of the still yellow areas with another substance. Bleaching does play a part in the production of bokolanfini but it is not the means through which the designs are initially achieved. It is solely through outlining a dark background color *around* the desired light areas that the patterning takes place.

Before the Imperato study was published, most scholars and students assumed that the light geometric designs on the dark background of mud cloth were the sole results of a bleaching—or *discharge*—process. It was assumed that certain natural materials were applied to the fabric in an organized design form. The chemical action of these materials on the previously dyed fabric then appeared lightened to pale yellowish-white decorative forms against the existing blackish rust-brown background. In many current textile sources, these bokolanfini cloths are still assumed to be covered with patterns achieved by the discharge method—that is, by discharging or releasing the dye from a dark fabric through a chemically induced bleaching process. (This is in contrast to other processes of dyeing—batik, tie-dye, and printing—where the light fabrics are patterned by the addition of a dark-colored dye, resulting in a dark-against-light background design.)

It is easy to see how the techniques of patterning bokolanfini became confused and mistaken. So little was known about dyeing techniques in Africa that whenever any information became available it was quoted and requoted until it was assumed that the few original—and often quite tentative—facts had been reliably studied and verified. As recently as 1971, references to the Malian mud cloth describe the designs as produced solely by discharge techniques or combined with resist methods.

Perhaps some of the confusion and resulting misinformation about bokolanfini can be traced to misquotation of information drawn from Henri Clouzot's *Tissus Nègres*, published in Paris in the early 1930s. A. Steinmann, in the 1947 issue of *Ciba Review* devoted to batiks, notes that:

> The Bambara, according to H. Clouzot, produce their patterns mostly by bleaching and reserving. The woman dyer prepares the dyebath by boiling the bark or leaves of certain trees for three hours. The cloth is then dipped for one day. The fabric thus dyed brown is then rinsed and the design is added by means of a scoop or spatula with "finiyenguele," which is a ferrous mud from certain ponds. When this has dried, the design is covered

> once more with a highly concentrated alkali soap which the natives produce themselves. The whole material is then rinsed in running water; and wherever the alkali soap has bleached away the color, the design (circles, squares, lines, zigzags) show up light on the dark ground.[2]

These comments are illustrated by a photograph captioned, "Cotton cloth ornamented in resist technique. Bambara, French Sudan. Musée de l'Homme, Paris."[3]

Actually, Clouzot recounts the observations of ethnographer François de Zeltner. In *Tissus Nègres,* Clouzot clearly states that the designs are *not* made by the reserve method, like batik.[4] Steinmann further confuses the issue by referring to the fabric as first being dyed brown, while in fact Clouzot notes that the fabric is immersed in a brownish liquid[5] (which we know dyes the fabric yellow). Steinmann may have been misled by Clouzot's description of the application of the soap mixture which sounds somewhat like a reserve technique, similar to applying starch resist in other parts of Africa (and in Asia as well). Clouzot himself creates confusion when he describes the use of the alkaline soap mixture as a form of mordanting,[6] which is not really accurate, as we shall see.

In contrast to these limited observations, scholars today have the benefit of Dr. Imperato's detailed, documented field study and of Mrs. Shamir's accompanying photographs. The two spent four years observing the process of producing this highly complex patterned cloth throughout the Bamana area. During one particularly concentrated study Dr. Imperato reports, ". . . we undertook an exhaustive study of the manufacturing process among the artisans of the Beledougou area, during which every step in the creation of this cloth was carried out in our presence."[7]

Dr. Imperato points out that the cloth, when patterned, may be called by various names, and that the Bamana refer to it as both bokolanfini, which means mud cloth, and *finignekele,* meaning designed cloth. Bokolanfini is very specific and is the one most frequently used, while finignekele can be applied to any designed cloth and routinely refers to printed cloth imported from either Europe or neighboring African countries.[8]

One recognizes the similarities in the word finignekele, employed by Dr. Imperato as a Bamana definition of any cloth with designs on it, and Henri Clouzot's use of the word *finiyeguele* in describing "ferrous mud from certain ponds," the mud/dye with which bokolanfini is patterned.

The actual process of preparing the cloth and creating the designs on bokolanfini cloth is lengthy and time-consuming, requiring a great deal of patience, skill, and precision. The unique manner of applying the mud/dye to the cloth has distinguished bokolanfini from other drawn and painted designs found in African textiles at the same time as it has caused confusion. The solution to the mystery lies in the main step in creating bokolanfini cloth. By isolating this process, one may see the complex procedure which confused both professionals and amateurs interested in how bokolanfini cloth was made. Dr. Imperato states:

> The technique on those cloths from Beledougou is essentially that of *outlining the designs and then painting in the backgrounds*[9] (italics mine).
>
> However, in the northeastern part of the Bamana country, near Mopti and Djenne, where artisans are less skilled, designs are black on a white background. These artists simply paint lines and dots and other configurations onto the cloth which has been made yellow through dyeing with *Wolo* (a solution made from the leaves and stems of *Wolo*—Terminalia auicennoides). When the *Wolo* is removed, the cloth emerges with black designs, the opposite of that from Beledougou. Artists in this area are aware that these cloths are lacking in quality and so they often recolor the white areas a deep orange, using a solution from the bark of *M'Peku* (Lannea velutina). More skillful artists of this region often fill in some of the background, and on these cloths it is difficult to perceptually determine what is background and what is design. The artists from Beledougou consider all of these cloths to be of inferior quality. To them, they demonstrate *an inability to paint around finely outlined designs*[10] (italics mine).

Rather than taking the usual approach and painting a *direct* line on the fabric, the true bokolanfini artist creates that line by painstakingly applying the coloring agent as an outline and then filling in the background *around* the desired design space. In effect, the artist has painted a dark background which creates in

Figure 88. *Handwoven strips of natural cloth are sewn together, washed, and dried.*

the remaining space a fine light line—as Clouzot simplistically described it—of "circles, squares, lines, zigzags." It is this fine, light line against a dark background that has made the method difficult to analyze, principally because the light-against-dark quality of bokolanfini cloth resembles other fabric-dyeing techniques which are familiar to most textile scholars through studies of Asian and Egyptian methods.

In any case, one must study the step-by-step process as presented in the Imperato/Shamir research project, to be able to understand all the implications of each part of bokolanfini production. Briefly, it is as follows,

1. (Figure 88) The narrow handwoven white cotton strips—finimougou—are sewn together, washed in ordinary water, and dried in the sun, primarily to allow for shrinkage of the fabric.

Figure 89. *Two different kinds of leaves are gathered to make the solution in which the fabric is first placed to absorb the liquid.*

2. (Figure 89) The leaves and attached branches of two trees—N'Galaman (*Andgeissus leiocarpus*) and N'Tjankara (*Combretum glutinosum*)—are gathered to prepare a solution sufficient to color the piece being worked on.

3. (Figure 90) After pounding with mortar and pestle, the small pieces of leaves and stems are placed in a calabash, then either soaked in water for twenty-four hours or boiled in water for a few minutes.

4. (Figure 91) The white cloth is then soaked in the resulting

Figure 90. *The leaves are reduced to small pieces by pounding with a pestle in a deep wooden mortar.*

solution, which colors the fabric a bright yellow. The cloth is spread out on the ground and any remaining solution is thrown over it. The cloth is then left in sunlight for half a day. When it is completely dry, the side of the cloth exposed to the sun is a much deeper yellow than the underside; the mud designs are applied to this top surface.

5. After this preliminary immersion the fabric is ready for the designing process. The artist uses "aged" mud that is collected from the central portions of large ponds that dried up during the

Figure 91. *The white fabric is soaked in the solution, which seems to condition the cloth, acting as a mordanting agent.*

previous April dry season. Placed in an earthen pot and covered with several inches of water, the mud is not moved for a year, during which time it turns from gray to grayish-black. When the artist is ready to use it, she takes out a small amount of mud, places it in a smaller earthen pot, and mixes it with water to a very thin consistency.

6. (Figure 92) The artist sits on the ground on a straw mat, places on her lap an inverted calabash, draped with the part of the cloth she is designing, and applies the preliminary outlines of the

Figure 92. *Without any preliminary sketching on the cloth, the artist applies the mud solution, resting the fabric over a large calabash.*

pattern. She uses the flattened edge of a pliant piece of bamboo, which she dips into the mud, stirring the solution from time to time.

7. (Figure 93) The artist outlines each pattern with the tip of a metal spatula and spreads the mud solution around the designs with the spatula's flattened surface (Figure 94).

8. As the artist works, the mud solution dries, changing from intense black to gray.

9. When the mud is thoroughly dry, the finished cloth is

Figure 93. *The artist meticulously outlines each pattern with a spatula.*

dipped in water, removing the excess mud and clearly revealing the yellow designs against the black background. When dry, the fabric is once more plunged into the solution made from leaves of the N'Galaman and N'Tjankara trees and dried in the sun.

10. (Figure 95) The first layer, in the foreground, is gray, but with the second application of the mud solution it stays black. When the entire piece is finished and dried, the cloth is again washed in plain water and dried in the sun. Although a third coating is sometimes requested by a client, the cloth at this second-layer stage is quite colorfast, fading only slightly after several washings.

Figure 94. *The designs are filled in by spreading the mud around the cloth with a spatula.*

11. (Figure 96) The cloth at this point has a completely black background with yellow designs. To bleach the yellow to the desired white, the artist applies a solution (of local origin) called *savon de sodani,* made of a heated and boiled mixture of ground peanuts, water, caustic soda (sodium hydroxide), and millet bran. The artist dips the tip of a thin stick into the savon de sodani and passes it over the yellow design areas, which turn brown on contact (Plate 7—see insert). When all the designs have been thus treated, the cloth is placed in the sun for a week. Most of the soap solution is then washed off by pouring ordinary water on the cloth, leaving the designs white against the black background. Water

Figure 95. *The first layer of mud in the foreground is gray; when the second layer is applied, the mud becomes permanently black and only lightens slightly after several washings.*

that has been used for washing millet, after the bran is removed, is thrown on the cloth, and a dash of plain water produces the final cloth.

An interesting study has been made by J. B. Donne, concerning the function of the preliminary dyeing—or "staining" as he calls it—with the brown solution which turns the white cloth bright yellow after several hours in the sun.[11] Mr. Donne suggests that the concoction made from the leaves and stems of the two trees contains tannic acid and actually serves as a mordant—that is, it reacts chemically with the iron present in the mud solution to

Figure 96. *The artist applies* savon de sodani *to the areas of the cloth which will later be bleached back to the natural color of the original fabric.*

produce a relatively stable dye which adheres to the textile's fibers. Mr. Donne supported his theory on bokolanfini with laboratory research and reported that chemical tests confirmed that tannic acid acted as a mordant and that cloth then painted with an iron oxide preparation turned black or dark brown.[12]

This would justify putting the fabric through several dippings in the yellow-producing dye and following this with complex bleaching of this same yellow coloring with savon de sodani. It would also answer Dr. Imperato's questions on the possibilities of chemical action between the yellow dye and the mud (he had no concrete proof to support his suspicions). Dr. Imperato notes, "The fact that the N'Galaman and the N'Tjankara solution is used widely among the Bamana and other groups raises the interesting speculation that the empirical discovery of bokolanfini was made after this dyeing process was already in use. We are unable to state whether or not some form of chemical reaction occurs between the dye and the mud, but it seems quite possible that it does, in view of the fact that mud is only applied in subsequent coats after the cloth has been redyed with the solution."[13]

The entire dyeing and design process involved in preparing bokolanfini is done by women and is still a relatively active enterprise in the villages of Beledougou. However, the young women who traditionally trained at their mothers' sides until they acquired the skills necessary to work on their own are no longer interested in following the long-term apprenticeships. Mud cloth production is further threatened by cheap and abundant factory-made cloths, as well as by imported European-style clothing, sought particularly by the urban young people.

Bokolanfini in its finished state is used mainly for men's shirts —either sleeveless or with long sleeves (preferred by hunters)— and for women's wraparounds, called *tafe*. In most cases, when a client wants patterns made on the original white fabric—finimougou—it must be presented to the bokolanfini artist already "cut, fitted, and sewn into the appropriate item."[14] Occasionally, however, the finished fabric with its various designs may be found in the marketplaces.

In addition to the complexity of bokolanfini production, the patterns on mud cloth are inherently significant to the Bambara peoples. In a publication entitled *Manding Art and Civilisation*, edited by Guy Atkins and published in conjunction with the presentation of a British Museum Exhibition "Manding: Focus on an African Civilisation," an interesting reference is made to the cloth of the Bambara in connection with language and script: "The paramount importance in Manding culture of secrecy and the guarded word has militated against the development of openly written forms of the language, in contrast to esoteric symbols. An interesting example of symbolic patterning is the so-called *bo-*

golafini cloth illustrated on another page."[15] We are reminded of David Dalby's study in which he notes that "among the many recorded usages of indigenous graphic symbols in West Africa, the most extensive and elaborate are the Bambara graphic systems of Mali and the *Nsibidi* graphic system of the Cross River tribes in Eastern Nigeria. The two graphic systems of the Bambara . . . are employed for ritual and mystic purposes, rather than for secular communication."[16] Dalby further notes:

> Another aspect of the Bambara graphic systems which is relevant to our present inquiry is their particular association with blacksmiths and other craftsmen . . . of greater interest at this point is the association of two of the modern scripts with another craft, namely, weaving and tailoring. . . . The Mende script was invented by a tailor. . . . The use by weavers and other craftsmen of the Mende script (or of some other graphic system?) was noted subsequently by Milburn. . . . All these links with weavers and tailors remain no more than circumstantial, but they are sufficiently numerous to be suggestive, and it is, of course, natural that workers in cloth—like workers in metal, wood, leather and clay—should concern themselves with the use of graphic symbols.[17]

This symbolism—in the form of the designs and patterns which represent it—is handed down to the young apprentice in the same manner as her technical skill is acquired by working with her mother or other women in the family group. In describing the patterns, Dr. Imperato said that most of the mud cloth designs are abstractions or semiabstractions of common objects and that simple patterns often used several designs together to represent a well-known historical event or commemorate a local hero. The names of the designs and patterns are fairly well known to most adults in the rural Bamana areas.[18]

Pictured on this exceptionally large bokolanfini cloth (Figure 97), which was commissioned by Dr. Imperato to include the widest possible variety of designs in the artist's repertoire, are examples of several important patterns. One which caters to the peoples' interest in historical events is the left-central motif entitled *Samory Ani Tieba Benyero* (*The War Between Samory and*

Figure 97. *The finished bokolanfini cloth (commissioned by Dr. Imperato) is much larger than usual and is covered with many designs from the artist's repertoire.*

Tieba). The design is analyzed as follows (refer to the chart as a guide to the form of each individual symbol, Figure 98):

Samory Ani Tieba Benyero is a much more complicated pattern, representing an alleged battle between Tieba, a nineteenth-century king of Sikasso, and Samory, an Imam warrior. There are a number of designs in this pattern, but for the artist the dominant ones are the series of lines terminating in diamonds. These lines represent the *tata* (fortified wall) of Tieba's capital of Sikasso. Enclosed within these lines are three main designs, the Mauritanian woman's cushion, a symbol of nobility, the house of calabash flowers, meaning the abode of an important person, and the drum of the king's *griot* (minstrel). Outside of the walls are zigzagging lines representing the paths of Samory's soldiers in attacking the city. The circles with the dots in the center represent the Wuiwayanko stream near Bamako where Samory was held in check by the French. The circles with the drums in the center represent

Figure 98. *Some of the individual designs used in bokolanfini cloth. Top to bottom:* 1. Gelike Be Wuowanyanko (*stream called the Wuowanyanko*). 2. Kolowi (*cowrie shells*). 3. Mali. 4. Fini N'Goloni Sirakele (*one twisted road*). 5. N'Tamani (*small drum*). 6. N'Kerenkan (*grasshopper neck*). 7. Souraka Moussa N'Kunkoro Talan (*Mauritanian woman's cushion*). 8. Woroso (*sickle*). 9. Samory's griot standing in the stream called Wuowanyanko. 10. Yiri Boulou (*tree leaves*). 11. Bara Fieri So (*house of the calabash flowers*).

> Samory's *griot* standing in the middle of the same stream, urging Samory to battle. While the principal theme of this pattern is a battle between two Malian kings, one sees that the artist has also incorporated portions of another historical event, the battle between Samory and the French.[19]

This large cloth also includes a design in the lower central portion of Figure 97 that focuses on a popular folk hero, Koumi Diosse, and Dr. Imperato explains the complexities of this design:

> *Doumi Diosseni Kandian* (Koumi Diosse, the long-necked) has as its essential elements a series of long parallel lines connecting diamonds. This pattern honors an extremely important folk hero of Beledougou, Koumi Diosse, who led an unsuccessful revolt against the French in 1915. He was killed in the course of a battle with the French garrison from Kati. Since the time of his death, Koumi Diosse has been immortalized in the songs of Bamana *griots*, and ranks as the greatest folk hero of the Beledougou area. He is said to have had an unusually long neck, which accounts for the nickname and also the abstracted representation in the pattern. The long parallel lines represent this hero's long neck, and the diamonds with the crosses the cushion of the Mauritanians, hence Koumi Diosse's nobility.[20]

Several other patterns may be seen on the large cloth as well. One of the most popular is the *Mali* pattern (far left), which is dominated by a continuous abstract representation of the human form, interspersed with the *n'kerenkan* (grasshopper neck), tree leaves, and drums. The cloth is bordered at intervals with a double row of serrated lines called *sajesera*, which means, appropriately, partition. Sometimes these double zigzags are coupled with a row of drum symbols, or varied with the inclusion of the cowrie motif. Many of the bokolanfini designs have names, but their meanings are difficult to trace. One of these, called *turusina* (a helping hand), appears on the cloth second from the far right and is distinguished by the unusual horizontal repetition of the design. At the far right is a pattern called *finingoloni sera fla*, meaning the two twisted paths, which has an interesting variation in the sizes of the symbolic lines as they march vertically up the designed area. The central pattern is made up of a repeat of a motif which is included in many of the previous designs: *Souraka*

Figure 99. *A large contemporary bokolanfini cloth collected by Marli Shamir.*

Mousso N'Kunkoro Talan literally means "that which holds up the head of the Mauritanian woman."[21] The central repetitive theme of this design is the square with the cross in the center, representing the cushion traditionally used by Mauritanian women. The entire pattern is effectively bordered by sajesera serrated lines combined with a continuous line of cowrie symbols. Figure 99 shows a contemporary cloth in the collection of Marli Shamir which illustrates various combinations of popular bokolanfini designs; Figure 100 shows some of the designs used on men's hunting tunics.

Identifying the designs and analyzing the symbolic content of patterns on older and usually much more finely designed cloths in museum collections is nearly impossible at this stage. One may

Figure 100. A *Bambara man wearing a recently designed tunic in bokolanfini motifs.*

Figure 101. *A bokolanfini cloth of the 1930s featuring many of the same motifs found on the contemporary fabric designed for Dr. Imperato.*

find similarities in older pieces, relating to the designs presented by Dr. Imperato and Mrs. Shamir, and hope to at least gain some insight into the relative continuity of designs as they pass on from generation to generation.

Among the bokolanfini cloths collected by François de Zeltner in the late 1920s, and acquired by the Musée de l'Homme in the early 1930s, is one which contains almost identical representations of three currently popular design motifs studied by Dr. Imperato and illustrated in this chapter. Looking at Figure 101, one can distinguish "The Mali Pattern," "Samory Ani Tieba Benyero," and "Koumi Dioseni Kandian." In this cloth, and in several others collected by de Zeltner at the same time, the final step of bleaching the first background dye in the design areas has not been carried out, and the fabrics have a strong orange pattern against the dark background, which might suggest that they are products of the less skilled artisans from the northeastern part of the Bamana country, near Mopti and Djene. These are not dyed yellow first, but rather are recolored a deep orange with the solution made from the bark of M'Peku. A sleeveless tunic acquired by the

Figure 102. *An unusually designed old bokolanfini cloth with more circular motifs than are seen in today's versions of the fabric.*

Musée de l'Homme in 1934, collected by Waterlot, shows a chevronlike central motif dominating the design, which corresponds to Dr. Imperato's identification of this pattern as *Woroso,* meaning "sickle."

It is not possible to find exact correspondences to Dr. Imperato's recorded motifs on the more finely designed pieces in the collection of the Musée de l'Homme (Figures 102 and 103). Perhaps these complex patterns are no longer being produced. The delicacy of the lines between each pattern may imply that such refined abilities belong to textile artists of a generation that has perished.

NOTES

1. Pascal James Imperato and Marli Shamir, "Bokolanfini—Mud Cloth of the Bamana of Mali," *African Arts* magazine, Volume III, Number 4, Summer 1970, pp. 32–41.
2. A. Steinmann, "Batik Work, Its Origin and Spread," *Ciba Review* #58, July 1947, p. 2109.
3. Ibid., p. 2109.
4. Henri Clouzot, *Tissus Nègres,* Librairie des Arts Décoratifs, Paris (no date), p. 5.

Figure 103. *A rare and intricately executed old bokolanfini cloth of extraordinary craftsmanship and fine detail.*

5. Ibid., p. 5.
6. Ibid., p. 5.
7. Imperato and Shamir, op. cit., p. 32.
8. Ibid., p. 34.
9. Ibid., p. 38.
10. Ibid., p. 40.
11. J. B. Donne, "Bogolanfini: A Mud-Painted Cloth," an unpublished paper delivered at the Conference on Manding Studies: Congrès d'Études Manding, School of Oriental and African Studies, London, 1972.
12. Ibid., p. 2.
13. Imperato and Shamir, op. cit., p. 40.
14. Ibid., p. 35.
15. Guy Atkins (ed.), *Manding Art and Civilisation*, London: Studio International, 1972, p. 4.
16. David Dalby, "The Indigenous Scripts of West Africa and Surinam: Their Inspiration and Design," *African Language Studies*, IX, 1968, p. 179.
17. Ibid., p. 181 (Dalby also adds his own footnote: "All the tribes mentioned in this paragraph . . . are speakers of Mande languages").
18. Imperato and Shamir, op. cit., p. 37.
19. Ibid., p. 40.
20. Ibid., p. 41.
21. Ibid., p. 41.

7

Korhogo Cloth of Ivory Coast

The handcrafted contemporary cloth from Korhogo, a town in northern Ivory Coast, is known for the stylized figures of humans and animals painted directly on fabric. They are applied in a blackish-brown dye on a coarsely woven, natural-colored fabric of narrow strips sewn together to form large, decorative cloths.

Until recently, very little has been published about the origins of contemporary Korhogo cloths or the significance of the designs, but some unpublished research from Mlle. Aminata Konaté is incorporated in this chapter. Mlle. Konaté was born in Korhogo, Ivory Coast, and lived there until she went to study at Abidjan's École des Beaux Arts and, later, the École des Arts Décoratifs, Paris.

The people of Korhogo seldom receive a Western education, Mlle. Konaté points out, but they may attend a form of Senufo "school of living" for men called Poro. Many years of study and a certain tuition are required to attend the school, which teaches the traditional ways thought necessary for maturity in the Senufo society of Korhogo—not the ways of the contemporary world. A similar, but (in her opinion) less important and less complete, school for women also exists.

Mlle. Konaté went to Korhogo in 1974 and gathered information on the history of contemporary Korhogo cloth, symbolism of designs, traditional and contemporary use of the cloths, dyes, colors, and processes of working on the cloth. Much of her information was given to her by an uncle—a Poro member—who told her all but the secrets kept from men outside the Poro society and from women.

The information she compiled concerning the original inspiration for contemporary Korhogo cloths differs from that of other sources and may seem surprising to some authorities on Senufo art and society. Still, it is interesting to examine her findings and consider them in relation to information from other sources.

Origins and Uses of Fabrics from Korhogo

Different kinds of fabric are made in Korhogo for various purposes, the best known of which are the popular cloths now being produced commercially as decorative wall hangings primarily for non-Ivorians. Mlle. Konaté's research indicates that these contemporary cloths are derived from cloths which were used by religious specialists (*fétichistes*) for religious purposes; they were never worn. Certain unpatterned cloths are worn or used as shrouds, and some differently dyed cloths—not the sacred ones—patterned either with figures or geometric forms, were worn on certain occasions. Finally, because of societal changes, Western influences, and commercialism, the meanings of some of these fabrics have been so distorted or misrepresented that uninformed people sometimes wear cloths that are still taboo.

The sacred unworn Korhogo cloths evolved from the needs of religious specialists to paint certain designs on the walls of their cult houses. These wall designs, painted with natural dyes, were usually worn away by the weather, so the religious specialists commissioned artists to interpret on cloth what they would have drawn on the wall. These cloths were hung when necessary and used by the religious specialist, who served as a priest for everyone in the village. No ethnic group other than the Senufo uses these cloths.

According to Mlle. Konaté, only white cloths are used in traditional funerals as shrouds. The cloths used for hunting and dancing and for Poro-initiate dance costumes are quite different from those used by religious specialists. Dance costumes were made of cloth dyed with geometric designs related to the type of mask worn. Hunting costumes were dyed black or brown and decorated with *gri-gris*—leather-covered amulets to protect the hunter —selected by the artisan. A special painted cloth is worn by initiates in the Poro dances.

Anita Glaze, an art historian who is specialized in Senufo society and did extensive fieldwork in the Korhogo area, believes that the contemporary Korhogo cloths are of recent date and inspiration, though they are based on traditional techniques, materials, and concepts. In her 1972 article, "Senufo Graphic Arts," which appeared in *Ba Shiru*,[1] she makes no reference to sacred cloths commissioned by religious specialists to hang on the walls of cult houses as replacements for eroded paintings. Instead, she names three pre-existing frameworks for Senufo graphic expression which serve as sources for the contemporary Korhogo cloth: "two-dimensional wall paintings in diviner's shrines, painted textiles of *fila* type worn as personal everyday clothing, and painted textiles of the type used for the costumes of certain masquerades of the Poro organizations."[2] (These latter two textiles are examined in the sections concerning motifs on traditional Senufo textiles and traditional dyeing techniques.) The wall paintings, she explains, are figurative designs which serve as a kind of advertisement—an announcement of the diviner's intelligence—and as aesthetically pleasing expressions of her professional ability and success. The paintings in some shrines are often embellished by younger family members and friends who are free to do whatever designs come to mind. She also notes that a pictorial representational mode is characteristic of the bas-relief figures molded in mud on the exterior walls of certain shrines and Poro schoolhouses.[3]

Glaze says that as late as 1965, she had seen no sign of contemporary Korhogo cloths in northern Ivory Coast markets. By 1969, however, she observed that hundreds of cloths were available throughout the region and that in the early 1970s, bolts of factory-printed material with lively Korhogan animal forms on them were being mass produced in the United States. "The designs were in fact faithful copies of original works by contemporary Senufo graphic artists in northern Ivory Coast, where a group of primarily Nafana-Senufo artists have created a new art form out of traditional media."[4]

Designs on Contemporary Korhogo Cloths

Studies of the contemporary cloths reveal a variety of concepts concerning the designs—their original size, source, and symbolic meaning. According to photographer/writer René Gardi, in *African Crafts and Craftsmen,* the rather large designs of human figures, animals, birds, and geometric ornamentations that decorate Korhogo cloths today were much smaller in their original traditional versions, which were sometimes only a few inches high. Gardi associates the designs with a Poro dance costume he purchased from an art dealer in Korhogo and a hunter he met, on a road outside Fakaha, who was wearing a pair of trousers made of the figured Korhogo cloth. The author and his translator also discovered used hunting clothes similarly decorated with figures, presumably as signs of good luck and protection.[5]

This information coincides with facts about Korhogo cloth found in a report by Mme. Jocelyn Etienne-Nugue entitled *Artisanats traditionnels en côte d'ivoire.* Mme. Étienne-Nugue states that the original designs were "emblematic and protective . . . reserved for the costumes of the Senufo initiates, hunters, and ritual dancers." The report also confirms that "on the very old woven cloths the designs are in general smaller and more regular than those which are currently being produced. . . ."[6] Mme. Étienne-Nugue refers the reader to an example in the collection of the Musée de l'Homme which may be seen in Figure 104. This cloth was collected in 1964 by M. Hugo Zemp, a young ethnomusicologist, who works at the Musée de l'Homme and who told me about Fakaha, the village where the cloth was made, and the artist who created it. He identifies the same artist as the one pictured in René Gardi's book, working in the same village, and said that at the time he alone was doing designs that are now considered typical of the entire Korhogo area. There were other artists painting, M. Zemp recalled, but their work was much more simplistic and childlike, rather in the nature of stick drawings.

Figure 104. *A Korhogo cloth in the early style, featuring small figures and geometric designs; collected in the 1960s.*

To acquire a cloth designed by this artist, M. Zemp was required first to purchase the plain, natural-colored handwoven cloth at the marketplace and bring it to the artist to be painted. M. Zemp remembers seeing large fabrics with figures on them that were much bigger than the scale of the designs on his small piece of fabric.

Mlle. Konaté agrees that Korhogo designs have gotten larger, saying that the older village people remember when the designs were small and that they consider the space left by larger and fewer designs to be "wasted." The current designs are deplored by the elders who no longer see meaning in them, but for commercial purposes, it is practical to have several cloths with large designs ready at the sound of the tourists' cars approaching a village.

Korhogo designs were once rich in meaning and carefully ordered by the customer, though they are now applied at the whim of the artisan. The following designs and their meanings are from a list brought by Mlle. Konaté from Korhogo in 1974:

The goat: Male sexual power
The guinea fowl: Feminine beauty
The chicken: Maternity
The tree: The sacred wood where the Poro ceremonies take place
The chameleon: Death
The fish: Life and water
The lion: Royal power
Fishbones: Drought
The hunter: The mysteries of the forest
The swallow: Trust
The crocodile and the lizard: Male fertility
The sun, moon, stars: First elements God put in the sky the first day of the creation of the world, according to the Senufo
The snake and the turtle: The earth

She was given the following explanations by relatives who have no Poro taboos:

1) *The crocodile and the big lizard:* "From the water shores." These symbols are found in Senufo ritual acts and show the definite transfer from land to water. (According to folktales, there was a sacred crocodile in the waters of Korhogo whose back was decorated with cowries. He appeared every ten years to announce the future events. The ten years correspond to the ten days of the creation of the world in the Senufo religion (Figure 104).

2) *The snake:* Symbol of the earth which he encircles with his tail in his mouth. This circle represents the world; the day the snake lets go of his tail the world will cease to exist. The snake is often represented in different Senufo art objects, especially jewelry such as bracelets and rings. The Senufo constantly remind us that our existence is tied to the slightest gestures of the snake (Figure 104).

Figure 105. *A Korhogo cloth (collected in the mid-1970s) with large masked figures.*

3) *The swallow:* A Senufo chief must always have swallows in his home. With the swallows he makes sacrifices to win the trust of the population and power over them. When there's a tribal war, a man's testicles are applied to this bird, which is sent to the enemy; the war will be won (Figure 104; Figure 107, central enclosed design, swallow lower left).

4) *The gray guinea fowl and the domestic chicken:* Birds in general have important roles, being animals associated with celestial powers. The guinea fowl and the chicken represent maternal virtues and feminine beauty. A bird in sculpture is the big "Senufo calao" that symbolizes hope and fertility (Figure 104; Figure 107, upper right).

5) *The lion and the leopard:* They share primacy. The religious specialist used lion eyes mixed with other elements

to inspire fear of the chief and submission of the people (Figure 107: leopard, left center; lion, center).

6) *Chameleon:* The messenger of death and the leprosy carrier. The Senufo have given the chameleon an important dual role as an animator, sometimes harmful, sometimes beneficial. Its evil side is the messenger of death and the leprosy carrier. (An initiated elder who meets a chameleon in the sacred woods will soon see the end of his days.) Its good side permits the chameleon to cure epilepsy (Figure 107, upper framed area, small figure at right).

7) *Turtle:* Considered one of the first animals created. It is believed that its slowness indicates its fear that the earth will crumble under its feet (Figure 106, lower center).

8) *The goat:* Evokes male sexual power: It is often a liturgical subject for the Senufo sculptor who makes the statue for certain propitiatory rites by the priestess of the Poro women's school (Figure 107, upper two enclosed animals).

9) *Fish:* Where there are fish, there's bound to be water—a vital necessity in a drought-prone area such as northern Ivory Coast—so the fish represents life to the Senufo.

10) *Fishbones:* Indicate inevitable drought, thirst, and famine.

11) *Tree:* Represents the sacred woods where Poro ceremonies take place (Figure 107, center).

Some examples of the meanings denoted by combinations of these designs are seen in Figure 107, where groups are outlined as if to imply that some special significance exists between them, such as:

Upper framed designs: *The goat, the chameleon, the swallow*
One must always trust male sexual power, even in death.

Central framed designs: *The lion, chameleon, guinea fowl*
Feminine beauty loves strength and strength is afraid of death.

Figure 106. *Another Korhogo cloth of the same vintage and size as Figure 105, also featuring masked figures.*

Mlle. Konaté found that the geometric designs are a hidden language and that the realistic figures represent protective gods in the eyes of the religious specialists. Cloths with geometric designs are worn at funerals, as part of a masked dance ensemble; the cloths with figures are never used but people are not too upset at selling these designs to tourists because they know the tourists are only interested in them aesthetically. Korhogans would feel sacrilegious if they revealed the secrets of the masks and animal designs, though they don't mind explaining the symbols.

More information on design symbolism was contributed by Helen Anderson-Bauer, with the help of Gora Thiam, a Wolof man who speaks the Senufo language. She said:

Figure 107. *A large Korhogo cloth distinguished by two groupings of animals and birds, each having a special symbolism. The design includes a tree representing the sacred forest and various other flora and fauna.*

"The men drawn on the cloths are religious specialists [fétichistes]. The leader is always distinguished by these two antennae [Figure 108, middle row, second to last]. He goes into the woods and the animals are attracted to him. The animals are thus shown on the canvases: *biches* [deer, antelope]; *pintades* [guinea hen]; another bird which was not given a French name; and snakes. Often a tree is painted to represent the sacred woods. Gora Thiam explained that one nonrepresentational design [Figure 108, top, eight-pointed "star"] was actually a symbol for the Senufo.

"There is a second special man-figure. He is also a religious specialist but is considered like an assistant. He is called 'Lubi.' He conducts the actual fetish act; he kills the animals to the sound of drums and to the movement of dance. Whether or not the animals are sacrificed or later eaten, I don't know.

"It is taboo for young women to attend this ceremony as it is said that if they see the religious specialist they will become sterile."

Anita Glaze examines several aspects of Senufo aesthetics and creative expression in her 1978 article, "Senufo Ornament and Decorative Arts,"[7] appearing in *African Arts* magazine. While her investigation is largely concerned with cultural themes too complex to be taken up here, she does offer an extensive exploration of Senufo imagery found in cast brass ornaments, architectural bas-reliefs, and fila mud cloth painting.

Motifs on Traditional Senufo Textiles

The motifs on fila textiles are depictions of several important themes permeating traditional Senufo art, primarily bush spirits, the python, and the chameleon. The nature of fila (an abbreviated form of *filafani wii,* meaning "a painted cloth") is somewhat complicated. Glaze outlines the factors that all fila textiles have in common, whether a child's cloth mask that appears at funerals, a woman's everyday skirt, a special shirt worn by wealthy men, or a two-piece ensemble commissioned by hunters. The designs on fila are created by mud dyeing; they include vertical or horizontal painted lines, called *kobigele,* the "design of paths" (sometimes combined with animated figures); and a fila textile is always "an object recommended by Sando diviners[8] as a protective charm and honorific device to appease or neutralize the potentially malevolent bush spirits."[9]

Glaze defines bush spirits (*madebele*) as "a generic term referring to any image of the human figure, whether it be ancestors, chiefs or warriors on horseback, favorite masquerade types, or the bush spirits themselves in human form. . . . Graphic representations of these spirits frequently include spots or circles, a characteristic motif of masquerades incorporating bush spirit and bush animal imagery. . . ."[10] "The Senufo believe that a spirit can take on the form of any animal . . . so that the tortoise, chicken, water lizard, cayman,* dog, bird, chameleon, mudfish, goat, and rabbit [and many other animals] are often represented. . . ."[11] According to Glaze's research, then, all the figures —both human and animal—appearing on Korhogo cloths illustrated in this chapter, could possibly represent bush spirits, particularly if dots and circles are incorporated in the design.

The relationship between bush spirits/Sando diviner/client is one of extreme complexity, intertwining and dovetailing to such an extent that it is sometimes difficult to determine where one begins and the other ends. Essentially, a person in Senufo society fears the all powerful madebele, whose duality they believe can inspire an artist or kill an opponent. The Senufo wishes to be in their good graces rather than receive their wrath. To accomplish this, he or she consults a diviner, who interprets, through her special abilities, just what steps should be taken to appease and please the bush spirits. Often, it is the commissioning of a fila garment which acts as a protection against a harmful presence or a past misdeed, or perhaps in connection with a special favor. Such clothing is termed *yarwiige*, literally, "things worn as protective medicine or charm."[12] Thus a full circle is reached and life becomes a continuous cycle of consultation/divination/protection. The diviners themselves want to please the madebele's aesthetic senses and this may account in part for the decorative wall paintings on their shrines, perhaps commissioned in their honor.

Although this is an oversimplified interpretation of the bush spirits, it serves as an introduction to bush spirit-related motifs on fila cloth (with some references to designs on masquerade costumes) and begins to show the relationship to figurative and nonrepresentational motifs on contemporary Korhogo cloth.

The python is almost as formidable a force in Senufo society as the bush spirits. Says Glaze: "Python is messenger and medium between spirits and diviner, just as the diviner is medium between spirits and her human clientele. . . . The python is also dominant on the figurative designs painted on divination-related textiles . . . and is noted for his power to change into human form."[13]

* A crocodilian similar to alligators but often superficially resembling crocodiles.

Symbolically, Fô, the python, is associated with sexuality, male-female relationships, and the protective role of the Sandogo society. Painted python bas-relief is seen decorating the exterior and interior walls of small Sando consulting chambers, shrines, altars, and Poro society storage houses. Glaze suggests that since the Senufo believe that "keeping in touch with the spirit world through Sando divination is the only safe route to health, vitality, and life itself . . . The Python is thus a metaphor for the life-sustaining communication channel with the spirits: Sando divination."[14]

The chameleon (*Gberi*) is also a prevailing motif on fila shirts, trousers, skirts, and tunics. As the third most common figurative theme in Senufo art, it is frequently seen atop the domed helmets of many Poro masks, as wood or brass freestanding sculpture in diviners' offices and painted on the interior walls of shrines. Glaze attributes the chameleon's importance in Senufo society to its folkloric prominence as the first primordial creature whose image "speaks of a knowledge that reaches back to the mysterious beginnings of the world and of an awareness of unpredictable and malevolent forces at work in the present."[15] Although the Senufo honor Gberi as an elder for his ancient wisdom, they are terrified of the chameleon and believe it has the power to kill, whereas in reality it is frightening but quite harmless. Glaze attributes this death threat to the realm of the supernatural: "Instability, unpredictability, extraordinary powers of vision, aggression, and above all, powers of transformation and expropriation (as demonstrated by the chameleon's changing color) are all attributes of witches and bush spirits."[16]

The hunter is an important culture hero in Senufo oral history, poetry, and song, respected not only as provider of game for protein and skins for drums and Poro display, but for his role as discoverer/founder of new village sites, his association with the magical powers of medicine, and his rise to prestigious positions in the Senufo sociopolitical and religious structure. The hunter wears clothing made of fila cloth and Glaze observes: "Although the primary theme of the *fila* cloth painting tradition concerns bush spirits and divination in general, *fila* shirts and matching

Figure 108. *A Korhogo cloth with designs of masked figures, animals, fish, birds, and a large snake.*

trousers are also associated with hunters (and by extension, with any elders of status and prestige). The elaborate dress not only gives aesthetic expression to the high prestige of the hunter but also reflects the hunter's greater exposure to bush spirits and dangerous animals, a recurrent theme in the oral literature."[17] Glaze also points out that waterbird motifs may also be represented in fila cloth designs commissioned by hunters, perhaps symbolically, since many of these birds are themselves expert hunters who catch not only fish but certain reptiles associated with spirits and witches.[18]

Mlle. Konaté's research shows that masks are apparently closely coordinated with the wearing of certain designs on fabrics. The mood of the occasion is enhanced and completed by the choice of fabric-designed masks. Masks that are taboo for women and noninitiates to see are announced by a drum so that those people can hide their eyes. Mlle. Konaté made phonetic translations of the names of the masks and explained their purposes. Some of the masks, appearing on the cloths photographed in Figures 106 and 108, can be positively identified:

1) *Koto:* From Kiembala, Djeli, Sonu (the Senufo being an ethnic group composed of several other smaller ethnic groups speaking the same dialect but often with different accents).

This mask can be seen by everyone—men, women, children, initiates or noninitiates.

2) *Korobila:* Can only be seen by men. There are a male and a female mask. During the ceremonies, bees come out of the male's mouth and lizards come out of the female's mouth to eat them. It's also one of the rare fire-breathing masks. Its wearer has the impressive role of setting fire to a large part of the woods and then dancing on the embers to put it out without getting burned. A pregnant woman who looks at him is believed to miscarry (Figure 105, upper left; Figure 106, upper left).

3) *Alatchon:* Can be seen by all, but can't be looked directly in the eyes. Behind his role as an animator, he hides his cruelty. It is the most powerful mask.

4) *Nauvière:* This mask can be seen by all, is essentially worn by young Poro beginners, and is inoffensive. It is supposed to make room for the other masks, to chase away the curious, and to put order in the ranks; it is the Poro police system.

5) *Kagba* (Nafara-Kiembaza): It represents a variety of cattle with spots on its back. This large mask is worn by two or three people and can only be seen by Poro initiates. It is believed that if anyone else looks at it, he is immediately paralyzed on one side.

6) *Quersegue:* A mask that announces death.

7) *Lafaragko:* The name of this mask means "diarrhea" and can only be seen by Poro initiates because it has the power to give diarrhea to anyone else.

8) *Wauibele:* This mask is at the end of the parade of masked characters. It can be seen by everyone, but it is rigorously forbidden to cross the street when its wearer passes, as it is believed one will immediately be struck by lightning (Figure 106, upper center).

9) *Teignan:* It precedes all the masks, announces the ones that follow, and can be seen only by Poro initiates.

Hans Himmelheber relates traditional Poro masks and masquerade costumes to contemporary Korhogo cloths in a fresh and insightful essay entitled "Moderne Negerkunst als Quelle für traditionelles Brauchtum—*Darstellung unbekannter Masken in modernen Stoffmalereien der Senufo*" ("Modern Negro Art as Source for Traditional Customs—*Unknown Masks in the Modern Textile Paintings of the Senufo*").[19] He offers a very detailed, extremely well-illustrated documentation of his relationship to several Senufo textile artists in the Korhogo area who are his source of knowledge about the commercial origins and development of the contemporary cloths. From the insights he gained talking to the artists about the masks, costumes, and ritualistic scenes they painted on the textiles, he is able to present a startling introduction to heretofore highly secret Poro society masks, costumes, and masquerading traditions. His very perceptive presentation is much too lengthy and detailed for summation here. However, it is important to describe the essence of his discovery not only to learn the basic facts, but because this information relates to, or further illuminates, material gathered by Aminata Konaté and Anita Glaze.

Himmelheber reports (with some amazement) that the artists readily explained the function and meaning of even the most secret masks and masquerade traditions (even those forbidden to non-Poro members and women, as Mlle. Konaté noted), clarifying much of his previous research and adding immeasurably to his total knowledge. "All of a sudden," he writes, referring to the textile artists in the Korhogo territory, "and for everyone to see, they are now painting creatures whom the Europeans do not get to see, whom one does not even speak about, in fact."[20] Poro masks with very special, secret functions—masks that relate surprisingly in appearance to other well-known, more regularly seen Senufo masks—appear readily on the contemporary Korhogo cloths. This is an astonishing revelation to a man of Himmelheber's nearly lifelong involvement in the art and culture of Ivory Coast. He describes this curious present-day phenomena—the evident acceptability to contemporary commercial Ivorian artists that a representation or a picture of a sacred object or event in no way compromises the sacredness of the original object or event. Says Himmelheber (with what can only be regarded as gracious good humor and perhaps a bit of bewilderment), "I myself had only been shown the Dje mask† after I had visited the Baule for more than 30 years!"[21] But of course, Himmelheber saw the *real* thing, the sacred object itself, not a representation of it (depicting as well the entourage of musicians and other special people associated with its presence), in a series of modern casts on sale at the Abidjan antique market.

A number of the masks Himmelheber documents have names that sound very much like those described by Mlle. Konaté, and some of their functions appear to be similar; others differ drastically. His written research and illustrations support Anita Glaze's observation that dotted designs appear frequently on Poro masquerade costumes. He also documents an abundance of checkered and gridlike patterns on mask-accompanied costumes, which correlates with Mlle. Konaté's reference to the use of geometric designs on cloth dance costumes worn with specific masks.

Dyes and Techniques for Contemporary Korhogo Cloths

The basic method for producing contemporary Korhogo cloth designs is a two-step process: first, the yellowish-brown mordant dye is applied in the desired motifs and, secondly, a thinned black mud dye is painted over the original design. (In the traditional method used to produce fila cloth, the second step is different: the entire cloth is dipped in the mud dye solution, the fabric is washed, and the dye adheres to the mordanted pattern, leaving a white background.) Mme. Étienne-Nugue summarizes the contemporary process as follows:

"*The natural dye:* It is in fact composed of two products applied one after the other. The first layer is of a light brown vegetal decoction (*kadayafour* and *nanganeman*); the second is of a thinning out of black mud taken from certain marshes. The chemical reaction of the mixture results in the very black lines of the final design.

"*The traditional technique*: The artisan works while seated on the ground. The woven cloth is stretched very flatly on a board in

† The most sacred mask of the Baule peoples of Central Ivory Coast, celebrated for their sculptural tradition.

Figure 109. *A Korhogo artist at work in front of his home, showing the bowl of dye and the tool used to create the designs.*

front of him by means of small pegs. Without any preliminary sketch, he traces the designs with his "knife" after having dipped it into the dye (Figure 109). The first lines are very fine; they are subsequently reinforced by new tracings.

"*The basic material* is a cloth in raw spun cotton made up of small sewn bands (in variable dimensions) on which the motifs are designed freehand, using a knife with a thick blade curved to the rear or a small stick fitted with a corncob handle."[22]

Most of the other sources offer similar information with slight variations or additional details, as the following paragraphs demonstrate.

Mlle. Konaté was told that the dye used in the first step is made of the bark and leaves of the *niganam* tree. These are cooked in large earthenware pots "a very long time or several

Figure 110. *In the village of Korhogo, cloths are hung to dry on clotheslines or are spread out directly on the ground.*

Figure 111. *A very large cloth suspended against a wall in the village of Korhogo.*

hours, but they do not ferment." The resulting bouillon is the dye which can be diluted for lighter shades, or be applied in layers for darker tones. The more layers, the darker the color. Many cloths with designs painted only yellowish-brown can be seen in market-places today. She also learned that the old way of dyeing was to fix the dye by immersing the cloth in a mud bath after the designs were drawn. This gave the blackish color most commonly associated with Korhogo cloth. Today a diluted mud dye is used in the method outlined by Mme. Étienne-Nugue.

Helen Anderson-Bauer described the process as she witnessed it in a letter to me:

"A small (6–7″ diameter) pottery bowl held the clearish liquid dye: next to the bowl was a series of blades about 4–8″ long used to apply the color. My Wolof friend suspects there are roots and

Figure 112. *Detail from a Korhogo cloth, showing two lively ducks within the body of a complacent antelope.*

leaves in the mixture. I asked if urine was used but the artisans refused to say. Gora Thiam said he was positive that animal excrement is *not* used, although I had heard of this possibility elsewhere. The paint or dye is definitely applied in 'layers'—perhaps two or maybe more. Some of the figures are light brown in color instead of black. When I persuaded one man to draw so I could photograph him, he applied the liquid on an already brown figure and the figure turned black."

René Gardi's description of the dyes and techniques is basically the same, although he notes a telling change: "At the market on my last visit, I was repeatedly offered cloth that was no longer painted with the old vegetable dyes, but with commercial black ink. And the fabric, too, came from Europe."[23]

In fact, today combinations of dyes are sometimes used. For in-

Figure 113. *Detail of an antelope eating a leaf with a fish beside him.*

stance, an Ivoirian art instructor from Korhogo found that people in the village still use the traditional dye made from tree bark, kola nuts, and corn, but that a few people producing for the tourist market do use chemical dyes. He added that originally only two villages—Napieoloudougou and Dikodougou—produced Korhogo cloth, but once the tourists began buying it, other villages joined in the rush to produce textiles for sale.

This mixture of natural and synthetic dyes calls into question the colorfast qualities of contemporary Korhogo cloths. Theoretically, the mordant/mud dye method forms an insoluble bond between dye and fiber, thereby rendering the fabric colorfast. Helen Anderson-Bauer has machine-laundered her Korhogo shirt successfully. However, attempts to wash Korhogo cloths purchased in Ivory Coast can prove disastrous, leading one to believe that either

Figure 114. *Detail of a large snake encircling a fish surrounded by masked figures.*

this process is not thoroughly reliable—that some mordants are stronger or more dependable than others—or that noncolorfast synthetic dyes and inks have been used.

The process for dyeing Korhogo cloth is strikingly close to the method used for dyeing the bokolanfini mud cloth of Mali described in the preceding chapter. The difference lies in the manner of applying the coloring matter to form the design. With bokolanfini cloth, the fabric is immersed in the first solution which then turns yellow as it dries in the sun. The second, dark mud substance is then applied to outline the yellow designs which are later bleached white. On contemporary Korhogo cloths, both the first application of yellow-brown dye and the second application of mud dye solution are stroked or painted onto the fabric—one directly upon the other—to form a final dark design against

Figure 115. *Detail of a lion (though spotted like a leopard, he has a mane) surrounded by masked figures, an antelope, and a fish.*

the natural, off-white color of the cloth. The first layer of the yellow-brown dye drawn on the Korhogo cloth serves the same purpose as the preliminary dyeing of the bokolanfini cloth, which is to react with the mud dye solution as a fixative, making the cloth colorfast.

Aminata Konaté learned that those men who traditionally worked on Korhogo cloth were sculptors—textiles were not a profession in a singular sense—and artisans participated in planting, harvesting, and the other village activities. No more prestige was attached to his artisanship than to that of a shoemaker. Women's roles were limited to spinning the locally grown cotton for the strips and to cooking the bark and the leaves for the dye. Men did the weaving and dyeing of the fabrics. Originally, clients brought fabrics to the artisan to be dyed, but today the artisan buys his

Figure 116. *An antelope with flamboyant bias-striped skin (detail).*

own cloth and dyes it for immediate sale. Today the artisan may be a professional in that the craft is his daily job and he may participate in only a few other village activities.

Mlle. Konaté's research includes the following natural dyes used to paint special scenes, the predecessors of Korhogo cloth, on the walls of cult houses:

Ochre: From wet earth, giving a liquid mush (the "mud bath").

Black: Made from crushed charcoal, diluted with water or added to karite butter (crushed seeds of a local tree).

White: Milk, animal (reptile, hyena, bird) droppings, or ground rice or millet flour.

Blue: Indigo (leaves).

Figure 117. *Detail of a masked figure with intricately patterned face.*

Red: Oxydized iron (rust) mixed in certain cases with sacrificial blood.

Yellow: Flour made from dried *nere* (a fruit).

Green: Made from horse, cattle, or sheep droppings (these animals being herbivores).

Dyeing Techniques for Traditional Senufo Textiles

As noted earlier, two types of traditional Senufo textiles—fila cloth and fabrics for Poro masquerade costumes—are designed and dyed in methods closely related to those used to create contemporary Korhogo cloths. Anita Glaze has documented both traditional procedures and points out the characteristics that distinguish one approach from the other. In describing the fila method, she observes:

"The critical point of the technique is that a yellowish solution including a dye from the *nigene* tree is painted directly without preliminary sketch on the cloth. The *nigeneme* dye makes fast or permanent the black dye (*fariga gii* or *feerege gii*), a black earth obtained from the *marigot*, a pool or muddy place in a stream bed. The entire cloth is immersed in this black earth dye and when washed later, only the surface covered by the *nigeneme* solution retains the black dye."[24]

Glaze reports that masters of the fila painting technique may achieve a widespread reputation which attracts clients from quite distant villages, and these clients bring cloths and clothing woven and sewn in still other villages. "This multiple-artist scene is characteristic of the Senufo artistic scene in general. In some cases the Sando diviner's prescription may necessitate the interaction of several different specialists and involve as many as six or seven different artisan and dialect groups."[25] Aminata Konaté has pointed out that before the making of contemporary Korhogo cloths developed into large-scale production, clients still brought their own fabrics to the artist. M. Zemp, also, had the same experience as recently as 1964.

Fabrics designed for use in certain Poro masquerade costumes differ from fila cloth in several ways. The fabrics are created by and for Poro initiates and the artist's services are confined to the family and family-related organizations. In a sense, his skills are "owned" and jealously guarded with restrictions to working only within the sphere of this special group. Some of the techniques and dyes also differ from fila. Glaze notes:

"The Poro costumes are painted directly with a mixture of dyes and *banga* (a strong solution which helps to "fix" the dye) and lemon juice. The favorite dye is *tyelisiire* which produces a rich magenta-red and burnt sienna hues when mixed with the other ingredients. This dye (literally "feathers of the Tyeli") has long been associated with the *tyelibele*, the leather-workers' artisan group."[26]

One sees a relationship between the two traditional techniques and the process used in creating contemporary Korhogo cloths. Fila cloth is first painted with a mordant dye and then dipped in a mud bath in much the same way Aminata Konaté reported Korhogo cloths were traditionally dyed. Masquerade fabric designs are painted on cloth in a one-step process with the mordanting agent included in one dye formula. Contemporary Korhogo cloth techniques incorporate aspects of both traditional sources in a two-step method: first, a mordant dye is painted on the cloth and then a second, mud-based dye is painted directly over each line to create a colorfast fabric.

Glaze also recognizes a relationship between fila dyeing techniques and those used to produce bokolanfini mud cloth. She indicates that there may have been some connection many, many years ago, "when the Senambele 'brought cloth from the Dyula' in order to practice the art of *fila*," but she questions this theory for several contrasting reasons. Women design bokolanfini motifs that are basically geometric patterns created by painting around the design area (negative design) while men create fila motifs that are more representational images formed by the lines themselves (positive design).[27]

Mme. Étienne-Nugue laments the large-scale commercialization of contemporary Korhogo cloths and the current deterioration of the designs. Commenting on the increased sales abroad, she notes that "the best village artisans receive orders and money directly, so that their entire production is reserved, and one would have difficulty finding quality pieces in the Ivory Coast." Aiming at speed and efficiency in production, no matter what the results, "the young artisans try to outdo each other by ingenuity in finding simpler and more rapid methods and by inventing dyes with an iron-oxide base (*logowo*) when they don't use the industrial inks of poor quality. . . ."[28]

Mme. Étienne-Nugue's closing comments reflect her sad appraisal of the situation in northern Ivory Coast:

> "These villages are now visited very frequently, although no signposts point them out. They will soon be part of tourist circuits of the region and it is unfortunately to be feared that, without control, and with their desire to please and to sell, artisans will allow themselves to be drawn into producing work that is more and more hybrid—a mixture of everything—without any relation to the delicate compositions which were their points of departure.
>
> "One can already observe, in addition to the disappearance of all symbolism, a distinct enlarging of the design and a more and more marked tendency toward overloading and organizing scenes in the style of comic strips!"[29]

Anita Glaze does not share Mme. Étienne-Nugue's negative feelings, nor does she dismiss the wave of commercially produced cloths as being merely a tourist attraction. "Indeed, the phenomenon appears as encouraging evidence of the flexibility and genius of the Senufo creative artist faced with economic and social change," she concludes.[30]

Today, dozens upon dozens of these stylized cloths are brought from Korhogo to the marketplaces of Abidjan, the dynamic capital of Ivory Coast (Figure 118). The cloth, dyes, and methods of stitching the rows of weaving together must be carefully analyzed to bargain and purchase wisely. Otherwise, one discovers zigzag machine-stitching holding the narrow bands together, smooth-textured, too closely woven cloth that might be factory-produced, or suspiciously strong black dyes that have a chemical look about them.

Since the large marketplaces are crowded and frenzied, one might choose to leave the haggling over prices and quality to

Figure 118. *Trader displaying cloths to tourist in Abidjan Plateau marketplace.*

Robert Clark, a former Peace Corps volunteer who now owns and operates Eburnea Exports, specializing in West African art. In his gallery in the Treichville section of Abidjan are neat stacks of Korhogo cloth, among them an unusually proportioned, narrow, border-designed cloth with traditional central motifs, but many of Mr. Clark's pieces are also machine-stitched. The designs on cloths of this quality may still be interesting, and they are popular items which are exported by various entrepreneurs for sale in other West African countries. Large examples of these zigzag stitched cloths may be seen on each of the nine floors of the new, ultramodern Hotel Terango in downtown Dakar, Senegal.

One hopes that ultimately the artists of the Korhogo area will reconsider the value of preserving some of the symbolism and techniques of the traditional designs. To maintain only old traditions could be societal suicide; to discard knowledge of them in the process would be a great loss, leaving a regrettable gap in development and continuity.

NOTES

1. Anita Glaze, "Senufo Graphic Arts," *Ba Shiru*, University of Wisconsin Department of Linguistics, Number 4, 1972, pp. 37–46.
2. Ibid., p. 38.
3. Ibid., pp. 41–42.
4. Ibid., p. 42.
5. René Gardi, *African Crafts and Craftsmen*, New York: Van Nostrand Reinhold, 1969, pp. 231–34.
6. Jocelyne Étienne-Nugue, *Artisanats traditionnels en côte d'ivoire*, unpublished manuscript, *ca.* 1972, p. 72.
7. Anita Glaze, "Senufo Ornament and Decorative Arts," *African Arts* magazine, Volume XII, Number 1, November 1978, pp. 63–71; 107–8.
8. In "Women Power and Art in a Senufo Village," *African Arts* magazine, Volume VIII, Number 3, Spring 1975, pp. 24–29; 64–67; 90–91, Anita Glaze defines Sando diviners (plural: *Sandobele*) as members of "Sandogo, a dual-level institution which includes a branch of divination specialists whose primary concern is with family relationships. . . . Under certain circumstances men can be trained as a diviner . . ." However,

"this skill is always considered an inheritance through the maternal line. In short, not all *Sandobele* are diviners, or for that matter, women . . . the sphere of Sandogo is more an inner, closed area where the individual grapples with daily problems, and his relationship with the unknown" (pp. 64–65).

9. Anita Glaze, "Senufo Ornament and Decorative Arts," p. 70.
10. Ibid., p. 65.
11. Ibid., p. 66.
12. Ibid., p. 65.
13. Ibid., p. 66.
14. Ibid., p. 67.
15. Ibid.
16. Ibid., p. 68.
17. Ibid.
18. Ibid., p. 70.
19. Hans Himmelheber, "Moderne Negerkunst als Quelle für traditionelles Brauchtum—*Darstellung unbekannter Masken in modernen Stoffmalereien der Senufo*," *Tribus*, Veröffentlichungen des Linden-Museums, Number 23, November 1974, Linden-Museum für Völkerkunde, Stuttgart, 1974, pp. 139–53.
20. Ibid., pp. 141–42.
21. Ibid., p. 140.
22. Jocelyne Étienne-Nugue, op. cit., pp. 71–72.
23. René Gardi, op. cit., p. 238.
24. Anita Glaze, "Senufo Graphic Arts," p. 42.
25. Ibid., p. 42.
26. Ibid., p. 44.
27. Anita Glaze, "Senufo Ornament and Decorative Arts," p. 71.
28. Jocelyne Étienne-Nugue, op. cit., p. 73.
29. Ibid.
30. Anita Glaze, "Senufo Graphic Arts," p. 44.

8

Traditions/Transitions: Working with African Textiles Today

African textile arts are still alive because of their immediacy. The fabrics were crafted by people who made remarkable use of all that was around them, who learned techniques from their elders who in turn had learned from others. Any materials or devices found or won or learned from other people were used whenever they seemed appropriate. The needs and lifestyles that wove vitality into the ancient African cloths cannot be duplicated, for the life in anything handcrafted must come from the reality around it. For our crafts to be vital, we must do the same. Our art must come from who we are, from what we learned yesterday, and from what we have and need today. And today we truly need to escape the passive role of allowing technology to entertain, feed, and transport us. We need to be part of the world we are spun about in. More and more people are seeking to modify the pace they find imposed on them by mechanization—not to return to the past, but to find some sort of compatibility with technology.

For some people, the exposure to African fabrics has provided a whole new vista—an enriching inner perspective coupled with a greater understanding of the complex societal changes affecting all the peoples of the world. Others have become involved in promoting economically profitable ventures that will provide others with employment and utilize the creative energies of the community. Many people find satisfaction in serving society directly—in schools and communal centers—furnishing stimulation and enlightenment through actual programs in African art and crafts, which include textile design. The vanguard artist expresses the essence of an African culture through a unique approach to its traditional textile arts. For scholars and students in universities and museums, research is a tool for assimilating knowledge and passing it on in the form of books, slide shows, various forms of the graphic arts, and special programs for community groups.

Each one finds that an involvement in the fabric arts of Africa invokes a special kind of international communication. Esther Warner Dendel considers this—the artist's inherent universal language—an expression of "the craftsman as diplomat." She says:

"When I lived in Liberia, West Africa, during the early 1940s, it was apparent to me that the extraordinary rapport which I enjoyed with certain of the people was possible because we were craftsmen. While we sat and worked, the things we did with our hands made our communication. At first, we had almost no words of a common language, yet we seemed to have a depth of understanding which is seldom achieved with speech.

"I went to the forest with the carvers when they selected a tree to be cut for the project at hand. I watched while they made an offering to the spirit of the wood for the blows which must follow. I went to the sacred swamp with the old women, who talked to the clay before they took it for pots. As I acquired more vocabulary, I began to understand the poetic richness of their lives.

"Our own terms, 'respect for materials,' for instance, began to seem coldly intellectual when compared to the tremulous emotions of my friends in supplication to living matter which they must disturb and alter, cut and bruise, put to fire. That the clay from the swamp had a unique life of its own seemed too obvious to them to need discussion. As for trees, their roots are anchored in the warm, moist earth from which all life springs. Their tops are in the sky where the spirits of the ancestors look down on their children below. Trees connect life here with life there. This

Figure 119. *Esther and Jo Dendel in the showroom of the Denwar Craft Fellowship studio salesroom, Costa Mesa, California.*

gives them a vitality that partakes of eternity and is vastly greater than the upward thrust of flowing sap and the outward thrust of new growth.

"In the fiber arts, the same reverence holds. The taboos and the folk sayings associated with carding, spinning, and weaving bear witness to the intimacy between craftsman and fiber. In Liberia it is said that a woman who 'spins her mad' (spins to work off a rage) will spoil the thread. The anger will stay in the thread and disturb the serenity of any who wears the cloth. Dye pots and their laboriously prepared contents are spoiled by anger, jealousy, and impatience, all of which are labeled 'heat.'

"During later years, when my husband and I established a craft studio and built our own house in California, we tried to perpetuate in our way of life the attitudes, the reverences, the serenities, we had learned in Africa. It seemed we might do this with more success if we were a part of a closely knit group trying to accomplish the same thing. Our Denwar Craft Fellowship grew from this impulse. We have now met and worked and talked together, sometimes sorrowed together, for ten years. We weave, we braid, we twine, we batik, we teach others. And those who can, travel with us to Africa.

"In our visits with African craftsmen, we began to see interconnections between different rhythmic expressions, whether these happened to be the repeats and the intervals between the crisp patterns dividing up the space of an adinkra cloth; or the pulse and the silences, when time is being sliced into beats by a drum. Space and time! Africa has made their relationship understandable in a way that is felt in the blood even when it can not easily be comprehended by the mind.

"The man, in the adinkra village in Ghana, who sits on the earth and swings his arm from a black dye pot to stretched yardage, a little carved gourd in his hand, seems to be dancing in place. His movements have the economy of concentrated purpose, the vitality of someone who knows what he is doing. The repeated and grouped motifs on the cloth advance in squares—regiments marching across the fabric. Each motif has a meaning and a wisdom-saying attached, a meaning which has come down through generations. The man is dancing meanings into cloth.

"Reverence and rhythm and meanings. We ask ourselves how these may be incorporated into our own crafts. The answers do not come easily. Rhythm stutters and motion stops because of our inner uncertainties. Reverence fails because in our haste we do not allow ourselves the luxury of deep feeling. It takes time for the hand to hear what the yarn is telling it. Meanings waver and are fragmented because we have not discovered valid symbols to articulate them. Achieving these qualities of reverence, rhythm, and relevance (or meaning) is a craftsman's life work, regardless of his medium. Each of us must seek as well as shape. We need to feel as well as fashion. We have learned this in Africa.

"Almost everyone who has traveled with us has commented on the skill with which the African craftsmen use whatever is at hand. A warp for weaving is prepared by a man walking through a field of cut corn stalks, thread in hand. The end of the spool is tied to one stalk. By meandering among the stubble and retracing his path, as many equal lengths of thread as needed for the project are measured. A warping wheel or warping paddle of the kind used here and in Europe is quite unnecessary, useful though it may be.

"An adire artist applying starch resist to fabric has no need of an expensive brush of natural fiber. She simply pulls a feather out of any nearby fowl. When one feather wears out, another is at hand for no more effort than chasing down a rooster. One could cite examples of this use of whatever is at hand which apply to every area of African crafts. We have learned we don't need quite as many things as we thought we did.

"The craftsman is, indeed, a diplomat between peoples of diverse cultures. In addition, the crafts objects he produces are in themselves vehicles of understanding."

Esther has observed that the people in the workshop group who had toured Africa with the Dendels seem to have developed a greater appreciation for natural fibers—jute and sisal and the earthy things. In her opinion, there is a real conflict between the superficial and the vital. The people who have gone to Africa seem to have a greater empathy for what's earthy instead of what's superficially elegant—the furnishings and colors within their own homes, most of the things they wear or respond to. Africa has had the same effect on her; she loves natural fibers with a great passion and hates shiny synthetics.

Esther has a profound effect on her workshop group. One member made very decorative tapestries when she first started weaving—pretty things with feathers and beads. When she met Esther and began working with her, she felt that she began to grow, not just as a weaver but even more as a person. She feels closer to nature, and now she *really* looks at trees and tree trunks and takes the time to notice the forms and designs of seashells. The workshops have brought her closer to people, too, she says; this seems to be the general feeling of the participants. One member said that being in the workshops and knowing the people in the group has completely changed her life, enriched it, and

Figure 120. *Helen Anderson-Bauer.*

given it a dimension she never dreamed of. Esther feels that this is partly due to encouraging a rapport with vital things of the earth, and that many members now enjoy people they formerly would not have made contact with if they hadn't incorporated this viewpoint into their lifestyle.

The Dendels sponsor a Craftsmen's Fair each summer, where workshop members set up booths and offer their work for sale. Most of the people sell their work to earn money to buy more materials to go on to new developments in their crafts. The Fair offers the feeling of sociability and exchange experienced in African and European *marchés* and is reminiscent of the American tradition of pot-luck dinners and county fairs. Esther feels that in a sense the workshop group is a big family, replacing the nourishing relationships of the traditional African or early American extended family, which could include a whole village.

The Dendels conceive of the workshops as an ongoing experience without specific time limitations. Even if people drop out for months or years, they come back and carry on as comfortably as if they'd never left. The Dendels have worked with thousands of people in their remarkable workshops, extending warmth and fellowship and a concept of crafts that is overwhelmingly human and beautifully related to the creativity that dwells in every individual's soul.

The transition from workshop to workroom—from cooperative effort for creative and social satisfaction to cooperative effort for financial gain—is not always an easy one. And if the purpose is to earn a living while maintaining a sense of independence and individual worth, it is even more difficult. These were some of the motives for establishing a cooperative in Dakar, Senegal, in 1972. Helen Anderson-Bauer, a Peace Corps volunteer assigned to Senegal, helped organize and run this cooperative for women textile dyers, which was formed to train young women in hand-dyeing techniques so they could eventually produce and sell high-quality textiles in Senegal and abroad.

The complexity of Helen's involvement—the number of organizations and people represented, and their various backgrounds, different interests, and degrees of understanding or animosity that each brought to the enterprise—offers an enlightening and sometimes painfully realistic view of the difference between crafts as a social, recreational, revitalizing experience and crafts as a viable business enterprise.

The dyers cooperative—to which Helen was loaned by the Peace Corps—was organized by a United Nations-sponsored company, SONEPI (Société Nationale d'Études et de Promotion Industrielle), which promotes small enterprises in Senegal. It was under the overall control of a governmental agency that had already organized cooperatives in agriculture and other areas but never before in handicrafts. Helen had a degree in textile design from the University of California and had considerable experience in community development work. She had requested assignment to West Africa because she spoke French and wanted to learn more about African textiles. She spent several months teaching in a kindergarten outside Dakar and learned Wolof, a local language.

Helen's immediate supervisor in the project was a Swiss expert assigned to SONEPI by the United Nations. Before Helen joined the cooperative, this expert and his Senegalese associate had made a study of the market for hand-dyed textiles, using both natural products (indigo and kola nut) and commercial dyes. They found that dyeing was generally done, on a small scale, by women working at home, who sold their products at a very low profit, to local street vendors.

This production was threatened with extinction because young people were not learning the traditional techniques, and local textiles were running into strong competition from three sources: machine-printed materials (made in Senegal and other West African countries) imitating the hand-dyed look and sold at low prices; factory-made, imported Western cloth; popular imported damask fabrics of good quality, hand-dyed by Africans (but sold at lower prices than the Senegalese handmades), which were smuggled into Senegal—often from Gambia, Sierra Leone, and Ivory Coast. Helen was well aware of this competition: "When I first got to Senegal, in 1971, there were perhaps three of the machine-made imitations out on the market. When I left a year later, there must have been at least one hundred and fifty."

The cooperative was definitely a success as far as production and sale of attractively dyed and patterned textiles was concerned. Planning and administration of the project, however, left much to be desired. Failure to meet promises to the cooperative's members and confusion as to who was actually responsible for making important decisions led to the cooperative's collapse. The original plan for the cooperative called for a teaching program covering literary skills, the rudiments of economics, and an understanding of how a cooperative works. But this program was never actually provided.

Helen firmly believes that any such venture, while it can be temporarily aided by foreigners, must be run by the women themselves; hence the pressing need for general as well as technical education. Even an alternative arrangement—a profit-making business rather than a cooperative, with the dyers being paid a wage—would require workers to have a certain level of education if they were to grasp notions of productivity and quality control necessary in producing goods for competition in an international market.

The cooperative was supposed to include four training and production centers, a showroom, and several sales outlets. But it began with only two centers and with only one volunteer (Helen) assigned to one of these. Also assigned to each center were Senegalese women who had been tie-dyeing for many years and who each bought at least one share of the cooperative (at about ten U.S. dollars a share); some bought two. In return, the women expected to be trained quickly and soon to be producing materials in exchange for a share of the cooperative's profits.

Initial financing was provided by the women's own investment, by a grant from the United States Embassy Self-Help Fund, and by gifts from the Senegalese National Cooperative Board and SONEPI. In addition, the company that provided the cloth used by centers—all of which was to be manufactured in Senegal from Senegalese cotton—donated about one thousand dollars' worth of material.

In theory, Helen was to be concerned only with the artistic and production side of the cooperative; the Senegalese government was to assign a manager to handle administrative and accounting work for each center as well as act as a liaison between the various agencies involved. However, it was Helen herself who had to do all the bookkeeping (a task for which she was not prepared) as well as set up the training program for the women for nearly the entire time the project existed.

Although she was familiar with hand-dyeing techniques, Helen learned a great deal by watching the experienced women work. She said it took "a lot of watching" and questioning to learn precisely how often something is put in the indigo dye, or when the indigo was ready, and that by recording this she verified the *science* that some of these women know.

Helen thinks the teacher in her center, Mme. Adja Awa Traoré, is an extraordinary person. While many experienced craftswomen tended to guard the secrets of their success, this woman openly shared everything she knew with Helen and with the younger trainees.

Helen has much praise for the women in the center and felt quite close to them, sharing meals and life experiences. These warm relationships didn't remove all misunderstandings, however, and a major problem was the matter of quality. Helen felt that certain slipups (for example, a tiny hole in the fabric, cut when the string is taken out, or a blotch of dye) that were acceptable to the women would not be to a foreign buyer. Another problem was to persuade the women to mark the outline of the designs with pieces of charcoal or pencils, which do not leave permanent lines, rather than pens, which do.

Helen understood the women's viewpoint: "Who's to say that a hole is bad?" Nevertheless she insists that "at times you can put things on crookedly and at times you can't, or a European won't buy it. So we're treading a thin line, trying not to ruin a creative process but to keep up a standard for export."

Gradually, with the help of those experienced in various techniques, Helen set up a teaching program and a system for keeping track of each trainee's progress. She also developed a teaching book, with diagrams illustrating various stages of the techniques covered—pleating, stitching, knot-tying, starch resist, and wax printing—and with exhibits of the finished products. And she timed the women as they completed tests on these techniques with three-yard pieces of fabric so she could work out a pay scale to use when the cooperative began to generate profits.

Helen's center was in Dakar, on the grounds of an old, tumbled-down house which had been used for storage, and her office was formerly a one-car garage. The women worked outdoors, where there were four big indigo vats, four wax-block printing tables, hibachis (charcoal burners) to heat the wax, and other necessary equipment. Newly dyed materials were hung outside to dry.

The high point of the cooperative's work was an exhibit held at the American Cultural Center in June 1972, and it was a huge success. The women were pleased with the exhibits. They were quite proud, Helen said. "This was really good, since they had started working in January but had actually been involved when they first paid in October. This was a long time, but the recognition was good." The fabrics in the exhibit, almost two thousand meters of cloth, were sold in the courtyard of the center, and a record was kept of each woman's sales.

Problems arose when the women at the cooperative asked to be paid, as promised. When Helen turned to the various agencies responsible for the cooperative, none wanted to make a decision on this matter. Finally, with a Senegalese assigned to the cooperative by SONEPI, she worked out a compromise payment of about ten dollars—the original investment—for each woman at the center.

Figure 121. *A young woman of fourteen at the Women's Cooperative in Dakar, Senegal, pounding kola nuts in preparation for the dyeing process.*

Figure 122. *Another participant in the Dakar Women's Cooperative cutting open the strings on a tie-dyed fabric.*

But it was clear at this point that no more money would be forthcoming; the earnings from sales, though considerable, were in a bank account which no one seemed to have the authority to touch!

Though Helen was responsible only for the production of dyed fabric, she found it impossible to limit her concern to this aspect of the center's operations. She sympathized with the women who made up the cooperative and was aware that they were unhappy about the way it was being run. Their attendance was beginning to fall off, and Helen could not really blame them for losing interest. The educational program that was to accompany training in dyeing techniques never materialized, and for many months the women had been working all day, five days a week, paying transportation and other expenses to do so.

Despite all these problems, the center continued to produce fabrics in preparation for an exhibit in Switzerland in August. With the help of a young Senegalese assistant and an American woman who ran a fabric business in Gambia, Helen was developing new designs for wax printing which were carved into wooden blocks (tampons) by local carvers. The women were dyeing the printed shirts that had been locally tailored and were of good-quality material. The Swiss exhibit was very successful.

But by this time the women were attending sporadically, and the cooperative was falling apart. When the pieces for the Swiss exhibit were labeled and shipped, Helen did one last inventory and gave the keys to the center back to the cooperative board. She also resigned from the Peace Corps, disappointed because they had not supported her when she tried to stand up for the cooperative members' rights.

In essence, Helen felt that the "cooperative" was such in name only, since the people responsible for it "were not willing to do the necessary work." Helen believes that, up to now, not many women in Senegal have that combination of technical ability, sufficient education to keep good records and understand modern business practices, and willingness to share knowledge and work with a group that a really successful cooperative venture requires. But, she says, "if someone offered me an assignment like that now I'd do it again." She looks back with obvious pleasure on her work with the women dyers of Dakar. She says she learned an enormous amount about the dyeing process and that the failure of the cooperative as such did not detract from what the women learned or from the richness of exchange they found in working together.

Postscripting this experience is the following letter written to me the year after her work with the cooperative. Helen says of the leading woman dyer, Adja Awa Traoré, the woman on the cover of this book: "Adja is to this day my mother substitute in this country . . . she is the kindest, gentlest woman I know and generous beyond belief. She had a very philosophical outlook on her trade and trade secrets, which are generally guarded with knives and nasty words! Although she never learned to read or write, she is an excellent businesswoman in her private trade. She sincerely felt that the cooperative would eventually benefit her. She was *never* paid during the months of work in the cooperative, and she worked like a dog. She put up with me asking her day in and out to repeat processes for me. She put up with young 'smart-alecky' girls who were being taught the *art* of tie dye in a very strange manner indeed. Adja's grandmother taught her. She started when she was about seven years old and for many years she was not ever allowed to touch the dye pots. She did the fabric stitching and pounding of kola nuts, the sweeping up, the building of fires, and other routine tasks. She went through the normal long and hard apprentice training."

Helen returned to the United States with her inner visions of Africa and Adja and indigo indelibly inked in her memory, her life, her lifestyle. Her disappointments echo the guilty conscience of a generation of utopian Peace Corps youth, who ventured into Africa (and elsewhere) with fervent high hopes and unrealistic ambitions to rapidly right the world's wrongs. They often failed, but this frequently resulted in a slow but symbiotic growth that changed their lives and ultimately gave them more to give the world. Perhaps the Senegalese government also gained some insights from the experiences of the Dakar Women's Cooperative. The Senegalese do want a more effectively organized artisanat. In 1975 after a successful exhibition of Moroccan handicrafts in Dakar, the government asked the official Moroccan artisanal organization to come to Senegal and help them. In the meantime, the women's cooperative of the Cap Vert region of Senegal has started commercializing their production of tie and dye and batik.

If the positive insights resulting from Helen's experiences at the Dakar center are being applied to the newly developing cooperatives, a profitable and satisfying situation can evolve for everyone.

Gloria Freeman and Melvin Deal are both intensely active people dedicated to the concept of human enrichment through community involvement in the arts. Both have worked in the same black inner-city area of Washington, D.C. Gloria is an artist who taught art at Adams Community School and now teaches at the Marie H. Reed Learning Center; Melvin, a dancer and choreographer, is director of The African Heritage Dancers and Drummers. Both have incorporated African art and culture into their personal and professional lives and find themselves and their work inseparable from its enriching influence.

Gloria's dedication and talent as an art teacher have won her the honor of being listed in the 1972 edition of *Outstanding Elementary Teachers of America.* She chose African textiles as a way to relate the cultural heritage of Africa to her students at Adams Community School, and added many of the fabric-decorating techniques first introduced in my Smithsonian classes to her own curriculum. She wanted to find as many ways as possible to help her students develop the feelings of black pride and cultural identity essential for a supportive self-image. When I asked her to summarize some of her feelings about this, she wrote:

"When I was a child, the world did not reflect my Black image. Those reflections that existed were quite often in caricature and negative stereotypes. There were, of course, 'super Negroes' who were allowed to penetrate the shield of hostility and aggression placed between the Black man and his natural right to relate in a positive manner to his environment. Early on I became aware that the only worldly image that seemed worthy of reflection had blue eyes and blond hair. In my early years of teaching (1961–63), images in children's readers reflected the same stereotyped blue-eyed blond being that I, myself, encountered as a child. A full ten years after the Supreme Court School Desegregation Decree of 1954, texts with multi-ethnic characters were just beginning to be published.

"My students often reflected their own images in shades and

tones that bore no relationship to their actual colorations! Imagine the ego detriment that has been suffered by a brown child who selects Nordic colorations for his self-portrait and says, 'This is me!' "

Gloria has tried to correct this negative image by creating an environment within her classroom that is multinational and reflective of her belief in universal understanding. She uses all aspects of African art and culture to encourage a more positive self-image and identification. She also hopes to introduce the children to the great variety of artistic roles both men and women often occupy in African society and to show how these differ from the more rigidly delineated cultural roles deemed appropriate for men and women in America. She hopes that this contrast will provide a different image of the artist's role in relation to everyday life in America as well as in Africa. She cites some of the benefits the children in her classes derived from the now-defunct New Thing Art and Architecture Center, a community cultural organization serving the inner-city youth of Washington, D.C.

"When the New Thing was in existence, it had many very strong programs. I bring as much as I possibly can into a focal point—into my classroom—but I do not want to convey to the children the feeling that art is something that must happen within the context of a particular classroom. I want them to constantly have the feeling that art can be found in many, many places. In this sense the New Thing served as an excellent auxiliary agent within the community. Exhibits often featured African artists and often male artists who had done stitchery and batik and other kinds of textile work that traditionally American boys feel is out of their realm. . . . I remember taking them to an exhibit that featured lovely wall hangings stitched by male artists from Africa. This was definitely a learning point for the students. I think it was much more relevant to see it in their neighborhood gallery than in the Smithsonian Museum, because the Smithsonian carries the aura of—well, we're not surprised at what we see here; it's such a vast establishment they can almost make anything happen here—a magical atmosphere as far as the students are concerned. With the New Thing, neighborhood children

Figure 123. *Gloria Freeman (center), artist and art teacher, working with students in tie-dye exchange between Adams Community School and the New Thing Art and Architecture Center, Washington, D.C.*

Figure 124. *Participant/assistant at Adams Community School/New Thing exchange, opening her tie-dyed cloth.*

Figure 125. *Gloria Freeman (center) with girls at Adams Community School tying fabric for dance program costumes.*

realized that art can be just down the street. They don't have to travel to a special building in which artistic things take place.

"Also, 95 to 99 per cent of the staff at New Thing were men. This was particularly important because youth in our Black culture is dominated by women. So, I was very happy for my students to see men working in a variety of artistic activities—from the visual to the performing arts. Also, the staff of New Thing was knowledgeable in their crafts and performances. As a result, the children in this school district got positive models from community people who projected sound character. Often, students in my classes who had worked with Melvin Deal (see next paragraph) in his dance classes would speak of the kind of discipline that he imparted to them—it seemed to make up for many deprivations in the life of a child from a lower economic level. It was the kind of caring that makes a person *self*-disciplined, not an external discipline in which I, the teacher, do this to you. No, this internal discipline makes one want to be a self-achiever, a self-sustained person. Melvin in particular gave this to his students, and it was one of the important contributions that the New Thing made to the community."

Figure 126. *Melvin Deal photographed before an invitational dance performance at the University of California, Los Angeles, wearing a gold adinkra cloth with brilliant Kente cloth appliquéd strips, designed and hand printed by the author.*

Melvin Deal, leader of The African Heritage Dancers and Drummers, was always very involved with African fabrics; he designed and executed all the costumes for the dancers and drummers and as a result was extremely knowledgeable about African textiles and dress. When I was involved in research on adinkra cloth, Melvin purchased dozens of adinkra stamps in Ghana and helped me unravel the mystery of their symbolic meanings. When we met recently, I asked him if he still found time for costuming now that his group is independent (due to lack of federal funding, it is now a self-supporting entity) and he has the added responsibility of administrative and managerial duties. He said that in general the group members do all the costuming, but that for certain productions, such as the forthcoming *The Coming of the Golden Stool,* special plans are being made. The drama, which is the Ashanti legend of the Golden Stool, includes all the traditional dances of the Ashanti which the group already knows. The adinkra cloths will be designed by Gregory McNight and sketches will then be made by Walter Neal. The designer will teach the members of the company how to use the adinkra stamps on the fabric and the group will do the actual hand-printing process. This is in keeping with their original hopes that the dance group use their own skills to decorate fabrics in the African tradition for their productions.

When I asked Melvin about his views on the New Thing—the loss to the community when it collapsed in 1972—he said:

"Basically, the New Thing organization was an outgrowth of the 1960s turmoil and very much related to the riots, the social upheavals, and the advent—the readvent—of Black consciousness. A lot of money was thrown into society for pacification purposes, and the New Thing was one of the organizations that flourished with that money. And as the New Thing progressed and developed, it had hopes of becoming an educational institution with municipal status. But one needs more scope to establish an educational institution than drawing-board plans. One needs professional research for a workable plan and some connection with financial ventures that are successful enough to support such an institution. So, I think, perhaps from disillusionment or perhaps from a failure to see all the intricacies in establishing an educational institution that was Black-based and Black-run and Black-owned—community-oriented but having a larger base—the director found it infeasible. Of course, there was less money in '69, '70, '71, and '72; it was increasingly difficult to get funds. Perhaps the New Thing could have survived by plugging into the educational system here in Washington.

"Unfortunately, the inner-city people of the New Thing community—the nonwhites—were pacifists in terms of arts programs for their children. They liked the New Thing organization; but they had no real idea of the long-term benefits it gave their children, whereas middle-class people do. People who are interested in communities understand that what looks like a recreational, or play, program incorporates and enhances real learning. The people in the New Thing community do not, so they're not amenable to fostering or pushing it—plus they don't have any political clout. They are people who are still struggling to survive.

"I feel that artists should have a commitment to their community. Art should exist within the community not only as artistic endeavor but as an enlightening and awakening force that goes beyond recreational aspects and brings vitality to a community and its people. When an organization like New Thing dies for lack of a leader, someone else should continue it. If I ever decide I want to give up African Heritage, I'm not going to simply let it die, because it means a great deal to a lot of people who may not realize it until it's not there anymore. That's why arts organizations are important. Many people who at first may not see how art can lift people out of ignorance and deprivation, realize it when it does. They see it working and they see that it helps do that. It is not only art; it is inter-relations of people; it is joy through entertainment, for all levels of people."

The vanguard textile artist as an international figure is perhaps best exemplified by Sheila Hicks,* an American currently living in Paris, who has traveled and worked in Mexico, Morocco, India, and Chile. She experiences complete involvement in the traditional textile arts of another culture, which she then reworks in an

* For a fascinating view of her life and art, read *Sheila Hicks,* by Monique Lévi-Strauss, Van Nostrand Reinhold, N.Y., 1973.

artistic statement incorporating that particular traditional aesthetic. She says:

"Essentially, it's the same point of view that I carry with me as my mental baggage in any country in which I travel—simple, straightforward statements that can be duplicated and repeated by local craftsmen within their own tradition. That is, allowing them to use the material they're accustomed to working with, the techniques they're accustomed to working with, and not imposing anything of a foreign nature or foreign culture or foreign image upon them. It is almost as though I am going into a garden that is growing and making a salad of the existing vegetables or herbs without adding anything that is not from the garden. Now you'll say, of course, I add my own ideas, my own vision to it. At the same time I try to make a kind of distillation—looking for the essence within that culture and allowing it to speak by itself. I consider myself as a vehicle, encouraging the strongest and most essential part of that culture to surge forth. Obviously I impose my own ideas because I cannot forget myself, but I try above all to let the culture and the materials speak for themselves.

"In Morocco when we are hand-knotting rugs, I familiarize myself with the local materials and techniques and become acquainted with the local craftsmen, and I try to adapt to their daily living habits in an essential way. I believe this is fundamental. I probably go to extremes, some people will say. I think that to know a culture and work within it you have to delve into it thoroughly—totally—and live, eat, sleep, and think that culture, and that's what I have done in Morocco—listen, observe, and wake up within that horizon. I put aside communications and connections with my own culture in order to do this. When you have gone through this seven or eight times, you begin to accumulate stratified experiences, like chapters in a book, which when gathered together comprise separate reference books. Inevitably, cross references creep in. However, I try to approach each completely unknown thing without any—or as few as possible—preconceived ideas. This means just looking and thinking and learning. Like that . . . I tried to smell the smells of Morocco, eat the food of Morocco . . . you know and live and think a culture when you eat the way they eat. A lot of people can't quite manage local diets, but I have a lead stomach—so far!

Figure 127. *Textile artist Sheila Hicks.*

"When I went to Morocco in 1970, I was very much taken by the architecture—by the souks, by the markets, by the things that people fabricated, sold, and traded daily. This made for a very lively atmosphere. Over the past six years, I've returned frequently and worked extensively, attempting to realize ideas that are utterly simple and in keeping with their traditional techniques of handcrafted rugs. I've built up the thickness of the wool pile a little beyond the customary limit in order to let shadows play a part in the work. Also, I've decided to use fewer colors and rely on a basic palette of three to four. I imagined the rugs sometimes hanging on walls as though they would be arches or architectural elements in themselves. An illusionary doorway. These are somewhat Islamic in feeling. When I hung one in the Bab Rouah National Museum of Rabat, it seemed as though it had grown on the wall itself.

"At the same time, people ask me, aren't you afraid of losing your own identity, or that people won't recognize this as an artist's work? I've always thought that was the least thing to worry about, my own identity. To me it's a success when the thing I make marries to the extent that it's not a foreign element, calling attention to itself as an artist's statement, but something integrated in the whole and enhancing, hopefully in a meaningful way, the total statement. . . . If one ingredient in cooking stands out much more than all the rest, it seems to me that you become tired of it after you've eaten the dish three or four times. As an ensemble, it should work harmoniously in a subtle way, inviting you to repeat the diet frequently—in other words, walking into the space frequently and discovering materials and shapes in terms of juxtaposition.

"A lot of artists—many of my colleagues—say they don't like to work for architectural settings or to have an architectural idea imposed upon them. To begin with, they like to work freely; I think that's important, too, to be able to dream freely, to wake up in the morning and to invent and dream in all senses. But at the same time, to live and work within a context and a world and to try to find something that improves it and combines with it is also a very enriching experience."

Describing her mode of working, her life as an artist who lives and creates in many different circumstances, in many different countries and cultures, she says:

"I'm very careful to say that I don't *have* studios. And I don't *own* looms or studios. Because, from the beginning, I have preferred not to accumulate and to own and to have. I've always thought that what I must have must be within myself, and that I must be completely mobile. And to be able to carry everything on my back or in my pockets or in my head, all things must be moving and growing with me—within me. I'm free to let things happen to me. If a silkworm eats mulberry leaves, it will secrete a certain kind of fiber. If it eats muga leaves, it will secrete another kind of fiber, and another thing happens to it. It has to do with its intake, its ingestion. What it produces and what comes out of it is a result of what it's taking in. I liken my life in thread in the same way. Whatever culture I find myself in or go to explore must affect what is going to come out of me."

She explains her penchant for working in large architectural space:

"The bigger the better. The more thread there is, the more color there is, the more tactile sort of sensuous statement you can invent to wrap yourself in. It's like living inside a complete thread kingdom. Of course I love that. At the same time I'm very happy to weave miniatures that are ten inches by six or seven inches. Very intimate, detailed needle work—almost like darning socks. Maybe I exaggerate in the sense of scales: I am drawn to either a very intimate format or a monumental scale."

Sheila Hicks is very much concerned about the increases in the prices of handwoven cotton textiles in India and Mexico and about the fact that the actual raw cotton from these countries is being bought before it is woven, so that soon there will be no more handwoven cottons from these countries. Linen canvas is not available on the open market. Silk, as well, is scarce in India, and orders from China and Thailand and other sources are so backed up and overpriced that they can only be obtained with difficulty at this time. This in turn affects the plastics industry. She says:

"If synthetic production is reduced, and textiles made of synthetics are also cut back, where are we? We will now have very expensive handloomed goods, and synthetics will start going up too because of their unavailability. All the prices of textiles, rugs, and clothing will probably increase. I wonder where we're going. The humble fiber-and-thread field will start becoming a luxury.

"Two years ago, every time I attempted to contact suppliers with whom I'd formerly worked, seeking to obtain silk thread, linen canvas, or rug wool, I had a terrible time tracking down and keeping up with them. They were slowly closing their workshops, they would tell me, because their pay scale had risen so that they could not afford to sell their linen and silk thread at the prices clients could accept. Their own sources for the raw materials had disappeared. So they were going out of business, broke, bankrupt. Treating these things in the spinning context, their own manpower was limited and prices became exhorbitant. All of the middle-sized and small workshops began closing, and we were frantically seeking replacements for these sources, but we've never been able to find them.

"These places will obviously never reopen because they've already sold or abandoned their equipment; they've sold their land; their workshops have been either torn down or converted into other activities. So these people who, say three years ago, were linen spinners, cannot reopen, even though it might be a very lucrative time to do so. They can't get themselves together again; they're all dispersed—the workers, the machinery—the wheels can't turn again. We've lost these supply sources, and we haven't replaced them with anything."

Still, Sheila Hicks manages to continue in her dynamic and creative way—substituting cotton for silk if necessary or taking out her cache of precious Chinese silk which she stacked away seven years ago, perhaps already anticipating the necessity to preserve the very fibers she loves in order to continue producing the magnificent and compelling creations of her thread kingdom.

Creativity in the field of African textile research flourished under the guidance of Dr. Joanne B. Eicher at the College of Human Ecology, Department of Human Environment and Design, Michigan State University, and continues at the University of Minnesota where Dr. Eicher now heads the Department of Textiles and Clothing in the College of Home Economics. Dr. Eicher is a sociologist who became interested in African textiles when she lived in Nigeria in the early 1960s. During that time, she collected fabrics first for her own pleasure and later acquired a representative collection of Nigerian textiles to be used for study and exhibition purposes. When she returned to Michigan State, a number of her students expressed an interest in her collection and soon these fabrics became the inspiration for masters and Ph.D. theses. These, in turn, stimulated further studies on handcrafted and machine-printed African fabrics. Some emerged in book form (including her own *African Dress: A Select and Annotated Bibliography of Subsaharan Countries*, and her book on Nigerian textiles), teaching kits with slides, an exhibition and accompanying catalogues, and various other studies in related fields. Dr. Eicher's interests are varied, but she tries to focus her commitments within the framework of her deeply felt humanistic beliefs. She says:

"I suppose my long-range goal is for more intercultural understanding of how similar life is around the world and how beauty appears everywhere. I think that one of the reasons I was attracted to African textiles is that I know that people know a great deal about sculpture and masks but—especially during the time we lived in Nigeria—very few people realized the extent of textile creativity. In recently looking at the old Dahomean appliqué hangings at the Musée de l'Homme, we saw that even though we don't know the age or full historical context of these textiles, they are marvelously beautiful.

"I try to work my African materials into particular courses. I use my Nigerian dress examples to show that Nigeria is a culture in transition—a society in transition from agrarian to industrial. We can see this by looking at Nigerian dress. The traditional, handwoven apparel is typical of an agrarian society, but the Western dress shows industrialization. People who are connected with industrialization often drop the traditional dress and wear Western clothes. An example is that the Japanese outlawed kimonos in factories because they were dangerous—the long sleeves could get caught in machinery. Usually men adopt Western dress first, not simply because they are men, but because they usually take the industrial jobs first. Women who take industrial jobs also wear the Western style of dress. Those who stay in the traditional jobs stay in traditional dress. Children also adopt Western dress when school uniforms are demanded because uniforms seem to be a Western idea.

"Much as I like the idea of traditional dress, I don't think we can mourn its passing in some places, because it's just not practical to keep it. I think that ties with the past are very good. But—as in the case of the kimono being dangerous in a particular setting—that doesn't mean that it can't be worn at home. I would hate to see a variety in life disappear. But some of the Nigerian robes for men are simply not practical in a work situation. And women, in offices, usually wear Western dress, but when they go home, they'll put on a traditional wrapper and blouse.

"In my senior course, 'Culture, Society, and Dress,' I analyze dress very specifically in sociocultural terms. We use the concepts from sociology and anthropology, and I use Nigerian dress as an example of stability and change. I show different kinds of dress that are very traditional and indicate the particular situations that encourage tradition—such as ritual dress. Or I show those kinds of clothing that are connected with change—examples of technology

Figure 128. *Dr. Joanne B. Eicher.*

Figure 129. *Aminata Konaté.*

illustrate this point when I show traditional looms juxtaposed with shots of modern textile plants in a country like Nigeria."

Joanne Eicher, through her supportive encouragement of her own students, her readiness to share insights and information with colleagues in America, Europe, and Africa, and her own tireless efforts to discover and disseminate information on African dress and textiles, is certainly fulfilling her desire to further intercultural understanding and appreciation throughout the world.

As an African student in Paris, Aminata Konaté is herself experiencing the transitional aspects of her culture. She is studying the traditional concepts and modern forms of graphics, which she coordinates into a form of communication that is both ancient and modern. In Korhogo, Ivory Coast, where she was born and spent her childhood, she learned that a major avenue of communication in the Senufo religion was achieved through a form of graphics. These were the drawings of the religious specialists (fétichistes) which were once applied to the walls of the cult house and later, since they were too easily eroded by weather, were transferred to cotton fabrics which could be hung more permanently. She left Korhogo to attend art school in Abidjan, the Westernized capital city of Ivory Coast, and ultimately specialized in graphics when she received a scholarship to study at the School of Decorative Arts in Paris. Although she has an interest and ability in various art forms such as painting and sculpture, she chose to develop her thesis in the field of African textiles—specifically, the graphic symbolism of the Korhogo cloths and the appliquéd fabrics of Dahomey. Her specific interest is to do animated drawings for television—a form of communication she feels would be well suited to her society since many of the older people in rural areas do not read. Animated drawings would be understood and respected, though the information they impart would be of a world other than that of the religious specialists.

In this era of industrialization, the transition from communication through inanimate drawings on a wall (which are later animated by a human being—the religious specialist) to communication via an electronic impulse—as is the case with animated cartoons (thereby eliminating the human element and substituting a technological one)—is both poetic and somewhat frightening. Aminata seems to regard it simply as a part of modern life, just as Abidjan, contemporary African metropolis, is complete with advertising agencies and newspapers, where she can use her graphic abilities when she returns to Ivory Coast. In a sense, Aminata is studying the ancient symbolism and technology of traditional African textiles as a means of developing a modern approach to the changing traditional society, which originally gave birth to these same symbols and techniques. The artist/craftsman, then, offers the key to the past as well as the keynote to the future.

Epilogue

To understand the various appeals that African textiles have had for Americans in the 1960s and '70s, it might help to have a brief look at the history of crafts in the United States.

Under the conditions of pioneer life, the crafts flourished magnificently. In their lonely, isolated farming settlements, pioneers found great enjoyment in socializing their mutual efforts while fulfilling life's needs. It gave their work the added grace of human contact. These needs for manual involvement and for individual expression within a group environment are integral parts of the tradition of communal enterprise which was the basis of life for the early settlers. The sewing bee, the quilting party, candle dipping, the raising of a roof, the gathering of maple syrup were based on cooperation by all who were able. And all shared the pride in the quality of goods produced.

After the industrial revolution, crafts remained but more as a leisure interest than as a necessity. As a result, they lost much of their vitality. With industrialization, too, standards of beauty and status changed. "Store-bought" became more prestigious than "handmade" and soon crafts became associated with eccentric old ladies who painted flowers on china plates. This dormancy was short, however.

During the Depression of the 1930s, government and private agencies stepped in with programs which, among other results, renewed participation in the arts and crafts. Most notable was the WPA, or Work Projects Administration, which enlisted thousands of unemployed artists and craftsmen in government endowed activities. Once again necessity forced people to work together cooperatively, and they found that they liked it.

Magnificent projects resulted from the WPA involvement in craft activities. One such WPA project is Timberline Lodge at Mount Hood, Oregon, where regional craftsmen and women constructed the entire edifice of native Oregon timber and stone. Everything—gates, furniture, draperies, lamps, bedspreads, even woodcarving tools—was handcrafted. The fireplace andirons were forged from discarded railroad tracks. The beautiful, sturdy hooked rugs in each room were fashioned from worn-out blankets and old CCC uniforms;* their olive-drab color was relieved by bits of colorful corduroy scraps salvaged from the cutting rooms of WPA garment sewing units that made clothing for welfare distribution. Timberline Lodge stands as a glorious tribute to the artisans of Oregon who, through the WPA's project sponsorship, saved the local wool and flax industries during the 1930s and preserved the traditional techniques for craftspeople of the 1970s to study and enjoy.

One of the private agencies sponsored by the WPA was the Southern Crafts Council. It developed out of the desperate situation of people living in the Ozark Mountains, an arid land with harsh winters. The Council sponsored such traditional craft forms as candlemaking and candlewick spreads—the forerunners of chenille bedspreads. This provided added earnings for these economically depressed families and kept alive an admirable skill.

With emphasis on industrialized products of the 1930s and 1940s, people soon wanted to escape the sameness they saw in the mass-produced things that surrounded them. "Handmade" once more became desirable. Americans began to treasure Grandma's rocker and highboy which had sat for years in the attic. People went to the farms of New England and Pennsylvania to reclaim the lovely old handcrafted furniture and household items of their ancestors. American patchwork quilts became scarce, then priceless.†

* CCC—another WPA group known as the Triple Cees—Civil Conservation Corps.

† By the 1970s, patchwork quilts warranted an international exhibition, one which charmed visitors to the Renwick Gallery in Washington, D.C., the Whitney Museum in New York, and the Musée des Arts Décoratifs in Paris. The Smithsonian Institution, once laughingly referred to as "the nation's attic," now offers a marvelous retrospective view of handmade, mostly anonymous, creations of an earlier America that was incredibly inventive.

By the late 1940s, and in the '50s and '60s, the return to the crafts was less out of economic necessity than as a reaction against the passivity produced by the technological era. How-to-do-it books flourished, and in the '70s threatened to inundate the bookshops. The 1970s brought a national awareness of the shortages of the world's natural supplies. Pollution, a by-product of mass production/industrialization, forced people to think about how they wanted to use the dwindling natural resources. Many people, shocked by the dual implications of waste and pollution in "store bought" goods, are turning again to the crafts, to "homemade."

Appendix: Indigo— The Legend and Technique

*How indigo dye came to Liberia—a folk tale**

In the long ago and far away when High God left the earth, he went to live in the sky. The sky was close to earth in those days, so close it rested on the hills and mountains and sagged into the valleys. Energetic women feared to beat their pestles too high lest they pierce the fabric of the sky just above their heads and poke the spirit of a departed elder. What calamity!

It was better, really better, that High God, after being whacked a few times by busy women, left the spirits of the departed elders and went higher and farther from people. At least the low-lying sky was left to blanket man and shield him from the fierce sun. The people in their loneliness for God made sacrifices to the spirits of the ancestors and gave them messages to carry to God.

The sky did more for man in those days than to shade him and to house the spirits. Bits of sky could be eaten. This was different from other foods. Rice and palm oil fill the belly. Sky fills the heart. With a scrap of cloud inside him, a person can float and

* Esther Warner Dendel, "Blue Goes for Down," Brooklyn Botanic Garden's *Natural Plant Dyeing*, Handbook II, 1974, pp. 23–28.

dream and find again the peaceful, joyous feelings that filled him before High God left the earth.

It was dangerous business, this eating of cloud. One had to come to cloud-food pure in thought and body. Even so, one could become cloud-drunk, sweetly drunk and unknowing. This is what happened to Asi, the seeress of Foya Kamara.

On a bright morning Asi came to the banks of the stream that flows past the town. She came with her girl child tied on her back under a pure white *lappa* of country cloth. On Asi's head was a raffia bag filled with rice which she must cook and eat on the sacred spot where an altar to the river spirit stood against a great silk-cotton tree. In her hands she held a hollow stick. In its hollow was the winking red eye of a lump of charcoal for lighting the sacred fire.

Asi walked calmly, her head high and straight as she neared the altar because one does not rush with unseemly haste to a sacred place. She collected sticks from the forest and lighted the fire between three rocks which held the sacred clay pot which was always left in the forest. After she had spread her lappa on the earth and made a cushion of leaves under it to soften the place for her child, she walked without clothes to the bank of the stream where she would rinse the pot and take water for cooking.

On sunny days strips of cloud came to lie down in the river. One could look down into the deep pools and see the beautiful blue color of the sky lying there in the sacred wetness. Asi had eyes and heart that were hungry for color. To Asi, the blue of the pools was the most beautiful color in all the world. Asi looked back at the bank of the stream where her child was lying on the white lappa. The color of the white lappa seemed a dead and lifeless thing that had never known sun or cloud or sky.

"Perhaps," thought Asi, "if I eat enough sky, the blue will come to my skin from inside me. With luck, my hair will be thunder-blue."

Asi shivered then because she knew that a seeress must not beg anything for herself at the holy pools; one must ask only for the entire people of the village. She had done a selfish, wicked thing just when she should have been most pure in her heart. Fear shook her body as she carried water for the rice toward the fire. What was done was done, the wicked thought had taken hold of her, she must beg forgiveness of the water spirit and think now of her sacred task.

When the pot of water had been set above the fire, Asi sat with her back against the great silk-cotton tree, waiting for the water to boil. "I will eat some sky now to make my heart lie down and be still," Asi told herself. Reaching up, she broke off a strip of sky as long as a plantain leaf and began to feed her lonely heart.

With the first swallow of sky, beautiful thoughts filled Asi. She felt herself within the roots of the trees far below her in the river-wet soil. The roots nuzzled the earth to drink the holy wetness the way a baby nuzzles a mother's breast to find milk. Asi's own breast ached with the nuzzling of the roots because her spirit was there inside the sacred roots.

When the roots had drunk their fill and were ready to sleep, Asi's spirit rose and entered the body of a *veda* bird dancing in the air before her. The veda is a blue so bright it is a hurting, a lovely hurting to the eyes. It dances in one spot in the air when it is ready to mate. It was from floundering in the sky where the blue rubbed off on its body that the veda became this trembling, beautiful blue. Once again, the woman Asi became jealous of possessing this color, blue. She shook herself to try to rid her longing for color. Perhaps if she asked for the blue for all the people, not just for herself . . . Asi rose and added the rice to the water in the pot which had begun to boil. She was calmer now and not so afraid since she had decided to make a begging for blue to come down to all the people of Foya Kamara. She saw that her baby was asleep on the white lappa. Asi was free to eat just one more bit of sky while the rice cooked. She would then leave her begging for blue along with some rice on the altar and go home before the forest was dark.

When Asi awoke, her head throbbed and she knew she had been drunk with sky. The forest no longer smelled sweet. No birds sang. In her nostrils was the stench of burned rice; she had spoiled the sacrifice she had come to make. The sun was low in the sky. Fear ate at Asi when she turned her aching head to look to her child. The baby had rolled off the lappa and was lying face down on the earth. Something strange about the lappa caught Asi's eye; there was a blue patch of color in the center where the baby had wet. One small patch of deep blue in the dead expanse of white. Asi did not stop to finger the lappa. She rose to her feet as quickly as she could get her joints together and ran to her baby. When she turned the child over, no breath came from its mouth.

Asi's baby was dead. This was the punishment for bringing selfish thoughts to that holy place. In a frenzy of grief Asi ran to the fire, now dead ashes, and loosened her hair to receive the grime of the ashes as is the custom with women in mourning. Tears streamed down her face, streaking the ashes she had piled on her head. Asi clutched her child to her, then wrapped the lifeless body in the lappa which was her own skirt. Her body rocked forward and back as she wailed and wept.

Finally, Asi felt the life and the grief going out of her. She fainted there at the base of the silk-cotton tree. And while she was in faint, the water spirit spoke to her, telling her about the blue spot on the white lappa. It was indigo, the spirit told her, and came from the leaves she had plucked to cushion her child. In order for the blue to stay, there must be urine and salt and ashes with indigo. It was necessary for the baby's spirit to leave its body; otherwise, Asi would not have added the salt of her tears and the ashes of her grief; the blue Asi had desired above all else would not have stayed on the earth.

Before Asi awakened from this trance, the spirit cautioned her that now since the color blue had come down to earth to stay, it was a sacred duty to guard the indigo and that only women too old to bear children should handle the indigo pots. Asi was to carry her new knowledge back to Foya Kamara and instruct the old women there how to make the blue juice live happily in the cloth for all the people. Only after that would Asi conceive again and the spirit of her child, just dead, return to live in her hut.

When the people of Foya Kamara awoke the next morning, they saw that the sky no longer rested on the hills or sagged to the roofs of the houses. High God, after having let women have the secret of blue for their clothes, pulled the sky up higher where no one could reach up to break off a piece for food. People look on the blue of fine cloth and have less need of a near sky, even though in their hearts they will always remain lonely for God.

Indigo Techniques

To be successful you must treat indigo gently and respectfully, even reverently, for you are quite literally coaxing the color to come out. If the current studies on plant life are right, and talking to leaves makes them respond, then I would suggest you whisper sweet nothings into indigo's ear, treating her as a heaven-sent soul with a mind of her own and the determination to keep her blueness to herself if you are not nice to her. I myself have the greatest respect for her, having on numerous (unsuccessful) occasions tried to woo away her deepest blues. I will admit that giving a nice girl caustic soda kisses is not the kindest treatment in the world, and so I am not surprised she rebuffed me with an uneven and chilly blue-gray. (Chemical analysis: too much sodium hydroxide—also called caustic soda—bleaches while indigo blues.) I tried to ferment her with sugared yeast and ammonia but she seems to reserve that favor for others and will yield only a few blue bubbles on my behalf. She won't reduce. She starts out enthusiastic—gurgly and effervescent like a giddy schoolgirl—but in the end she rests sullenly on the bottom of a bubbleless bath, stubbornly blue but only for her own sake. To the liquid above, she offers nothing but an occasional yeasty and contemptuous burp. She seems happier when showered with washing soda and apparently yields herself in utter abandon to dainty sprinklings of sodium hydrosulphite. She turns yellow with jealousy, green with envy, and finally, free in the fresh air from whence she came, Paris sky blue—streaked and cloudy. (Chemical analysis: too little dyestuff, too small a dyebath for the fabric to circulate freely.) I dip into the deep wealth beneath her horizon but she is whimsical, elusive, and full of trickery—is that why she so often adorns Eshu, the Yoruba trickster god? She has a sense of humor but it is deceptive and malicious; often the second dip is lighter than the first one. (Chemical analysis: "The concentration of the sodium hydroxide redissolves what has already been deposited." So says

Fred Gerber, the indigo expert, and he ought to know.) Is it any wonder that she is so mysterious, has a goddess of her own, and performs miracles before your eyes if she so desires? Tread softly and, when you try the indigo formula, keep a cautious heart and a blue thumb.

There are many formulas for indigo—some take several days (or weeks) of fermentation, others require the use of strong and often dangerous chemicals. I spent some time, during the past few years, experimenting with various indigo formulas in an effort to understand some of the dye's complexities and arrive at a simple approach suitable to a workshop situation. But indigo is not a simple dye, and my efforts to find an easy approach have often been frustrating and disappointing in the extreme.

Fred Gerber has written a small but insightful book entitled *Indigo and the Antiquity of Dyeing*, which I recommend to everyone interested in indigo. It is a slender volume, covering historical and contemporary considerations of indigo dyeing. I was struck by his statements about the difficulties encountered by most of his students in using the available formula instructions: "This general inability of the dyer to build up deeper blues is seldom, if ever, mentioned in the instructions." He explains some of the complications facing the modern craftsman working with indigo—the problems inherent in the strong chemicals proposed by most of the contemporary formulas; the difficulties of obtaining darker shades from redipping in these same formulas; the necessity to use weaker sources of alkalies to prevent redissolving the indigo on the previously dyed fabric, when the second or third dips are made to achieve a darker tone; the need to return to the traditional urea (urine) formulas of antiquity.

All of this has lead me to try to formulate a one-dip approach to indigo—to achieve, in a workshop situation, a deep dark blue that offers the necessary contrast to the protected white areas of cloth in tie and dye. This has not been easy and, in fact, much of my work is still in the experimental stage. Sometimes I am successful and sometimes my efforts are (quite literally) clouded with failure. I am still seeking solutions to some of these dilemmas. In spirit I can agree with Fred Gerber's philsophical approach and his desire to return to the ancient formulas which require dozens of dippings to achieve a deep strong blue. While this is the true nature of indigo dyeing in antiquity—a gradual buildup of color—I feel this approach is not suitable to a workshop situation where people want to see results in a few hours.

My experiments have taken me in the direction of using larger amounts of indigo dye when working with cotton fabric (wool presents no problem as indigo takes to it with wondrous affinity). This approach has made me vastly uncomfortable in view of the smaller amounts of dyestuff recommended by most existing formulas. However, a letter from Fred Gerber offers me some comfort. He says, "Natural indigo only runs about 40%. So, you see, precise measurements may be pure self-delusion when it comes down to working with the stuff. . . ." Perhaps, then, the variables in my success/failure affair with indigo are to some extent accountable to the very nature of indigo itself—an inherent inconsistency, almost a fickleness. And perhaps the Africans in their ancient wisdom recognized this capricious quality long ago and continue to placate indigo's whimsical and inconstant nature with prayers and offerings. I cannot say that I have not offered a mute prayer every now and then, but perhaps it was too self-centered, wishing only for my own success and forgetting that it is indigo that should be rewarded, not me.

It should be understood, therefore, that these formulas are to be regarded as simply a series of ongoing inquiries into the nature of indigo, which you yourself may want to continue if you are sincerely interested in understanding this complex and fascinating dye.

Making a Hydrosulphite Vat with Natural Indigo:†

(Note: This is one quarter of a full formula which I recommend

† Retail sources of indigo are few and frustratingly elusive. No sooner does one find a supplier who sells indigo in small quantities than the vendor mysteriously disappears. The best recommendation I can make is that you check all the ads in magazines like *Fiberarts* and *Craft Horizons* plus all the books on natural dyes listed in the Bibliography. You may also get more information from your local library, bookshop, or craft center. (Chemicals are available from chemical supply stores.) Also, some of the craft colleges and universities with active textile departments buy powdered indigo by the barrel and might be willing to sell you some, especially if you sign up for a course. So search out all the sources you can find in your own vicinity and then check with friends and artist/craftspeople around the country, especially anyone traveling to the West African countries or even Europe or Asia.

for the first experiments, since indigo is expensive and it may require several tries before perfecting the technique. Later, the ingredients can be doubled or quadrupled according to your needs.)

You may want to protect your hands by wearing plastic gloves; also, try to work in a well-ventilated place and keep chemicals out of your eyes. (Use separate equipment for cooking and dyeing.)

1 cup cold water
1 tablespoon powdered natural indigo
1 tablespoon sodium hydrosulphite
4 tablespoons washing soda (also called sal soda, soda ash, or sodium carbonate)
½ cup warm water
6½ cups warm (120° F) water
1¼ teaspoons sodium hydrosulphite

1) Measure 1 cup cold water into a 2-cup Pyrex measuring cup. Sprinkle 1 tablespoon indigo over the water, allowing it to settle. Stir gently with glass rod.
2) Sprinkle 1 tablespoon sodium hydrosulphite over indigo mixture, stirring gently with glass rod.
3) Let stand for ten minutes.
4) Dissolve 4 tablespoons washing soda in ½ cup warm water, mixing thoroughly and crushing with a spoon until no lumps remain. Add to indigo solution, stirring gently.
5) Place the measuring cup of indigo solution in a pot of hot water double-boiler fashion. Put these two containers—the cup within the pot—on the stove at medium-low heat, insert a cooking thermometer into the indigo liquid, and bring to 120° (about ten minutes).
6) Remove measuring cup of indigo solution from the stove, cover tightly with Saran Wrap, and let stand one hour.
7) When the indigo is ready, measure 6½ cups warm (120° F) water into a large Pyrex-glass vat, bowl, or stainless-steel pot; sprinkle 1¼ teaspoons sodium hydrosulphite over this water. Stir slowly with glass rod. Place on the stove over very low heat to maintain 120° F for ten minutes.
8) Add indigo solution by sliding the cup beneath the surface and easing this liquid into the dyebath (to avoid causing air bubbles). Stir gently to mix thoroughly.

9) The solution looks dark yellowish-green in the vat, but when you trickle a few drops down the side of a glass or a plate, it is yellow and very shortly turns green and then blue. The mixture is ready to receive the fabric.

Dyeing the Fabric:

1) Wet samples to be dyed; squeeze out excess moisture and air bubbles.
2) Slip fabrics gently into dyebath for twenty minutes, maintaining 120° F temperature.
3) Stir continually and keep fabrics completely submerged.
4) Remove fabrics and hang by clothespins to air for twenty minutes.
5) After five to ten minutes of the airing time have passed, remove from the clothespins and cut ties on pieces, to allow inside of pieces to oxidize. Hang from opposite ends so that the area first covered by clothespins can be aired; complete the full twenty-minute period of oxidation.
6) Rinse pieces in warm water. Wash in soapy warm water, rinse again, hang to dry. Iron damp-dry.

Making a Hydrosulphite Vat with Synthetic Indigo 60 Percent Grains:

Follow the above instructions for natural indigo, substituting
1 tablespoon synthetic indigo 60 percent grains

Dyeing the Fabric:

Follow the instructions for natural indigo as above.

Using the Fermentation Method with Natural Indigo:‡

1¼ teaspoons powdered natural indigo (5 grams)
⅓ cup clear nondetergent household ammonia (75 ml)

‡ Fermentation Formula courtesy Fred and Juanita Gerber, The Arachnid—Early American Crafts, Ormond Beach, Florida. This formula has many variables. I have never been able to achieve the results I sought and even the Gerbers have had problems with it. *They attribute the failures to poor temperatures for good yeast growth or the use of synthetic indigo which never seems to perform the way that natural indigo does.* (Italics requested by Fred Gerber)

1 package dry active yeast (or one cube fresh yeast)
1 tablespoon sugar
1 gallon of water at about 95° F

1) Soak 1¼ teaspoons powdered natural indigo in ⅓ cup clear ammonia for one hour.
2) Place one unit of yeast plus 1 tablespoon sugar in a gallon of water at about 95° in a narrow-mouthed jug or vat (plastic can be used). Fermentation (disintegration of yeast into bubbly, soft, heatproof substance) should be active in five to fifteen minutes.
3) Add the indigo/ammonia mixture to the active yeast bath, sliding the cup under the surface of the liquid and emptying the contents underwater to avoid introducing air bubbles. Stir gently with glass rod.
4) Place the entire mixture in an assured warm place (95°–100°—over a pilot light or lowest stove burner with asbestos plate beneath vat) and leave it alone. In approximately twelve to eighteen hours, the liquid will start to clear from the bottom upward.
5) When the bottle is mostly yellowish (a few more hours may be needed for the full process to take place), well-washed and wetted cotton or wool fabric can be entered, weighted down to prevent the yeast bubbles from bringing it to the surface.
6) After from twenty minutes to overnight, the fabric can be removed. It will be a yellowish-green color which will—on exposure to air—reoxidize to permanent blue indigo. (You can test the time for removal by taking the fabric out and airing it for fifteen minutes; if it oxidizes properly, it's ready.)
7) For a darker shade, redip the fabric until it acquires the depth of tone desired.

Some of my experiences with indigo may be of interest to you while you are preparing your first endeavors. I had difficulties in getting an even color distribution on many of my tied pieces. I tried various ways to correct this and sometimes was successful; more often not. Sometimes, for no apparent reason, the classic circular tie which I used most regularly in my small experimental pieces would come out beautifully even. I have no explanation for this phenomenon except indigo's inexplicable nature; for other times, with the same formula and careful preparation, the area surrounding the central tied design formed an unattractive grayish pattern. By analyzing the markings in this area, I realized that the indigo was not penetrating into the crevices and crinkles created by the ties. This has not been the case with other commercial dyes I have used. It was suggested that I add wallpaper paste to the dye vat for a more even color distribution. I did this with a very concentrated natural indigo formula and produced the most beautiful, even, deep blue I have ever achieved—and in only one dip. Indigo is expensive, but you may wish to experiment with it all the same and see if it gives you the same excellent results I experienced. The formula is very similar to the one for natural indigo, with a few additions. Add to the list of ingredients:

¼ teaspoon lye (caustic soda)
¼ cup warm water
4 tablespoons wallpaper paste
¾ cup warm water
Dyebath: 3 cups water

After Step 4 (p. 228), when you have dissolved the washing soda, add ¼ teaspoon lye to ¼ cup warm water and stir till dissolved. Add to the indigo mixture after mixing in the washing-soda solution. Stir thoroughly. Proceed to the next steps. After Step 6 (p. 228), while the indigo is being dissolved, slowly add the 4 tablespoons of wallpaper flour to ¾ cup warm water so that it makes a smooth paste. Gently stir this mixture into the indigo solution, a little at a time, making a smooth, slightly thickened mixture. For Step 7, add this mixture slowly to 3 cups of warm water, stirring gently and steadily so that all the solution is mixed evenly into the dyebath. This small dyebath has a murky, yellowish-pea green color—unappetizing, but the most successful of my experiments in terms of deep, strong color and even dyeing. There is one curious side effect of the paste, and that may explain some of its effectiveness.

When I removed the pieces from the dyebath and hung them to oxidize, I was chagrined to see that they failed to turn blue except for one or two tiny (albeit *very* deep blue) spots. I waited nervously the entire twenty-minute period, then thirty, then an hour, finally a disillusioned hour and a half. I thought, as I had read can happen, I had put in too much sodium hydrosulphite, and that the pieces were a failure. I had noticed that the thickened dye/paste rested heavily on the pieces, and after taking them outside to get more oxygen and finding that they still didn't oxidize, I returned to my workspace (the kitchen, of course) and tentatively dabbed at the fabric with paper towels, blotting off some of the excess dye/paste. Miraculously, the air hit the cloth and the most startling midnight blue appeared. I proceeded to blot each piece with paper towels and after the appropriate twenty minutes of oxidation had elapsed, I rinsed and washed all the pieces, allowed them to damp-dry, and ironed each sample. Imagine my delight to find that the deep, rich blue had not totally disappeared with the washing (as it frequently does; alas, indigo often deceives you with its first enthralling, metallic midnight blues).

In the late spring of 1978, my husband and I visited Fred and Juanita Gerber at their home in Ormond Beach, Florida. Stimulated by Fred Gerber's book on indigo and our exchange of letters over the years, I arrived with a folder full of indigo samples, seeking his advice on some of my failures, his opinion of some of my successes. Why had the paste formula worked so well? What caused the unsightly grayish streaks in the circular ties? How can one achieve an even color systematically with indigo? Does each batch of powdered natural indigo differ in quality and content? The Gerbers received us graciously and after a delicious luncheon of local crabmeat salad and cool white wine, we were able to talk. Fred Gerber, a botanist, is a loquacious, likable man, his intellectuality complemented by a wry sense of humor. His wife, Juanita, shares Fred's interests and is as warm and hospitable as he is.

Anticipating our arrival in the late morning, Fred had prepared a miniworkshop to show me his method of working a hydrosulphite vat, using ammonia as the alkali to dissolve the indigo rather than a strong one like caustic soda because he believes that the weaker alkaline content of ammonia, though slower acting than caustic soda, permits the old practice of redipping the cloth in indigo for a deeper shade to be carried out successfully. It is successful, Fred says, because it does not redissolve the indigo already deposited on the fabric in the first (and each successive) dipping which is what happens with a strong chemical like caustic soda.

Fred showed me his collection of indigo: natural powdered indigo from India, indigo balls from Nigeria and Mexico, indigo paste, indigo in liquid form, and synthetic indigo crystals from I.C.I., America (a subsidiary of the British firm, I.C.I. International, Ltd.). We dashed into the yard where he surprised us with a beautiful growing indigo plant with tiny buds about to blossom. In another part of the tropical growth surrounding his home was an indigo plant in full bloom. He had planted the seeds at random and some grew to maturity. (This was living proof of the history we had just read of the thriving indigo plantations in early colonial days, a crop second only to rice in the Carolinas.) We snapped a picture and hurried back inside. With casual aplomb, Fred began mixing his indigo "formula." He wanted me to see exactly how easily it's done, and sure enough, with quick, deft movements (no gloves, no apron, no scales, no glass rods—but a chopstick—no measuring cups or spoons), he mixed a teaspoonful of synthetic indigo crystals with some cold water in a jelly jar, swished it around a bit, then added a teaspoonful of sodium hydrosulphite (Fred still believes it is the best reducing agent for indigo and is not opposed to its use) and mixed it round a bit again. Then he poured in about a cup of plain household ammonia and set the whole thing down to get itself together.

He had been soaking some old, well-washed muslin in washing soda (as a wetting agent) long before we arrived and he now invited me to tie up a few samples to dip in his ammonia concoction. I was a little taken aback by his invitation, since I usually tie my designs on dry cloth, but I plunged in and began tying. I made a few ineffective-looking pieces and Fred plunged them into the dyebath he had prepared in a gallon jar, which had previously housed kosher dill pickles or quantities of cole slow (he asks the local supermarket to save him all the gallon jars from the delicatessen department, a wonderful idea). I can't remember seeing him prepare the dyebath, it all happened so fast; I see by my notes that another teaspoonful of sodium hydrosulphite went in before he added the indigo/ammonia liquid. One thing that really impressed me was that the flecks of indigo floating around in the jar were actually white; mine are always a sludgy greenish-yellow, even when the vat itself turned a clear yellow, as Fred's had. When I mentioned this to him, he suggested I send him a sample of my natural indigo so that he could test it. He uses synthetic indigo (British), but I never get white with my synthetic, either. He also pointed out that the undissolved bits of indigo that eventually settle to the bottom of both the jelly jar and the gallon jar are saved; ammonia is added, and the concoction is allowed to sit until it dissolves. The liquid is then added to the dyebath and the same process is repeated thriftily until all the indigo has been dissolved and used.

In any case, after a short interval, Fred popped in my tied pieces, and to my amazement, in about a minute and a half, he popped them out again. Then of all things, he *rinsed* them *before* they had oxydized—strictly *verboten* in all the indigo instructions I had been reading over the years. When I opened the tied samples, of course, the designs were miserable-looking, partly from my inept, nervous tying, partly because the pieces hadn't been in the vat (pickle jar) long enough. "These haven't been in the dye long enough," I said accusingly to Fred, hoping to defend my sometime status as a tie-dye specialist. I can't remember that it fazed Fred, but later, he appeared with a remaining tied piece I had hoped he would forget and unfurled it before me. It was darker than the pale sky-blue pieces that preceded it, the design was slightly more passable, but it was no award-winner either. "Oh, did you leave it in the dye longer?" I asked innocently. Fred nodded and smiled knowingly.

Later we discussed some of the principles behind his actions. As I mentioned before, Fred firmly believes in using a weak alkali (such as ammonia or urine) to dissolve the indigo, and repeated dippings—as many as two dozen or more—to build up a darker tone. He mentioned that the dyeings of dark blues for Oriental rugs were often done with as many as fifty overlays of blues. However, he does not really disapprove of my seeking a one-dip solution with a relatively large amount of indigo powder, stating that the old dye formulas show that the dyers used a particular amount of the same dyestuff for one shade of blue and a greater (or lesser) amount of the same dyestuff for another shade of blue. As to his seemingly casual approach to measurements and methods while mixing his dyebath, he feels that, again, the old dye records show that the dyers used methods of measuring dyestuffs and chemicals which were not calculated in exact quantities. And the dyestuff itself—indigo particularly—was highly variable in its content, so that consistency of measurement did not particularly mean scientific exactness in a formula. Fred feels these principles are equally valid today. As to the glass rod (used to minimize introducing air into the dyebath), he feels it's inevitable to get air bubbles into the indigo vat, unavoidable by the sheer nature of dyeing fabric which captures air (particularly tie and dyes, according to my observations). In fact, when I told him my analysis of the streaky grays on my circular ties—that the dye was not penetrating (at the same rate) into the crinkles and crevices in the fabric caused by the tying, that the fabrics were, in fact, sometimes sticking together and causing a "resist" in the area where no resist was desired—he answered that the old dye formulas recommend that the fabric be "worked," that is, manipulated by hand during the indigo-dyeing process. I had made some guilty forays into this forbidden realm during a particularly frustrating session, but perhaps I didn't work the fabric enough, because my streaks remained. When I showed Fred these samples of my experiments and asked him what he thought caused them, he said quite frankly that he was not experienced with indigo dyeing on cotton, or resist techniques. He showed me some skeins of wool he had dyed in the ammonia/hydrosulphite formula, using a buildup of blues—a lovely variety of medium indigo tones. But, he suggested, perhaps my problem was caused by the depth of the blue achieved in one dipping. I feel that this would not explain why some of the circular ties were successful, and most of all, why the most concentrated dyebath, used with the wheat wallpaper paste addition, came out the most even, purest, and darkest color. Fred said that the use of various starches in a dye vat was very common in the old formulas, the reason being that it held the indigo in suspension and kept it on the surface of the fabric. And as we know from my experience, it delays oxidation and prolongs the contact of indigo with the fabric, thus encouraging a more even distribution of the color.

Fred had some other suggestions for further experimentation. He thought it might be a good idea to plunge the dyed pieces into an acid bath—white vinegar and water would do—to stop the action of the alkalies on the fabric and perhaps contribute to a more evenly dyed cloth. This would be done after a quick rinse in cold water immediately upon removal from the dye vat, which he feels also aids in achieving an even color distribution. I had already taken some of the tips Fred had given me by letter several weeks before our luncheon meeting; one was from his book. He suggests a twenty-four-hour oxidation period, rather than the relatively short twenty-to-thirty-minute period usually allowed. It seemed to make no difference with my regular formula, but perhaps the one using the wallpaper paste would have eventually oxidized by itself (without blotting off the excess dye/paste mixture with paper towels). It seems a good idea to try this. I also took Fred's advice to scour the fabric, that is, boil it for two hours in a solution of washing soda and soap, and when this made little difference in the evenness of the dyeing, I took it upon myself to mordant the fabric in alum. This, too, had changed nothing significantly.

I showed Fred some of the other samples I had made in my experiments and pointed out that to my way of thinking, the type of tying seemed to be the determining factor in the evenness of color distribution. Pieces that were folded in an accordion-pleated fashion, refolded and tied in various ways, inevitably came out evenly (although of course there would be variations in the actual design part such as all tied pieces have). I attribute this to the fact that the fabric is held firmly in place, and moreover, it is held flat. This seems to allow an even flow of dye, and because the piece rests in the dyebath a full twenty minutes, the dye has time to penetrate to the interior of the tied area. Too thick a piece would not allow this penetration, and this should be kept in mind when tying large amounts of fabric in this folded style.

The afternoon with the Gerbers was too short, and we had to leave with only a swift look at his library and a tantalizing glance at his extensive files. The Gerbers are lovely people and it was a delight to meet them at last and have a firsthand exposure to Fred's research and techniques. Fred Gerber's unorthodox approach to indigo will open up even more avenues of experimentation for me and for you.

Glossary

ACID A substance containing hydrogen which, when the hydrogen is replaced by a metal, forms a salt. Acids taste sour, and to test or prove the acidity of a solution, litmus paper is used. Litmus paper is a specific blue-colored matter which turns red if dipped in an acid solution. Conversely, an alkali will turn the red, acid-soaked litmus paper back to the original blue. An alkali neutralizes an acid as is so simply seen with the litmus paper test.

ALKALI Any substance that has the ability to neutralize acids. Originally, these were obtained from the ashes of plants. Lime, magnesia, and other vegetable alkalies are also included.

ANILINE An oily, poisonous, colorless liquid produced from coal tar, discovered (accidentally) in 1856 by Sir William Henry Perkin. The first synthetic used for dyeing purposes, it revolutionized the dyeing industry. The discovery of the original purplish color was followed by the other colors until natural dyes were no longer valued in the industrialization of dye production.

BOU-BOU A garment for men, women, and children in Africa, cut from a length of cloth placed on the straight of the goods, with a simple slash from neck to chest forming a head opening. The length varies, depending on whether a shirt, tunic, or ankle-length robe is desired. Side seams can be sewn, looped at the waist, or can hang loose without sewing. The neck opening and sleeve endings are often decorated with hand- or machine-stitched embroidery; sometimes the garment has pockets in the chest area.

CALABASH The fruit of certain plants of the gourd family, principally the hard-shelled bottle gourd (*Lagenaria vulgaris*); when cleaned and dried, the shell can be cut in half and used as a dipper, drinking vessel, storage bowl, et cetera. Whole gourds serve as bottles of various sizes. Decorative designs are frequently incised, scratched, or burned into the outer skin's surface. Broken bits of the dried and hardened calabashes are carved into printing blocks for adinkra textiles in Ghana.

CAMWOOD A wood found in West Africa, one of the three (the others are Barwood from Sierra Leone and Sanders from parts of tropical Asia) known by their Latin names (*Baphia nitida* and varieties of *Pterocarpus*) and which all share a common dye principle, santalin. Depending on the mordant and the dyeing methods, various shades of red, orange, and purple are produced.

CASSAVA A root plant that grows in tropical countries and is the basic starch in the local diet. It is served boiled and mashed and is also used to make the starch for paste resist patterning in Nigeria. (In French-speaking West Africa it is called *manioc.*)

COWRIE The small shell of a marine gastropod (*Cypraea*), used extensively in Africa as currency; because of its prestige and attractive appearance, it is used to decorate clothing and religious objects such as masks, statues, weaponry, and utensils.

FÉTICHISTE A religious specialist who establishes values and powers of cult objects (fetishes) and often administers them or gives lay people the sanctioned permission to use them.

FETISH A name given certain cult objects believed by cult followers to possess positive metaphysical or magic powers—such as to save its owner from harm, disease, or death.

GELE (geh-lay) The stylish head tie of the Yoruba women of Nigeria. Originally a covered head denoted bridal, then marital, status; currently it is a popular fashion used by all Yoruba women, in fabrics ranging from inexpensive cottons and traditional handwoven raw silks and cottons to luxurious laces, velvets, and damask imports, thereby denoting wealth and status. Skill in tying the several-yard length of fabric is required; each style has a name and a meaning which reflect the wit and ingenuity of market women, who frequently set the trend.

GLUCOSIDE A sugar product, usually glucose, obtained by adding water to certain compounds which activates a specific type of chemical composition resulting in the sugar product.

KARITÉ A kind of nut, ground into a butter. It is not exported or cultivated but is gathered from wild trees in northern Togo, Ivory Coast, Mali, Upper Volta, and other African countries.

KOLA NUT A brown narcotic-containing seed produced by various African trees (*Cola nitida*). It is commonly chewed in Subsaharan Africa to fight fatigue and diminish hunger, much the way Westerners drink coffee. When crushed and combined with water, it yields an attractive rust-colored dye very popular throughout West and Central Africa.

LAPPA See PAGNE, below.

LONCHOCARPUS The Latin name for one of the fifty or more indigo-producing plants; the leaves of this shrubby vine found in West Africa are the source of the blue coloring matter.

LOST-WAX CASTING Called *cire perdue* in French, it is a method of casting gold, copper, brass, or bronze. The creativity could be said to lie in the sculpting of the wax which is then covered with clay and *melted*, or lost, when the clay hardens. The clay is then a mold, or a negative, of the original wax creation which now no longer exists. Into this mold is poured the heated metal, and when it hardens, the clay form is chipped off. The creativity is combined with intuition and timing, however, as once the wax has been melted, this original inspiration is truly lost. If the metal is too hot or not sufficient when it is poured, or if the cast is imperfect or not hard enough or cracks before the metal has cooled properly, the casting is lost as well as the wax. Thus the whole creation and its method is a precarious one.

LYE Caustic soda (Sodium Hydroxide—$NaOH$), used in vat and fermentation methods to make the alkali solution necessary to dissolve indigo, which is insoluble in plain water. In Nigeria, the traditional method for achieving lye is by leaching wood ashes.

MORDANT A substance which fixes, or makes fast, a color on a textile by causing the fibers of the fabric to open and become more receptive to the dyestuff, thereby forming an insoluble compound—hence the word "colorfast." Mordants can also affect the hue and intensity of colors in dyestuffs.

OXIDATION The act of oxidizing, or combining with oxygen.

PAGNE (pah-nya) A free-form, wraparound skirt, usually ankle-length, made of a single length of fabric approximately 2½ yards long, sometimes held at the waist by a string over which the rather loose fabric is folded inside, but which also can be fastened by simply tucking the loose end over the wrapped parts at the waistline. In English-speaking Africa, the same type of garment is called a wrapper or a *lappa*.

RADIO-CARBON DATING A method of archaeological dating of organic prehistoric materials. Two kinds of carbon are absorbed into the systems of everything living; one is stable (Carbon-12) and one is not (Carbon-14). Both can be measured and when anything dies, unstable Carbon-14 decays and stable Carbon-12 does not. By measuring the rate of decay according to the half-life of surviving Carbon-14 against the constantly existing amounts of Carbon-12 in bone, wood, charcoal or shell, one can approximate the age of the object, plus or minus a hundred years or so. Radio-carbon dating is used for periods over 40,000 years.

RAFFIA The fiber from the raffia palm used for making baskets, mats, fans, hats, et cetera. For tie and dye techniques in Africa, it is readily available as a local natural product and is traditionally used instead of string, though string has become common.

SLAKED LIME WATER Hydrated Calcium Hydroxide—$Ca(OH)_2$—used to make an alkaline solution for dissolving indigo which is insoluble in plain water.

SOLVENT Any substance—usually liquid—in which another substance, such as indigo, can be dissolved.

WOAD (*Isatis tincotia*) A plant that was, in antiquity, the principal source of blue coloring matter. European in origin and grown mainly in Holland and France, it lost its popularity with the importation of indigo in the sixteenth century. Woad contains indigotin (a sugar and indigo compound) and, like indigo, requires the same lengthy dyeing procedure but yields a less intense blue, which accounts for its diminishing usage once indigo became available.

Bibliography

Adams, Monni. "Kuba Embroidered Cloth," *African Arts*, November 1978, Volume XII, No. 3, pp. 24–69.

Antubam, Kofi. *Ghana's Heritage of Culture*. Leipzig: Kehler and Amelang, 1963.

Atkins, Guy (ed.) *Manding Art and Civilisation*. London: Studio International, 1972.

Bailey Film Corporation. *The Ashanti—African Craftsmen* (documentary film).

Barbour, Jane. "Nigerian 'Adire' Cloths," Baessler-Archiv, Neue Folge Band XVIII (1970), (XLIII Band), Heft 2, Ausgegeben am 31 Mai, 1971, pp. 363–426.

———, and Simmonds, Doig. *Adire Cloth in Nigeria*. University of Ibadan, Nigeria: The Institute of African Studies, 1971.

Boser-Sarivaxévanis, Renée. *Aperçus sur la teinture à l'indigo en Afrique Occidentale*. Sonderabdruck aus den Verhandlungen der Naturfoschenden Gesellschraft in Basel, Band 80/1, 1969.

———. "Les tissus de l'Afrique Occidentale à dessin réservé par froissage," *Ethnologische Zeitschrift Zurich*, January 1972.

———. *Les tissus de l'Afrique Occidentale*. Band 13, Basler Beiträge zur Ethnologie, 1972.

Bravmann, René. *Islam and Tribal Art in West Africa*. London: Cambridge University Press, 1973.

Bowdich, T. E. *Mission from Cape Coast to Ashanti*. London: John Murray, 1819.

Brooks, Lois. "Workshop: Adire Eleko," *Craft Horizons*, August 1971; pp. 12–15.

Bühler, A. "Primitive Dyeing Methods." *Ciba Review: Dyeing Among Primitive Peoples*, No. 68, July 1948, pp. 2485–2500.

Chives, E. M. "Nineteenth Century Trade in the Bamenda Grassfields, S. Cameroons." *Afrika und Übersee*, Band XLV, Heft 4, 1962, pp. 233–57.

Clouzot, Henri. *Tissus Nègres*. Paris: Librairie des Arts Décoratifs.

Dalby, David. "The Indigenous Scripts of West Africa and Surinam: Their Inspiration and Design." *African Language Studies*, IX, 1968, pp. 156–97.

Dendel, Esther Warner. "Blue Goes for Down," *Natural Plant Dyeing*, Handbook II. Brooklyn, N.Y.: Brooklyn Botanic Garden, 1974, pp. 23–28.

———. *African Fabric Crafts*. New York: Taplinger, 1974.

Donne, J. B. "Bogolanfini: A Mud-Painted Cloth," unpublished paper, Conference on Manding Studies: Congrès d'Études Manding. London: School of Oriental and African Studies, 1972.

Dugast, I., and Jeffreys, M. D. W. "L'Écriture des Bamun," I.F.A.N. Mémoires, Série: Populations, No. 4, 1950.

———. "Ivory Coast: Bouake: Loin-cloth dyeing, a traditional art." *Entente*, No. 1, July 15, 1969, pp. 52–55.

Eicher, Joanne B. *African Dress—A Select and Annotated Bibliography of Subsaharan Countries*. Michigan State University, African Studies Center, 1970.

———. *Nigerian Handcrafted Textiles*. Ile-Ife, Nigeria: University of Ife Press, 1976.

Étienne-Nugue, Jocelyne. *Artisanats traditionnels en côte d'ivoire*, unpublished manuscript.

Gardi, René. *African Crafts and Craftsmen*. New York: Van Nostrand Reinhold, 1969.

Gerber, Frederick H. *Indigo and the Antiquity of Dyeing*. Ormond Beach, Florida: Gerber Publications and the Arachnid, 1978.

"Making an 'Adinkrah' Cloth." *Ghana News*, Vol. 2, No. 2, March/April 1970, pp. 3–4.

Glaze, Anita. "Senufo Graphic Arts," *Ba Shiru*, University of Wisconsin Department of Linguistics, Number 4, 1972, pp. 37–46.

———. "Women Power and Art in a Senufo Village," *African Arts*, Volume VIII, No. 3, Spring 1975, pp. 24–29; 64–67; 90–91.

———. "Senufo Ornament and Decorative Arts," *African Arts*, Volume XII, No. 1, November 1978, pp. 63–71; 107–8.

Glover, E. Ablade. *Adinkra Symbolism*. Kumasi, Ghana: University of Science and Technology.

Hale, Sjarief. "Kente Cloth of Ghana." *African Arts*, Spring 1970, Vol. III, No. 3, pp. 26–29.

Heathcote, David. "Hausa Embroidered Dress." *African Arts*, Winter 1972, Vol. V., No. 2, pp. 12–19; 82.

Imperato, Pascal James, and Shamir, Marli. "Bokolanfini—Mud Cloth of the Bamana of Mali." *African Arts*, Summer 1970, Vol. III, No. 4, pp. 32–41.

Kayper-Mensah, Albert W. *SANKCFA—Adinkra Poems.* Tema, Ghana: Ghana Publishing Corp., 1976.

Kennedy, Jean. "New Heirs to Talent in Oshogbo." *African Arts*, Summer 1971, Vol. IV, No. 4, pp. 24–27.

Kyerematen, A. A. Y. *Panoply of Ghana.* New York: Praeger, 1964.

Leuzinger, Elsy. *Africa—The Art of the Negro Peoples.* New York: Crown, 1960.

Lévi-Strauss, Monique. *Sheila Hicks.* New York: Van Nostrand Reinhold, 1973.

Menzel, Brigitte. *Goldgewichte aus Ghana.* Berlin: Museum für Völkerkunde, 1968.

———. *Textilien aus Westafrika*, Volumes I, II, and III. Berlin: Museum für Völkerkunde, 1972–73.

Meyerowitz, Eva L. R. *The Akan of Ghana.* London: Faber and Faber, 1958.

———. *At the Court of an African King.* London: Faber and Faber, 1962.

Nielsen, Ruth. *The History and Development of Wax-printed Textiles Intended for West Africa and Zaïre.* Unpublished master's thesis, Michigan State University, 1974.

———. *African Wax-Prints—An Exhibit from the Nielsen and Eicher Collections.* Michigan State University: Kresge Art Gallery, 1977.

Plumer, Cheryl. *African Textiles—an outline of handcrafted Subsaharan fabrics.* Michigan State University: African Studies Center, 1970.

Quarcoo, A. K. *The Language of Adinkra Patterns.* University of Ghana, Legon: Institute of African Studies, 1972.

Rattray, Robert S. *Ashanti.* London: Oxford Press, 1923.

———. *Religion and Art in Ashanti.* London: Oxford Press, 1927.

Robinson, Stuart. *A History of Dyed Textiles.* London: Studio Vista, 1969.

Samassa-Mayer, Emerico. *Adinkira Cloth.* Accra, Ghana: Ghana Museum and Monument Board.

Smith, Shea Clark. "Kente Cloth Motifs." *African Arts*, October 1975, Vol. IX, No. 1, pp. 36–39.

Stanfield, Nancy. "Dyeing Methods in Western Nigeria," in Jane Barbour and Doig Simmonds (eds.) *Adire Cloth in Nigeria.* University of Ibadan, Nigeria: The Institute of African Studies, 1971, pp. 7–42.

Steinmann, A. "Batik Work, Its Origin and Spread." *Ciba Review, Batik*, No. 58, July 1947, pp. 2102–9.

Talbot, P. A. *In the Shadow of the Bush.* London: William Heinemann, 1912.
Thompson, Robert F. *African Art in Motion.* Berkeley: University of California Press, 1974.
Trowell, Margaret. *African Design.* New York: Praeger, 1966 (Revised Edition).
Wenger, S., and Beier, H. U. "Adire—Yoruba Pattern Dyeing." *Nigeria Magazine,* No. 54, 1957.

Recommended Reading

AFRICAN HISTORY AND CULTURE

Ajayi, Ade, and Espie, Ian. *A Thousand Years of West African History* (Revised Edition). Nigeria: Ibadan University Press, 1969.
Biobaku, Saburi O. (ed.) *The Living Culture of Nigeria.* Lagos, Nigeria: Thomas Nelson (Nigeria) Ltd., 1976.
Boahen, Adu. *Topics of West African History.* London: Longmans, Green, 1966.
Bohannan, Paul. *Africa and Africans.* New York: Natural History Press, 1964.
Davidson, Basil. *Black Mother* (Paperback edition: *The African Slave Trade*). New York: Little, Brown, 1961.
———. *The African Past.* New York: Universal Library, 1964.
———. *A History of West Africa.* New York: Anchor Books/Doubleday, 1966.
———. *The African Genius.* New York: Little, Brown, 1969.
DuBois, W. E. B. *The World and Africa* (originally published in 1947). New York: New World, 1965 (Enlarged Edition).
Gidal, Sonia, and Gidal, Tim. *My Village in Ghana.* New York: Pantheon Books, 1969.
The Horizon History of Africa. New York: American Heritage, Inc., 1971.
Oliver, Roland, and Fage, J. D. *A Short History of Africa.* Baltimore: Penguin Books, 1962.
Paulme, Denise. *Women of Tropical Africa.* Berkeley: University of California Press, 1971.
Robinson, A. L.; and Foster, C. G.; and Ogilvie, D. H. *Black Studies in the University.* New Haven: Yale University Press, 1969.

AFRICAN ART

African Arts magazine. University of California Press (All Issues).
Beier, Ulli. *Contemporary Art in Africa.* New York: Praeger, 1968.

Biebuyck, Daniel. *Tradition and Creativity in Tribal Art.* Berkeley: University of California Press, 1969.

Cole, Herbert M. *African Arts of Transformation.* Santa Barbara: The Art Galleries, University of California Press, 1970.

———, and Ross, Doran H. *The Arts of Ghana.* Los Angeles: Museum of Cultural History, University of California, 1977.

d'Azevedo, Warren L. (ed.) *The Traditional Artist in African Societies.* Bloomington: Indiana University Press, 1975.

Fagg, William. *The Art of West Africa.* New York: The New American Library, 1967.

———. *African Tribal Images.* The Cleveland Museum of Art, 1968.

———. *The Living Arts of Nigeria.* New York: Macmillan Publishing Co., 1972.

———, and Plass, Margaret. *African Sculpture.* London: Studio Vista, 1964.

Fraser, Douglas, and Cole, Herbert M. *African Art and Leadership.* Madison: University of Wisconsin Press, 1972.

Goldwater, Robert. *Primitivism in Modern Art.* New York: Vintage Books, 1967.

Gunn, Harold D. *A Handbook of the African Collections of the Commercial Museum.* Philadelphia.

Redfield, R., Herskovits, M., and Ekholm, Gordon F. *Aspects of Primitive Art.* New York: Museum of Primitive Art, 1959.

Rubin, Arnold. "Accumulation: Power and Display in African Sculpture." *Artforum,* May 1975, pp. 35–47.

Sieber, Roy, and Rubin, Arnold. *Sculpture of Black Africa: The Paul Tishman Collection.* Los Angeles: Los Angeles County Museum of Art, 1969.

Thompson, Robert F. *Black Gods and Kings.* Los Angeles: Museum of Cultural History, University of California, 1971.

Trowell, Margaret. *African Arts and Crafts.* London: Longmans, Green, 1937.

———, and Wachmann, K. P. *Tribal Crafts of Uganda.* London: Oxford University Press, 1953.

Wahlman, Maude. *Contemporary African Arts.* Chicago: Field Museum of Natural History, 1974.

AFRICAN TEXTILES, DRESS, AND RELATED CRAFTS

Anquetil, Jacques. *L'Artisanat Créateur—Afrique Noire 1.* Paris: Dessain et Tolra, 1977.

Boser-Sarivaxévanis, Renée. *Textilhandwerk in West-Afrika.* Fuhrer durch des Museum für Völkerkunde und Schweizerische Museum für Völkskunde, Basel, Sonderausstellung, Dezember bis April, 1972–73.

Eicher, Joanne B. *Nigerian Handcrafted Textiles.* Bulletin Vol. VII, No. 2, November. Kresge Art Center, Michigan State University, 1973.

Joseph, Marietta B. "West African Indigo Cloth." *African Arts,* Vol. XI, No. 2, January 1978, pp. 34–37; notes, p. 95.

Kent, Kate. *Introducing West African Cloth.* Denver: Denver Museum of Natural History, 1971.

Lamb, Venice. *West African Weavers.* England: Duckworth Press, 1975.

———, and Lamb, Alastair. *West African Narrow Strip Weaving.* Washington, D.C.: The Textile Museum, 1975.

Newman, Thelma R. *Contemporary African Arts and Crafts.* New York: Crown, 1974.

Nigeria in Costume (Third Edition). London: Shell Company of Nigeria, 1965.

Nordquist, Barbara K., and Aradeon, Susan B. *Traditional African Dress and Textiles.* Washington, D.C.: Howard University School of Human Ecology and the Museum of African Art, 1975.

Picton, John M. *African Textiles.* London: British Museum Publications, 1979.

Roach, Mary Ellen, and Eicher, Joanne B. *The Visible Self: Perspectives on Dress.* Englewood Cliffs, N.J.: Prentice-Hall, 1973.

Seiber, Roy. *African Textiles and Decorative Arts.* New York: The Museum of Modern Art, 1972.

Wass, Betty, and Murnane, Barbara. *African Textiles.* Madison: Elvehjem Art Center, University of Wisconsin, 1978.

Williams, Geoffrey. *African Designs from Traditional Sources.* New York: Dover, 1971.

TEXTILES, DYES, AND DESIGNS: HISTORICAL BACKGROUND

Abrahart, E. N. *Dyes and Their Intermediates.* New York: Pergamon Press, 1968.

Ash, Beryl, and Dyson, Anthony. *Introducing Dyeing and Printing.* London: Batsford, 1970.

Batty, J. W. *Textile Auxiliaries.* New York: Pergamon Press, 1967.

Bühler, Alfred. *Ikat Batik Plangi Band* 1, 2, 3. Reservemsterungen auf Garn und Stoff aus Vorderasien, Zentralasien, Sudosterupa und Nordafrika, Museum für Völkerkunde in Basel.

Clarke, Leslie J. *The Craftsman in Textiles.* New York: Praeger, 1968.

Hornung, C. P. *Hornung's Handbook of Design and Devices.* New York: Dover, 1959 (Second Edition).

Humbert, Claude. *Ornamental Design*. New York: Viking, 1970.
Kornerup, A., and Wanscher, H. H. *Methuen Handbook of Colour*. London: Methuen & Co., 1967 (Second Edition).
Larsen, Jack Lenor; Buhler, Alfred; Solyom, Bronwen; and Solyom, Garrett. *The Dyer's Art—Ikat, Batik, Plangi*. New York: Van Nostrand Reinhold, 1976.
Lehner, Ernst. *Symbols, Signs and Signets*. New York: Dover, 1969.
McIntyre, J. E. *The Chemistry of Fibres*. London: Edward Arnold, 1971.
Petterson, Richard B. *Native Threads—International Weavings and Embroideries*. Clark Museum, Scripps College, 1973.
Piper, Brenda. *Fibres and Fabrics*. London: Longman Housecraft Series, 1968.
Robinson, Stuart. *A History of Dyed Textiles*. London: Studio Vista, 1969.
———. *A History of Printed Textiles*. London: Studio Vista, 1969.
Sonday, Milton, and Smith, Paul J. *Fabric Vibrations: Tie and Fold-Dye Wall Hangings and Environments*. New York: Museum of Contemporary Crafts, 1972.
Tirtaamidjaja, N. *Batik—Pattern and Motif*. Indonesia: Penerbit Djamatan, 1966.
Victoria and Albert Museum. *Batiks* (booklet). London, 1969.

TEXTILES, DYES, AND DESIGNS: PRACTICAL GUIDES

Adasko, Laura, and Huberman, Alice. *Batik in Many Forms*. New York: William Morrow, 1975.
Adrosko, Rita. *Natural Dyes in the United States*. Washington, D.C.: Smithsonian Institution Press, 1968.
———. *Natural Dyes and Home Dyeing*. New York: Dover, 1971 (paperback revision of above).
Belfer, Nancy. *Designing in Batik and Tie Dye*. Worcester, Mass.: Davis, 1972.
Brooklyn Botanic Garden. *Dye Plants and Dyeing—a handbook*. Brooklyn, N.Y., 1964.
———. *Natural Plant Dyeing—Handbook II*. Brooklyn, N.Y., 1974.
Clark, W. *An Introduction to Textile Printing*. London: Butterworth (in association with I.C.I. Dyestuffs Division), Third Edition, 1971.
Cockett, S. R. *Dyeing and Printing*. Bath: Sir Isaac Pitman and Sons, 1964.
Davidson, Mary Frances. *The Dye Pot*. Published by the author, 1950.

Dendel, Esther Warner. *Needleweaving . . . Easy as Embroidery.* New York: Countryside Press, 1971.

———. *The Basic Book of Fingerweaving.* New York: Simon & Schuster, 1974.

Fiberarts magazine. "A Special Issue: Dyes and Dyeing." Volume 5, No. 1, January/February 1978.

Gerber, Frederick H. *The Investigative Method of Natural Dyeing.* Ormond Beach, Florida: Gerber Publications and the Arachnid, 1978.

———. *Cochineal and the Insect Dyes.* Ormond Beach, Florida: Gerber Publications and the Arachnid, 1978.

Grae, Ida. *Nature's Colors—Dyes from Plants.* New York: Macmillan, 1974.

Hobson, June. *Dyed and Printed Fabrics.* Leicester, England: Dryad Press, 1970.

Inkodye. Screen Process Supplies, 1199 East Twelfth Street, Oakland, California.

Jameson, Norma. *Batik for Beginners.* New York: Watson-Guptill, 1970.

Johnston, Meda Parker, and Kaufman, Glen. *Design on Fabrics.* New York: Reinhold Book Corp., 1967.

Keller, Ila. *Batik: The Art and Craft.* Rutland, Vermont: Charles E. Tuttle, 1966.

Krevitsky, Nik. *Batik/Art and Craft.* New York: Van Nostrand Reinhold, 1964.

Lesch, Alma. *Vegetable Dyeing.* New York: Watson-Guptill, 1970.

Maile, Anne. *Tie and Dye as a Present Day Craft.* New York: Taplinger, 1963.

———. *Tie and Dye Made Easy.* New York: Taplinger, 1973.

Meilach, Dona Z. *Contemporary Batik and Tie-Dye.* New York: Crown, 1973.

Monk, Kathleen. *The Craft of Fabric Printing.* New York: Ballantine, 1969.

Murray, Aileen. *Design in Fabric and Thread.* New York: Watson-Guptill, 1969.

Nea, Sara. *Tie-Dye.* New York: Van Nostrand Reinhold, 1969.

———. *Batik.* New York: Van Nostrand Reinhold, 1970.

Proud, Nora. *Textile Printing and Dyeing.* New York: Reinhold Book Corp., 1965.

Russ, Stephen. *Fabric Printing by Hand.* New York: Watson-Guptill, 1964.

Thurston, Violette. *The Use of Vegetable Dyes.* Leicester, England: Dryad Press, 1972.

Photography Credits

	Source	*Credit*
Figure 1	Claire Polakoff	Claire Polakoff
Figure 2	Helen Anderson-Bauer	Helen Anderson-Bauer
Figure 3	Helen Anderson-Bauer	Helen Anderson-Bauer
Figure 4	Helen Anderson-Bauer	Helen Anderson-Bauer
Figure 5	Helen Anderson-Bauer	Helen Anderson-Bauer
Figure 6	Smithsonian Institution, National Museum of Natural History, Washington, D.C.	John Philibert
Figure 7	Courtesy of the Photothèque, Musée de l'Homme, Paris	
Figure 8	Claire Polakoff	Claire Polakoff
Figure 9	Photothèque, Musée de l'Homme, Paris	Dr. Pales
Figure 10	Smithsonian Institution, National Museum of Natural History, Washington, D.C.	John Philibert
Figure 11	Photothèque, Musée de l'Homme, Paris	D. Destalle
Figure 12	Courtesy of the Photothèque, Musée de l'Homme, Paris	
Figure 13	Courtesy of the Photothèque, Musée de l'Homme, Paris	
Figure 14	Courtesy of the Photothèque, Musée de l'Homme, Paris	
Figure 15	Photothèque, Musée de l'Homme, Paris	Albert Robillard
Figure 16	Courtesy of the Photothèque, Musée de l'Homme, Paris	

	Source	*Credit*
Figure 17	Courtesy of the Photothèque, Musée de l'Homme, Paris	
Figure 18	Claire Polakoff	Claire Polakoff
Figure 19	Courtesy of the Museum für Völkerkunde, Basel	
Figure 20	Claire Polakoff	Claire Polakoff
Figure 21	Claire Polakoff	Claire Polakoff
Figure 22	Claire Polakoff	Claire Polakoff
Figure 23	Courtesy of the Musée Royal de l'Afrique Centrale, Tervuren, Belgium	
Figure 24	Claire Polakoff	Claire Polakoff
Figure 25	Claire Polakoff	Claire Polakoff
Figure 26	Claire Polakoff	Claire Polakoff
Figure 27	Claire Polakoff	Claire Polakoff
Figure 28	Claire Polakoff	Claire Polakoff
Figure 29	Claire Polakoff	Claire Polakoff
Figure 30	Courtesy of the Musée Royal de l'Afrique Centrale, Tervuren, Belgium	
Figure 31	Cooper-Hewitt Museum of Design, Smithsonian Institution	
Figure 32	Helen Anderson-Bauer	Helen Anderson-Bauer
Figure 33	Helen Anderson-Bauer	Helen Anderson-Bauer
Figure 34	Paul Polakoff	Paul Polakoff
Figure 35	Paul Polakoff	Paul Polakoff
Figure 36	Claire Polakoff	Claire Polakoff
Figure 37	Claire Polakoff	Claire Polakoff
Figure 38	Helen Anderson-Bauer	Helen Anderson-Bauer
Figure 39	Helen Anderson-Bauer	Helen Anderson-Bauer
Figure 40	Henri Aougah	Henri Aougah
Figure 41	Claire Polakoff	Claire Polakoff
Figure 42	Rita Warpeha	Rita Warpeha
Figure 43	Courtesy of the British Museum	
Figure 44	Claire Polakoff	Claire Polakoff
Figure 45		Photographer unknown
Figure 46		Photographer unknown
Figures 47–77	Hand printed by Claire Polakoff	
Figure 78	William Lawrence	William Lawrence

Figure 79	Rita Warpeha	Rita Warpeha
Figure 80	Rita Warpeha	Rita Warpeha
Figure 81	Rita Warpeha	Rita Warpeha
Figure 82	Rita Warpeha	Rita Warpeha
Figure 83	Claire Polakoff	Claire Polakoff
Figure 84	Adele Scheele	Adele Scheele
Figure 85	Rita Warpeha	Rita Warpeha
Figure 86	Rita Warpeha	Rita Warpeha
Figure 87	Adele Scheele	Adele Scheele
Figure 88	Marli Shamir	Marli Shamir
Figure 89	Marli Shamir	Marli Shamir
Figure 90	Marli Shamir	Marli Shamir
Figure 91	Marli Shamir	Marli Shamir
Figure 92	Marli Shamir	Marli Shamir
Figure 93	Marli Shamir	Marli Shamir
Figure 94	Marli Shamir	Marli Shamir
Figure 95	Marli Shamir	Marli Shamir
Figure 96	Marli Shamir	Marli Shamir
Figure 97	Marli Shamir	Marli Shamir
Figure 98	*African Arts*	Dr. Pascal James Imperato
Figure 99	Marli Shamir	Marli Shamir
Figure 100	Marli Shamir	Marli Shamir
Figure 101	Photothèque, Musée de l'Homme, Paris	D. Destalle
Figure 102	J. Oster	J. Oster
Figure 103	J. Oster	J. Oster
Figure 104	Courtesy of the Photothèque, Musée de l'Homme, Paris	
Figure 105	Paul Polakoff	Paul Polakoff
Figure 106	Paul Polakoff	Paul Polakoff
Figure 107	Paul Polakoff	Paul Polakoff
Figure 108	Courtesy of the Musée Royal de l'Afrique Centrale, Tervuren, Belgium	
Figure 109	Helen Anderson-Bauer	Helen Anderson-Bauer
Figure 110	Helen Anderson-Bauer	Helen Anderson-Bauer
Figure 111	Helen Anderson-Bauer	Helen Anderson-Bauer
Figure 112	Helen Anderson-Bauer	Helen Anderson-Bauer
Figure 113	Helen Anderson-Bauer	Helen Anderson-Bauer

	Source	*Credit*
Figure 114	Helen Anderson-Bauer	Helen Anderson-Bauer
Figure 115	Helen Anderson-Bauer	Helen Anderson-Bauer
Figure 116	Helen Anderson-Bauer	Helen Anderson-Bauer
Figure 117	Helen Anderson-Bauer	Helen Anderson-Bauer
Figure 118	Claire Polakoff	Claire Polakoff
Figure 119	Claire Polakoff	Claire Polakoff
Figure 120	Helen Anderson-Bauer	Patrick Bauer
Figure 121	Helen Anderson-Bauer	Helen Anderson-Bauer
Figure 122	Helen Anderson-Bauer	Helen Anderson-Bauer
Figure 123	Percy Martin	Percy Martin
Figure 124	Percy Martin	Percy Martin
Figure 125	Claire Polakoff	Claire Polakoff
Figure 126	Adele Scheele	Adele Scheele
Figure 127	Steve Murez	Steve Murez
Figure 128	Courtesy of the Minneapolis Star and Tribune Company	
Figure 129	Paul Polakoff	Paul Polakoff

Index

Abeokuta, 62
Abidjan, 171, 183ff., 217
Accra, 117, 125
Acids, 30, 31, 40, 236. *See also* specific substances
  defined, 239
Adams, Monni, 49–50, 54
Adams Community School (Washington, D.C.), 201–5
Adentin, Kwamin Frimpon, 86
Adinkera, King, 88ff.
Adinkira Cloth (Samassa-Mayer), 129
Adinkra cloth, 61, 83–130, 190, 206, 207
  charts available on, 252
Adinkrahene motif, 101–5, 123
Adinkra Symbolism, 129
Adire. *See* Tie and dye
Adire Cloth in Nigeria, 25, 53, 62
Adire eleko. *See* Batik
African Art in Motion, 53
African Arts, 12, 49, 53, 66, 82, 165, 185–86
  Imperato and Shamir in, 152, 154
African Crafts and Craftsmen (Gardi), 158, 185, 186
African Design, 54
African Dress (Eicher), 213
African Fabric Crafts, 12
African Heritage Dancers and Drummers, 201, 206, 207
African Language Studies, 53–54, 154
African Studies Association, 252
African Textiles (Plumer), 129, 130
African Wax-Prints, 4n
Afrika und Übersee, 54
Ahinful, Charles, 119
Airing of cloth, 125
Akan, the, 89
Akan of Ghana, the, 130
Akenten, Oti, 96
Akoma, 112
Alatchon mask, 169
Alkalies, 30–31, 40, 133, 226, 232–33, 234. *See also* specific substances
  defined, 239
Alum, 58, 69, 78
American Crafts Council, 251
Americans. *See* United States and Americans
Ameyaw, Nana Akumfi, III, 94
Ammonia, 31, 225, 229, 230, 232ff.
Anderson-Bauer, Helen, 17, 69–71, 77–78, 163–65, 174–75, 176, 192, 193–201
Andgeissus leiocarpus. *See* N'Galaman
Anena, Kwabena, 121
Anilines, 40
  defined, 239
Animal designs. *See* Korhogo and Korhogo cloth; specific animals
Animated drawings, 217
Annatto, 40
Antelope, 175, 176, 178, 179

Antubam, Kofi, 91, 92n, 94, 97–98, 129, 130
Aperçus sur la teinture à l'indigo . . . See Boser-Sarivaxévanis, Renée
Appliqué, 127, 128. *See also* Kente cloth Dahomean, 214, 217
Arabic script, 89
Artisanats traditionnels en côte d'Ivoire. See Étienne-Nugue, Jocelyn
Art of the Negro People, The, 129
Asantehene. *See* Adinkra cloth
Ashanti. *See* Ghana
Ashanti (Rattray). *See* Rattray, Robert
Ashanti—African Craftsmen, The (film), 130
Asokwa, 125
Atkins, Guy, 144, 154
At the Court of an African King. See Meyerowitz, Eva L. R.
Avocado seeds, 50
Aya, 109

Bab Rouah National Museum, 210
Badie tree, 95, 121
Badu, Kwasi, 125
Baiden, Kojo, 125
Bambara, the (Bamana), 59, 131–54
Bamileke, the, 41
Bamun, the, 33, 35ff., 41–48
Banjul, 74
Baphia nitida. See Camwood
Barbour, Jane, 25, 54, 63, 82
Bark cloth, 41
Barwood, 240
Basel, 12
  Museum für Völkerkunde, 56, 59, 77
Ba Shiru, 157, 185
Bata Fieri So, 147
Batik, 48, 55–82
Baule, the, 171
Beating or pounding cloth, 70–71, 80
Beier, H. Ulli, 32–33, 53
Beledougou, 131, 133, 144, 148
Bells, 43–44
Benne River, 41
Berlin, 12
Beving Collection, 24
Bibliography, 243–53
Bi-nka-bi, 105
Birds, 161, 168
Birisi cloth, 91, 92
Black, 91, 92, 98, 157, 179. *See also* Bokolanfini
Blanket, 113
Bleaching. *See* Bokolanfini
Blue, 50, 98, 179. *See also* Indigo; specific techniques
Blue Men, 31
Bokolanfini (Bogolafini), 131–54
Bolivia, 15
Boma, 54
Bono-Tekyiman, 94
Bonsu-Panyin, Nana Osei, 88, 89
Bonwere, 96
Boser-Sarivaxévanis, Renée, 12, 15–16, 24, 41, 52ff., 56–57, 82
Bottle gourd. *See* Calabash
Bouaké, 80
Bou-bou, 239
Bowdich, T. E., 83–86, 90, 95, 125, 129
Bravmann, René, 89, 129
British Museum, 13, 24, 83, 86, 90, 125
Brocade, 96
Bronze sculpture. *See* Lost-wax casting
Brooks, Lois, 69, 82
Brooms, 77
Brown (russet; terra-cotta), 41, 88, 91, 128, 157. *See also* Bokolanfini
Bühler, A., 24, 52
Bulongongo, Shamba, 54
Bushongo, the, 49
Bush spirits, 165–66ff.
Butterfly, 47

Calabash
  defined, 239
  stamps. *See* Adinkra cloth
Calcium hydroxide, hydrated, 242
California, University of, at Los Angeles (UCLA), 12, 126, 206
Cameroon, 33, 41, 48, 60
Camwood, 38–41, 49–50, 240
Cape Verde Islands, 15–16

Cap Vert, 200
Carbon dating, radio-, 242
Cartoons, 217
Cassava, 16, 52, 58, 63, 64, 240. *See also* Batik
Caustic soda. *See* Sodium hydroxide
CCC, 219
Chameleon, 162, 165, 167
Checkerboard, 114
Chicken, 161
China, 15, 55, 212
Chives, E. M., 48, 54
Ciba Review, 52, 82, 132–33
Circles, 46
Cire perdu. *See* Lost-wax casting
Clark, Robert, 185
Clay. *See* Paste
Clothing pattern book, 252
Clouzot, Henri, 132–33ff., 152–54
Cola nitida. *See* Kola nut
Color. *See also* specific cloths, colors
  symbolism in Ghana, 97–98
Coloring book, 252
Combretum glutinosum. *See* N'Tjankara
Combs (comblike tools), 60, 69, 77, 95, 117ff., 123
Community, sense of, 8
Congo River, 54
Corn flour, 58
Costa Mesa, Calif., 189ff.
Cotton, 16, 96, 212, 213, 227. *See also* specific cloths, techniques
Cowries (cowrie shells), 112, 147, 148, 240
Craft Horizons, 69, 82, 227n
Cremieux, Mme., 74
"Crocking," 31–32
Crocodile design, 160
Cross River, 46, 47, 145
Cushion, Mauritanian woman's, 147, 149
Cypraea. *See* Cowries

Dagwumba, 90
Dahomean appliqué, 214, 217
Dakar, 16n, 17ff., 61, 69ff., 77, 185, 193–201
Dalby, David, 47–48, 53–54, 145, 154
Damask cloth, 23, 50
Dancing, 156–57, 158
Deal, Melvin, 126–27, 201, 205, 206, 207–8
Death, 162. *See also* Funerals; Mourning
Debrah, Ebenezer, 127, 129
Delafosse, *Haut Sénégal*, 56n
Dendel, Esther Warner, 12, 38–41, 53, 188–93, 221n
Dendel, Jo, 189ff.
Denkyira, 89
Denwar Craft Fellowship, 189, 190
Depression (1930s), 218–19
Designs. *See* specific cloths, techniques
Dikodougou, 176
Diosse, Koumi, 148
Disorientation, 7–8
Djeli, 168
Dje mask, 171
Djenne, 134, 151
Donne, J. B., 142–43, 154
Dono ntoasua. *See* Drums
Drawings. *See also* Painting
  animated, 217
Drums, 110, 123, 147, 148
Ducks, 175
Dugast, I., 47, 53
Dupuis, Joseph, 89
Dutch, the, 13
Dweninini aben. *See* Ram's horns
Dyes, 24–41, 49–50. *See also* specific cloths, colors, substances
  dyers' cooperative, 193–201

Eburnea Exports, 185
Egypt, 55–56
Eicher, Joanne B., 12, 213–16
Ejagham, the (Ekoi), 46, 47
Elu. *See* Indigo
Embroidery, 23–24, 42, 86, 91, 95ff., 117, 118, 123, 128, 129
Entente, 80, 82
Epilepsy, 162
Étienne-Nugue, Jocelyn, 158, 171–74, 182–83, 185, 186
Excrement, 175
Eye, 115

Factory cloth. *See* Machine-made cloth

Fakaha, 158–59
Fashion, 6–7
Feathers, 62, 90, 191
Fern, 109
Féticistes, 156, 164–65, 217
  defined, 240
Fetish, defined, 240
Fiberarts, 227n
Fihankra, 113
Fila cloth. *See* Korhogo and Korhogo cloth
Fingers, to make designs, 77ff.
Finignekele. *See* Bokolanfini
Finimougou, 131
Fini N'Goloni Sirakele, 147
Fishbone design, 162
Fish designs, 162, 168, 176ff.
Fofoo flower, 103, 107, 123
Foulbé, 77
Foumban, 41, 42, 46, 48
4-H Youth Program, 251
Fouta Djallon, 77
Freeman, Gloria, 201–5
French, the, 146–48
Froissage, 16
Funerals, 89, 156, 163. *See also* Mourning
Fututam cloth, 92

Gambia, 15, 16, 50, 74, 194
Gardi, Bernhard, 12
Gardi, René, 158, 175, 185, 186
Gberi. *See* Chameleon
Gele, 240
Gelike Be Wuowanyanko, 147
Genya, the, 49
George, King, 66
Gerber, Fred, 29–32, 226, 229n, 232–37
Gerber, Juanita, 229n, 232, 236–37
Ghana, 57, 60, 61, 77, 83–130, 190, 207
Ghana News, 89–90, 129, 130
Ghana's Heritage of Culture. *See* Antubam, Kofi
Gibson, Gordon D., 54
Glaze, Anita, 157, 165–68, 170, 171, 181ff., 185–86
Glossary, 239–42
Glover, E. Ablade, 89, 98, 101n, 125, 129, 252
Glucoside, 29, 240
Goat design, 162
Gold, 117
  weights, 116
Gold Coast, 117
Gold color, 98
Golden Stool, 88, 89, 115, 207
Goldgewichte aus Ghana, 116, 130
Goudouma, Christophe Zemana, 80
Gourd. *See* Calabash
Grasshopper neck, 147, 148
Gray, 98
Green, 98, 117, 181
Guinea, 16, 50, 77ff.
Guinea-fowl design, 161, 162
Gyaman, 88ff., 96, 97. *See also* Ivory Coast
Gye Nyame, 109

Harris, Catherine, 252
Hausa, the, 41ff.
Haut Sénégal, 56n
Heart, 112
Heathcote, David, 53
Hicks, Sheila, 208–13
Himmelheber, Hans, 170–71, 186
History and Development of Wax-printed Textiles Intended for West Africa and Zaïre, The 4n
Holland, 13
House, circular, 113
House of the Calabash Flowers, 147
How-to-do-it books, 220
Hunting and hunters, 156ff., 167–68
Hydrosulphite. *See* Sodium hydrosulphite

Ibadadun designs, 63, 64
Ibadan, 17–23, 27–29, 32, 52, 62–63
I.C.I., America, 233
Imperato, Pascal James, 131ff., 143–44ff.
India, 15, 55–56, 212
Indican, 29
Indigo, 24–33, 41ff., 50, 91, 92, 98, 194, 196. *See also* Batik; Tie and dye
  legend of, 221–24
  techniques for, 225–27. *See also* specific techniques

Indigo and the Antiquity of Dyeing, 226
Indigofera. *See* Indigo
Indigotin, 242
Indonesia, 13, 15, 55, 60
Inla, 90
In the Shadow of the Bush, 47, 53
Ironing, 71
Iron slag, 95, 121
Isatis tincotia. *See* Woad
Islam and Tribal Art in West Africa, 89, 129
Iva Mapo, 32–33
Ivory Coast, 16, 50, 57, 61, 72, 80, 155–86, 194, 216–17

Janus, the, 46
Japan, 15, 55, 214
Java. *See* Indonesia
Jeffreys, M. D. W., 47, 53
Jeune Afrique, 56n
Journal of a Residence in Ashantee, 89
Jubilee Design, 66, 68

Kagba mask, 169
Kano, 25, 42
Karamoro-kioyolingo cloth, 89
Karité, 240
Kasai area, 49
Kennedy, Jean, 66, 82
Kente cloth (Kente strips), 88, 96, 97, 129, 206
Kiembala, 168
Kiembaza, 169
Kobene cloth, 88, 91, 92
Kola nut, 33, 50, 74–75, 80, 194, 197, 241
Kolowi. *See* Cowries
Konadu, Francis, 120, 121
Konaté, Aminata, 155–56, 159, 160, 163, 168, 170, 171, 178, 179, 181, 216–17
Koran, 89
Korhogo and Korhogo cloth, 154–86, 216–17
Korobila mask, 169
Koto mask, 168–69
Kraban, Ota, 96
Kuba, the, 49
Kumasi, 84, 89, 96, 97
Kuntinkantan, 106
Kuntunkuni cloth, 88, 91, 92
Kuntunkuni tree, 91, 95
Kwame, Osei, 89
Kwasida adinkera, 91, 92
Kyerematen, A. A. Y., 91, 92n, 96–97, 129, 130

Lafaragko mask, 169
Lagenaria vulgaris. *See* Calabash
Lagos, 67–68
Lannea velutina. *See* M'Peku
Lappa, 241
Leopard design, 161–62
Leopard society. *See* Ngbe society
Leprosy, 162
Leuzinger, Elsy, 129
Lévi-Strauss, Monique, 208n
Liberia, 16, 33, 34, 38–41, 50, 188
  indigo legend, 221–24
Liberia (Johnson), 39
Limes, 39, 40
Lime water, slaked, 242
Linen, 97, 212
Lion design, 161–62, 178
Lizards, 68, 160
Lock, 110
Lonchocarpus, 241. *See also* Indigo
London. *See* British Museum
Lost-wax casting, 57, 241
Lye. *See* Sodium hydroxide

Machine-made cloth (factory cloth), 5, 13, 123, 124, 127–28
McNight, Gregory, 207
Madebele. *See* Bush spirits
Mali (Sudan), 16, 24, 131–54
Malinké, the. *See* Manding, the
Mali pattern, 147
Mampong, 89
Manchester, England, 13, 96
Manding, the (Malinké), 16, 24
Manding Art and Civilisation, 144–45, 154
Manioc. *See* Cassava
Mapo Hall, 63
Mary, Queen, 66
Masks, 47, 156–57, 163, 168–71, 177, 178, 180
'Ma te, 112

Mauritanians, 148, 149
Mauritanian woman's cushion, 147, 149
Mauve, 50
Mbala, the, 54
Meanings, 190
Mende script, 145
Menzel, Brigitte, 12, 116, 130
Mexico, 212
Meyerowitz, Eva L. R., 94, 129, 130
Mframa-dan motif, 98–100
Michigan State University, 12, 57, 213
Milburn, and Mende script, 145
Millet bran, 141, 142
Minnesota, University of, 12, 213
Mission from Cape Coast to Ashanti. *See* Bowdich, T. E.
Mmra Krado, 110
Mohun, R. Dorsey, 49, 54
Moon, 111, 115, 130
Mopti, 134, 151
Mordant, defined, 241
Morocco, 201, 209–10
Mount Hood, Oregon, 219
Mourning, 88, 91, 93, 95, 97, 127, 128
M'Peku, 134, 151
Mud cloth, 131–54
Musée de l'Homme, 33, 47, 59, 133, 151, 152, 158–59
Musée des Arts Décoratifs, 219n
Musée d'Ethnographie (Basel), 12
Musée Royal de l'Afrique Centrale. *See* Tervuren, Belgium
Museum für Völkerkunde. *See* Basel; Berlin
Museum of Modern Art, 251
Museums, 5. *See also* specific museums
Muslims, 89
Mustard color, 117
Musuyidie, 103, 107

Nafana, the, 89, 157
Nafari, 169
Napieoloudougou, 176
Natural Plant Dyeing, 53, 221n
Nauvière mask, 169
Ndiaye, Iba, 5n
Neal, Walter, 207
New Thing Art and Architecture Center, 202–5, 207–8
New York City, 6, 7, 219n
N'Galaman (tree), 136, 140ff.
Ngbe society, 46, 47–48
Niang, Mme., 74
Nielsen, Ruth, 4n
Niganam tree, 172–74
Nigene tree, nigeneme dye, 181
Niger River, 59
Nigeria, 57, 61, 62–69, 145, 213–14, 240. *See also* Tie and dye
Nigeria Magazine, 53
Night school, 9
Njoya (king), 41–42, 43, 46, 48, 53
Njoya, Ibraham, 41–42
N'Kerenkan. *See* Grasshopper neck
Nkotimsefuopua, 106
Nordquist, Barbara K., 252
Nsaa, 113
Nsibidi, 47–48, 145
Nsirewa. *See* Cowries
Nsoroma. *See* Stars
N'Tamani, 147
Ntesie-matemasie, 112
Ntieya, 42, 48
N'Tjankara (tree), 136, 140ff.
Ntonso, 117, 121, 123–25
Nwumu cloth, 88, 91, 92, 96–97
Nyombos, 20, 21

Obi nka obie, 105
Ochre dye, 179
Ohene nwa, 108
Okra (gumbo), 77–78, 114, 115
Oladepo, Jinadu, 66
Oladepo, Kekelomo, 66
Olatunde, Asiru, 66
Olokun design, 64, 65
Oloyede, Senabu, 66
Orange, 134, 151
Oregon, 219
Ormond Beach, Fla., 229n, 232–37
Oshogbo, 66
Osrane ne nsoroma, 111
Ouagadougou, 80
Oxidation, defined, 241
Ozark Mountains, 219

Pagne, 241
Painting (drawing), 44, 45, 90, 217
on walls, 156, 157, 179–81
Palestine, 56
Panoply of Ghana. *See* Kyerematen, A. A. Y.
Paris, 208, 219n. *See also* Musée de l'Homme
Paste, 44, 55ff. *See also* Batik; Cassava
wallpaper, 231, 236
Patchwork quilts, 219
Pattern book, 252
Patterns of Traditional African Dress, 252
Peace Corps, 80, 193, 199, 200
Peanuts, 141
Pebbles, 114
Perkin, Sir William Henry, 239
Person, Yves, 56n
Perspiration, 31–32
Peru, 15
Peters, Jackie, 126
Philippines, 15
Pile cloth, 49
Plastics, 212
Plumer, Cheryl, 129, 130
Poku, Mathiew Jacob, 98–100
Pollution, 220
Poro society. *See* Korhogo and Korhogo cloth
Portuguese, 15–16
Pounding or beating cloth, 70–71, 80
Prempeh, King, 86
Prempeh II Jubilee Museum, 97
Printing. *See* Resist; specific cloths
Pterocarpus, 49, 240
Pueblo Indians, 15
Python designs, 165, 166–67

Quersegue mask, 169

Rabat, 210
Radio-carbon dating, 242
Raffia. *See also* Tie and dye
defined, 242
Ram's horns, 108, 116
Rattray, Robert, 86–88, 89, 91, 92n, 95–96, 101n, 121, 127, 129
Rayon, 96
Rectangles, 44
Red (rust; vermilion), 49–50, 88, 94, 98, 116–17, 128, 181. *See also* Kobene cloth
Redwood, 49–50
Reed, Marie H., Learning Center, 201
Religion, 32–33. *See also* Adinkra cloth; Korhogo and Korhogo cloth; specific peoples
Religion and Art in Ashanti, 88, 92n, 95, 129
Renwick Gallery, 219
Reserving, 132–33. *See also* Batik
Resist, 32, 55–82. *See also* Bokolanfini; Tie and dye
Reverence, 190
Rhythm, 190
Rice paste, 58, 59
Rosenthal Art Slides, 251
Rufisque, 74–77
Rugs, 209, 210
Russia, 15
Rust color, 50. *See also* Brown; Kola nut; Red

Sahara, the, 57
Sahel, the, 57
Salt, 40
Samassa-Mayer, Emerico, 89, 129, 252
Samory, 146–48
Samory Ani Tieba Benyero, 145–50
Samory's griot, 147
Sanders, 240
Sandogo and Sando diviners, 166, 167, 185–86n
Sango, 32
Santalin, 240
Sarakolé, the. *See* Soninké, the
Savon de sodani, 141, 143
Sculpture. *See* Lost-wax casting
Seiber, Roy, 89
Semitic-Syrians, 56
Senegal, 15ff., 50, 59–60, 61, 70ff., 193–201. *See also* Dakar
Senufo. *See* Korhogo and Korhogo cloth
Shamir, Marli, 131, 133, 135, 149ff.
Shawl, tie and dye, 33
Sheila Hicks (Lévi-Strauss), 208n

Shrouds, 156
Sickle, 147, 152
Sierra Leone, 50, 194
Sikasso, 146
Silk, 96, 97, 212, 213
Simmonds, Doig, 25, 62
Singer Education and Training Products, 251
Sketchbook of Traditional African Dress, 252
Slaked lime water, 242
Slides (kits; modules), 251–52
Smithsonian Institution (Museum), 48–49, 219n
Snake designs, 160, 168, 177. *See also* Python designs
Soap, 133, 141
Sodium carbonate. *See* Washing soda
Sodium hydrosulphite, 225, 227–29, 232ff.
Sodium hydroxide (caustic soda; lye), 141, 225, 231, 241
Solvent, defined, 242
SONEPI, 193, 195, 196
Soninké, the (Sarakolé), 16, 24, 59, 77ff.
Sonu, 168
Souraka Moussa N'Kunkoro Talan. *See* Mauritanian woman's cushion
Spider, 101
Stamps. *See* Adinkra cloth
Stanfield, Nancy, 25, 26, 53
Stanley Falls, 49
Starch, 27, 77–78, 79, 191, 235
Stars, 111, 123
Steinmann, A., 59, 82, 132–33, 152
Stencils, 66–69
Stoessell, Pamela Becker, 252
Stuckenrath, Barbara, 49
Sudan. *See* Mali
Sulphuric acid, 31
Sun, 115
Swallow design, 161, 162
Swastika, 105, 106, 116, 130
Switzerland, 199. *See also* Basel
Syrians, 56

Tables Synoptiques des Alphabets, 53
Tailoring, 145
Talbot, P. A., 47, 53
Tampons, 61, 69ff., 199
Tannic acid, 142–43
Tapestry, 96
Tardits, Claude, 41, 44, 46
Teachers Publishing Corporation, 252
Technology, 8–9
Teignan mask, 169
Tekyiman, 90
Tekyiman-Brong, 94
Television, 217
Terminalia auicennoides, 134
Tervuren, Belgium, 49, 64
Textilien aus Westafrika, 12, 130
Thailand, 212
Thiam, Gora, 163, 164, 175
Thompson, Robert, 46, 47
Tie and dye, 15–54, 55, 116, 198, 203, 204, 230–32, 233–34, 236
Tieba, 146–48
Timberline Lodge, 219
Tissus de l'Afrique Occidentale, Les. *See* Boser-Sarivaxévanis, Renée
Tissus Nègres (Clouzot), 132–33ff., 152–54
Tjantung, 60
Tjap, 61
Traoré, Adja Awa, 19, 61, 78–79, 195, 200
Traoré, Zita, 79–80
Tree design, 162, 164
Tree-leaf pattern, 147, 148
Trees, 188–89. *See also* specific colors, trees
Treichville, 50, 72, 80
Triangles, 46–47
Tribus, 186
Trowell, Margaret, 54
Turtle design, 162
Tyelisiire, 182

Unicorn—Books for Craftsmen, The, 253
United Nations, 193
United States and Americans, 1–10, 218–20. *See also* specific persons
United States Embassy Self-Help Fund, 195

Upper Volta, 60, 80
Urine, 30–31, 175, 234

Van Geluwe, H., 49

Wall decorations (hangings, paintings), 156, 157, 180–81, 217
  Dahomean appliqué, 214
Wallpaper paste, 231, 236
War Between Samory and Tieba, The, 145–50
Ware, Opuku, II, 98–100
Warp, corn-stalk, 191
Warpeha, Rita, 125
Washing soda, 225, 228, 231
Washington, D.C., 201–8, 219n
Waterlot, tunic collected by, 152
Wauibele mask, 169
Wax printing, 4n, 196, 199. *See also* Batik
Weaving, 56, 57, 96, 145, 178, 191
Wenger, Susanne, 32–33, 53
Wheat paste, 58
White, 98, 179. *See also* specific cloths
White, Katherine Coryton, 53
Whitney Museum, 219n
Woad, 29, 242
Wolo, 134
Wolof, the, 16, 24, 79
Wolof language, 193
Wood carving, 188–89
Wool, indigo and, 227
Workshops, 9. *See also* Denwar Craft Fellowship; specific techniques
Woroso, 147, 152
WPA, 218–19

Yeast, 225, 229n, 230
Yellow, 117, 181. *See also* Bokolanfini
Yiri Boulou. See Tree-leaf pattern
Yoruba, the, 51, 52, 58, 62ff., 240. *See also* Tie and dye

Zaïre, 48–49
Zeltner, François de, 59–60, 77, 133, 151
Zemp, M. Hugo, 158–59, 181